HISTORY OF THE GREAT WAR

BASED ON OFFICIAL DOCUMENTS

BY DIRECTION OF THE HISTORICAL SECTION OF THE COMMITTEE OF IMPERIAL DEFENCE

ORDER OF BATTLE
OF DIVISIONS

• PART I •

The Regular British Divisions

Compiled by
MAJOR A. F. BECKE
R.F.A. (Retired), Hon. M.A. (Oxon.)

The Naval & Military Press Ltd

Reproduced by kind permission of the Central Library,
Royal Military Academy, Sandhurst

Published by

The Naval & Military Press Ltd

Unit 10, Ridgewood Industrial Park,

Uckfield, East Sussex,

TN22 5QE England

Tel: +44 (0) 1825 749494

Fax: +44 (0) 1825 765701

www.naval–military-press.com

www.military-genealogy.com

© The Naval & Military Press Ltd 2007

ORDER OF BATTLE OF DIVISIONS

Part 1 The Regular British Divisions

Part 2a The Territorial Force Mounted Divisions and
The 1st-Line Territorial Force Divisions (42-56)

Part 2b The 2nd-Line Territorial Force Divisions (57th-69th),
with The Home-Service Divisions (71st-73rd)
and 74th and 75th Divisions

Part 3 New Army Divisions (9-26 and 30-41)
and 63rd (R.N.) Division

Part 4 The Army Council, G.H.Q.s, Armies, and Corps 1914–1918

*In reprinting in facsimile from the original, any imperfections are inevitably reproduced
and the quality may fall short of modern type and cartographic standards.*

Printed and bound by Antony Rowe Ltd, Eastbourne

*L'organisation actuelle en divisions est excellente,
chacune possédant ses organes complets. C'est
comme la légion.*

N.

PREFACE

It was stated in the preface to the volume dealing with the Military Operations in France up to the 1st July, 1916, that, as orders of battle take up much space and would be much the same for all the volumes covering 1916, 1917, and 1918, they would, following in this the example of the French Official History, be provided in a separate volume, and would give in addition the compositions of staffs and other details. To prevent such a volume being too cumbersome, it has been decided to give the divisional orders of battle, arranged uniformly as far as circumstances permit, in four parts, dealing with (1) the Regular British Divisions, now published ; (2) the Territorial Force Divisions ; (3) the New Army Divisions ; and (4) the Australian, Canadian, New Zealand, and Indian Divisions.

In the lists of Commands and Staffs, absence on short leave, at short courses, and at schools of instruction is not shown.

In the divisional tables the organization is given for each year in which the division served in a theatre of war ; the particular month selected being the one which shows the composition of the division at one of the most important periods of its history : as it first went overseas, followed by its organization in 1915 for the Battle of Loos, in June, 1916, for the Battles of the Somme, and in 1917 for the great battles of the latter part of that year, and completed by the organization of the division in its final reduced 1918 shape.

In order to make clear the development and changes which took place between 1914 and 1918 in the War Establishment of a British Division, a table is given in Appendix 1 which shows the authorized establishment for each year of the War.

An examination of the original six divisions of the B.E.F. shows that they kept strictly to the War Establishment then in vogue, but the composition of the five divisions of Regulars which were improvised between August and December, 1914, shows a variety of establishments insofar as the artillery is concerned. This variation from 1914 War Establishments was chiefly due to the lack of a reserve of 4·5-inch howitzers. To allow each division to be despatched to the theatre of war as soon as possible, the divisional artillery had to be made up with the artillery *matériel* which was available when the particular division was being assembled. These five divisions had three quite different artillery establishments,[1] and the composition of their artillery differed considerably in every case from the artillery establishment of the first six divisions.

The numerous and often involved reorganizations and changes in nomenclature of the field artillery brigades and field batteries are given in the notes to the various tables.

In the lists of Battles and Engagements, in which a division fought, the periods when the divisional artillery, engineers, and pioneers were left in the line after the relief of the division have not been given ; and the attachments to divisions in 1917 and 1918 of Army field artillery brigades (formed on the reorganization of divisional artilleries in 1917) and R.G.A. brigades are not given in the general notes to the order of battle tables. These were so numerous, and often of such short duration, that their inclusion would have been misleading.[2] All other attachments are given in the order of battle itself or in the general notes which precede it. In order that the table itself shall be as clear as possible, the numbered notes are printed on the page following it.

---

[1] Originally it was intended that the 28th Division artillery should include two heavy (4·7-inch) batteries (124 and 125) as well as one 4·5-inch howitzer battery (459) ; but these three batteries did not accompany the division abroad.

[2] The total number of attachments of A.F.A. Brigades to the regular divisions in 1917 and 1918 varies between 34 and 12.

In the lists of Battles and Engagements, occasional deviations have been made from the list given in the *Report of the Battles Nomenclature Committee* (published in 1921) so as to allow the inclusion of actions of which a division was particularly proud. In every case after the name of the battle in which a division fought there is given in square brackets the corps and Army in which it was serving at the time. In the rare cases when, during a whole year, a division did not happen to be engaged in any specific battle or engagement, only the year itself is shown ; this entry signifies that the division was on active service in the field during the period thus covered. In the lists, the words " Action " and " Affair," of the Battle Nomenclature classification, have been omitted, and only the date and name are given of these engagements.[1]

Each divisional story was submitted for comment to the general officer who commanded the particular division in the field at the conclusion of the Great War, and I wish to express my gratitude to divisional commanders and staff officers for the help they have given me in checking and correcting the charts and tables.

I am also greatly indebted to the staff of the Historical Section (Military Branch) for the specialised help given to me so freely and so often. Throughout the preparation of this part, Mr. P. F. L. Wright, in particular, has been untiring in helping me in every way.

Any correction or amendment thought necessary to these tables, etc., should be sent to the Secretary, Historical Section, Committee of Imperial Defence, 2 Whitehall Gardens, S.W.1.

A. F. B.

April, 1934.

---

[1] The Action of Hooge is shown as " 19th July, Hooge."

CONTENTS

LIST OF ABBREVIATIONS

NOTE.—For the period of the Great War the titles of regiments have been taken from the 1914-1918 Army Lists.

A.

(A.-A.)	(Anti-Aircraft).
A.-A. & Q.-M.-G.	Assistant-Adjutant & Quarter-Master-General.
A. & S.H.... ...	Argyll & Sutherland Highlanders.
A.F.A. Bde. ...	Army Field Artillery Brigade.
A.H.Q.	Army Head-Quarters.
Amb. or Ambce.	Ambulance.
Ammn. Coln. ...	Ammunition Column.
Ammn. Park ...	Ammunition Park.
A.R.O.	Army Routine Order.
Arty.	Artillery.
A.S.C....	Army Service Corps.
A.T.	Army Troops.
Aux.	Auxiliary.

B.

B.A.C.	Brigade Ammunition Column.
Bde.	Brigade.
Bedf.	Bedfordshire Regiment.
Bedf. Yeo.... ...	Bedfordshire Yeomanry.
B.E.F.	British Expeditionary Force.
B.F.T.	British Forces in Turkey.
B.-G., R.A. ...	Brigadier-General, Commanding Royal Artillery.
B.-G., R.H.A. ...	Brigadier-General, Commanding Royal Horse Artillery.
Bn.	Battalion.
Bord.	Border Regiment.
Br.-Gen.	Brigadier-General.
Bty.	Battery.
Buffs	Buffs (East Kent Regiment).
B.W. ... ...,	Black Watch (Royal Highlanders).

C.

Camb.	Cambridgeshire Regiment.
Cam. H.	Cameron Highlanders.
Cav. or Cavy. ...	Cavalry.
C.B.	Cavalry Brigade.
C.C.S.	Casualty Clearing Station.
cd.	command.
C.D.M.T. Coy. ...	Cavalry Divisional Mechanical Transport Company.
Cdn.	Canadian.
C.G.	Coldstream Guards.
Ches.	Cheshire Regiment.
C.I.	Central India.
Col.-Cdt.	Colonel-Commandant.
Comp.	Composite.
Conn. Rang. ...	Connaught Rangers.
Coy.	Company.
Cos.	Companies.
C.R.E.	Commanding Royal Engineers.
C.R.H.A.	Commanding Royal Horse Artillery.

D.

d.	died.
D.A.C.	Divisional Ammunition Column.
D.C.L.I.	Duke of Cornwall's Light Infantry.

D.—Continued

D.E. Coy.	Divisional Employment Company.
Detnt.	Detachment.
Devon	Devonshire Regiment.
D.G.	Dragoon Guards.
Dgns.	Dragoons.
Disembkd.	Disembarked.
Div.	Division.
Divnl....	Divisional.
D.L.I.	Durham Light Infantry.
d. of w.	died of wounds.
Dorset	Dorsetshire Regiment.
Duke's	Duke of Wellington's (West Riding Regiment).

E.

E.	East.
E. Lanc.	East Lancashire Regiment.
Embkd.	Embarked.
Emplnt. or Emplynt.	Employment.
Essex	Essex Regiment.
E. Surr.	East Surrey Regiment.
evacd.	evacuated.
E. York.	East Yorkshire Regiment.

F.

Fd.	Field.

G.

Garr. Bn.	Garrison Battalion.
Gds.	Guards.
G.G.	Grenadier Guards.
G.H.Q.	General Head-Quarters.
Glouc.	Gloucestershire Regiment.
G.O.C.	General Officer Commanding.
Gord. H.	Gordon Highlanders.
Gr. How.	Green Howards (Alexandra, Princess of Wales's Own Yorkshire Regiment).
G.S.O. 1.	General Staff Officer (1st Grade).

H.

(H.)	(Howitzer).
H.A.C.	Honourable Artillery Company.
Hants.	Hampshire Regiment.
H.A.R.	Heavy Artillery Reserve.
H.B.	Heavy Battery.
Herts....	Hertfordshire Regiment.
H.L.I....	Highland Light Infantry.
Home Co's. ...	Home Counties.
Househ'd.	Household.
How. Bde.	Howitzer Brigade.
How. Bty.	Howitzer Battery.
H.Q.	Head-Quarters.
Hsrs.	Hussars.
H.T.	Horse Transport.
H.T.M.B.	Heavy Trench Mortar Battery.
Hy. Bde.	Heavy Brigade.
Hy. Bty. A.C. ...	Heavy Battery Ammunition Column.

LIST OF ABBREVIATIONS

I.

I.G.	Irish Guards.
Ind.	Indian.
Inf.	Infantry.
Ir.	Irish.

K.

K. or Kd.... ...	Killed.
K.G.O.	King George's Own.
King's	King's (Liverpool Regiment).
K.O.	King's Own (Royal Lancaster Regiment).
K.O.S.B. ...	King's Own Scottish Borderers.
K.O.Y.L.I.... ...	King's Own (Yorkshire Light Infantry).
K.R.R.C.	King's Royal Rifle Corps.
K.S.L.I.	King's (Shropshire Light Infantry).

L.

Lcrs.	Lancers.
Leic.	Leicestershire Regiment.
Leic. Yeo. ...	Leicestershire Yeomanry.
Leins. ...	Leinster Regiment.
L.F.	Lancashire Fusiliers.
L.G.	Life Guards.
L.I.	Light Infantry.
Linc.	Lincolnshire Regiment.
L.N.L.	Loyal North Lancashire Regiment.
L. of C.	Line of Communications.
Lond.	London Regiment.
Loyal	The Loyal Regiment (North Lancashire).
L.R.B.	London Rifle Brigade.
L.S.	London Scottish.

M.

Manch.	Manchester Regiment.
Med.	Medium.
M.G.C.	Machine Gun Corps.
M.G. Coy.... ...	Machine-Gun Company.
M.G. Sec.	Machine-Gun Section.
M.G. Sqdn. ...	Machine-Gun Squadron.
M.I.	Mounted Infantry.
Midd'x.	Middlesex Regiment.
Mk.	Mark.
M.M.G.	Motor Machine Gun.
Mon. or Monm'th	Monmouthshire Regiment.
M.T.	Mechanical Transport.
Mtd.	Mounted.
Mtn.	Mountain.

N.

N.	North.
Newf'dld.	Newfoundland.
N.F.	Northumberland Fusiliers.
N. Irish H. ...	North Irish Horse.
N.M. Fd. Coy. ...	North Midland Field Company.
Norf.	Norfolk Regiment.
Northants. Yeo.	Northamptonshire Yeomanry.
North'd.	Northumberland.
North'n.	Northamptonshire Regiment.
N. Som.	North Somerset.
N. Staff.	N. Staffordshire Regiment.
N.S.W.	New South Wales.
N.Z. & A. ...	New Zealand and Australian.

O.

O. & B.L.I. ...	Oxfordshire & Buckinghamshire Light Infantry.

P.

(P.)	(Pioneers).
P.P.C.L.I.	Princess Patricia's Canadian Light Infantry.

Q.

Q.O.O. Hsrs. ...	Queen's Own Oxfordshire Hussars.
Queen's	Queen's (Royal West Surrey Regiment).

R.

R.	Royal.
R.A.F.	Royal Air Force.
R.A.S.C.	Royal Army Service Corps.
R.B.	Rifle Brigade.
R. Berks.	Royal Berkshire Regiment.
R. Cdn. H.A. Bde.	Royal Canadian Horse Artillery Brigade.
R.D.F.	Royal Dublin Fusiliers.
R.E.	Royal Engineers.
Regt.	Regiment.
R.F.	Royal Fusiliers.
R.F.A.	Royal Field Artillery.
R.G.A.	Royal Garrison Artillery.
R.H.A.	Royal Horse Artillery.
R.H.G.	Royal Horse Guards.
R. Innis. F. ...	Royal Inniskilling Fusiliers.
R. Ir. F.	Royal Irish Fusiliers.
R. Irish Regt. ...	Royal Irish Regiment.
R. Ir. Rif.	Royal Irish Rifles.
R.M.F.	Royal Munster Fusiliers.
R.M.L.I.	Royal Marine Light Infantry.
R.N.A.C.D. ...	Royal Naval Armoured Car Division.
R.N.D.	Royal Naval Division.
R. Scots	Royal Scots (Lothian Regiment).
R.S.F.	Royal Scots Fusiliers.
R. Suss.	Royal Sussex Regiment.
R.W.	Royal Warrant.
R. War.	Royal Warwickshire Regiment.
R.W.F.	Royal Welsh Fusiliers.
R.W.K.	Queen's Own (Royal West Kent Regiment).

S.

S.	South.
S.A.A. Sec. ...	Small-Arm-Ammunition Section
S.B.	Siege Battery.
S.B.A.C.	Siege Battery Ammunition Column.
Sco. Rif.	The Cameronians (Scottish Rifles).
Sea. H.	Seaforth Highlanders.
Sec.	Section.
S.G.	Scots Guards.
Sher. For. ...	Sherwood Foresters (Nottinghamshire & Derbyshire Regiment).
Sig.	Signal.
S. Irish H.... ...	South Irish Horse.
S. Lanc.	South Lancashire Regiment.
S.M. Fd. Coy. ...	South Midland Field Company.
Som. L.I.	Somerset Light Infantry.
Sqdn.	Squadron.
S. Staff.	South Staffordshire Regiment.
Suff.	Suffolk Regiment.
S.W.B.	South Wales Borderers.

T.

T. & S. Coln.	...	Transport & Supply Column.
Tempy.	... ...	Temporary.
T.F.	... ...	Territorial Force.
T.M. Bty.	... ...	Trench Mortar Battery.
Trp.	... ...	Troop.

U.

U.K.	... ...	United Kingdom.

V.

Vety.	... ...	Veterinary.

W.

W.	... ...	West.
War.	... ...	Warwickshire.
W.E.	... ...	War Establishments.
Welsh	... ...	Welsh Regiment.
W.G.	... ...	Welsh Guards.
Wilts.	... ...	Wiltshire Regiment.
Worc.	... ...	Worcestershire Regiment.
w. or wd.	... ...	wounded.
W. York	... ...	West Yorkshire Regiment.

Y.

Y. & L.	... ...	York & Lancaster Regiment.
Yeo.	... ...	Yeomanry.

THE CAVALRY DIVISION
then
1st CAVALRY DIVISION

G.O.C.

Mobilization... ... ... Major-General E. H. H. ALLENBY.
12 October, 1914 ... ... Major-General H. DE B. DE LISLE.
27 May, 1915 ... ... Major-General Hon. C. E. BINGHAM.
24 October, 1915 ... ... Major-General R. L. MULLENS.

G.S.O. 1.

Mobilization ...Colonel J. VAUGHAN.
15 Sept., 1914...Lt.-Col. G. DE S. BARROW.
12 Oct., 1914...Lt.-Col. A. F. HOME.
23 Aug., 1915...Lt.-Col. B. D. FISHER.
18 Jan., 1918...Lt.-Col. S. F. MUSPRATT.
20 June, 1918...Lt.-Col. R. E. CECIL.

A.-A. & Q.-M.-G.

Mobilization ...Colonel E. R. O. LUDLOW.
1 Feb., 1915...Major R. L. MACALPINE-
LENY (acting).
8 Feb., 1915...Lt.-Col. P. O. HAMBRO.
15 Dec., 1915...Major R. L. MACALPINE-
LENY (acting).
23 Dec., 1915...Lt.-Col. S. F. MUSPRATT.
18 Jan., 1918...Lt.-Col. J. BLAKISTON-
HOUSTON.

B.-G., R.H.A.

Mobilization ...Br.-Gen. B. F. DRAKE.
(On the formation of the Cavalry Corps, on 10/10/14, the B.-G., R.H.A., was transferred from the division to the corps.)

C.R.E.

(The division had no C.R.E., but the O.C. Field Squadron, R.E., acted as such.)

C.R.H.A.
(and Offr. Comdg. VII., R.H.A.)

12 Oct., 1914...Lt.-Col. G. H. A. WHITE.
10 April, 1916...Major E. J. SKINNER
(acting).
29 April, 1916...Lt.-Col. A. B. FORMAN
(wounded, 15/9/16).
16 Sept., 1916...Lt.-Col. E. HARDING-
NEWMAN (tempy.).
22 Sept., 1916...Major W. J. S. POSTON
(acting).
26 Sept., 1916...Lt.-Col. W. E. CLARK.

THE CAVALRY DIVISION

1st CAVALRY BRIGADE

Mobilization...Br.-Gen. C. J. BRIGGS.

2nd CAVALRY BRIGADE

Mobilization...Br.-Gen. H. DE B. DE LISLE.

3rd CAVALRY BRIGADE

Mobilization...Br.-Gen. H. DE LA P.
GOUGH.
(Bde. transferred to 2nd Cav. Div.
on 13/9/14.)

4th CAVALRY BRIGADE

Mobilization...Br.-Gen. Hon. C. E.
BINGHAM.

1st CAVALRY DIVISION
(16/9/14.)

1st CAVALRY BRIGADE

[Mobilization] Br.-Gen. C. J. BRIGGS.
7 May, '15...Lt.-Col. T. T. PITMAN
(acting).
15 May, '15...Br.-Gen. E. MAKINS.
16 April, '18...Br.-Gen. H. S. SEWELL.

2nd CAVALRY BRIGADE

[Mobilization] Br.-Gen. H. DE B. DE LISLE.
12 Oct., '14...Br.-Gen. R. L. MULLENS.
26 Oct., '15...Br.-Gen. D. J. E. BEALE-
BROWNE.
16 April, '18...Br.-Gen. A. LAWSON.

4th CAVALRY BRIGADE

[Mobilization] Br.-Gen. Hon. C. E.
BINGHAM.
(Bde. transferred to 2nd Cav. Div. on
13/10/14.)

9th CAVALRY BRIGADE

(Formed 14/4/15.)
14 April, '15...Br.-Gen. W. H. GREENLY.
15 Nov., '15...Br.-Gen. S. R. KIRBY.
25 Oct., '16...Lt.-Col. G. D. FRANKS
(acting).
31 Oct., '16...Br.-Gen. D'A. LEGARD.

GENERAL NOTES

At 11 a.m. on the 24th March, 1918, the 1st Cavalry Division formally constituted a " Dismounted Division," under Br.-Gen. D'A. Legard. Each cavalry brigade and machine-gun squadron furnished a regiment. The " Dismounted Division " returned on the 26th March, 1918.

On many other occasions the 1st Cavalry Division formed dismounted units for service in the trenches—each cavalry brigade forming a regiment under the command of the brigadier.

—————

The following units also served with the 1st Cavalry Division :—

Q.O. Oxfordshire Hussars, from 31/10/14–11/11/14 (then transferred to 4th Cav. Bde., 2nd Cav. Div. (see note 4)).

No. 9 Sanitary Section, landed at Havre on 25/12/14 ; joined 1st Cav. Div. on 9/1/15, and served with it until the Armistice.

1st Cav. Div. Fd. Ambulance Workshop, joined 14/5/15, and served with the 1st Cav. Div. until 6/4/16, when it was absorbed into the 1st Cav. Supply Column.

1st CAVALRY DIVISION[1] ORDER OF BATTLE, 1914 - 1918

	CAVALRY		ARTILLERY		Light Armoured Cars	Engineers	Signal Service	Cavalry Field Ambces.	Mobile Veterinary Sections	Divisional Emplymt. Company	ARMY SERVICE CORPS			
Dates	Brigades	Regiments and attached Units	R.H.A. Brigades and Ammn. Colns.	R.H.A. Batteries		Field Squadron	Signal Squadron				H.Q. 1st Divnl. A.S.C. Company	1st Cav. Supply Column Companies	1st Cav. Divnl. Aux. (Horse) Coy. Company	1st Cav. Ammn. Park Company
1914 August	1st Cav.	2/D.G. (Queen's Bays), 5/D.G., 11/Hsrs.; 1st Signal Troop.	III,5 & III Bde. Ammn. Coln.	D,5 E5	...	1st	1st	1st	1st	...	27 (H.T.)	57 (M.T.)		45 (M.T.)
	2nd Cav.	4/D.G., 9/R. Lcrs., 18/Hsrs.; 2nd Signal Troop.						2nd8	8th10			58 (M.T.)		
	3rd Cav.2	4/Hsrs., 5/R. Ir. Lcrs., 16/Lcrs.; 3rd Signal Troop.	VII,6 & VII Bde. Ammn. Coln.	I,6 L7				3rd	9th11					
	4th Cav.3	Comp. Regt. of Househ'd Cav.,4 6/D.G. (Carabiniers), 3/Hsrs.; 4th Signal Troop.						4th9	10th					
1915 Sept.	1st Cav.	2/D.G. (Queen's Bays), 5/D.G., 11/Hsrs.; I Bty., R.H.A.;13 1st Signal Troop.	VII, & VII Bde. Ammn. Coln.	...	...	1st	1st	1st	1st	...	27 (H.T.)	57 (M.T.)	57421	45 (M.T.)
	2nd Cav.	4/D.G., 9/R. Lcrs., 18/Hsrs.; H Bty., R.H.A.;14 2nd Signal Troop.						3rd	10th			58 (M.T.)		
	9th Cav.12	15/Hsrs.,15 19/Hsrs.,16 1/Bedf. Yeo.;17 1/War. By., R.H.A.;18 9th Signal Troop.						9th19	39th20					
1916 June	1st Cav.	2/D.G. (Queen's Bays), 5/D.G., 11/Hsrs.; I Bty., R.H.A.;22 1st Cav. Bde. M.G. Sqdn.;23 1st Signal Troop.	VII, & VII Bde. Ammn. Coln.	...	No. 8 Bty.25 (M.M.G.)	1st	1st	1st	1st	...	27 (H.T.)	57 (M.T.)	574	45 (M.T.)
	2nd Cav.	4/D.G., 9/R. Lcrs., 18/Hsrs.; H Bty., R.H.A.; 2nd Cav. Bde. M.G. Sqdn.;23 2nd Signal Troop.						3rd	10th			58 (M.T.)26		
	9th Cav.	15/Hsrs., 19/Hsrs., 1/Bedf. Yeo.; Y Bty., R.H.A.;24 9th Cav. Bde. M.G. Sqdn.;23 9th Signal Troop.						9th	39th					
1917 June	1st Cav.	2/D.G. (Queen's Bays), 5/D.G., 11/Hsrs.; I Bty., R.H.A.; 1st Cav. M.G. Sqdn.; 1st Signal Troop.	VII, & VII Bde. Ammn. Coln.	...	No. 8 Bty.29 (M.M.G.)	1st	1st	1st	1st	771st30	27 (H.T.)	57 (M.T.)	574	45 (M.T.)31
	2nd Cav.	4/D.G., 9/R. Lcrs., 18/Hsrs.; H Bty., R.H.A.; 2nd Cav. M.G. Sqdn.; 2nd Signal Troop.						3rd	10th					
	9th Cav.	15/Hsrs., 19/Hsrs., 1/Bedf. Yeo.;27 Y Bty., R.H.A.;28 9th Cav. M.G. Sqdn.; 9th Signal Troop.						9th	39th					
1918 March	1st Cav.	2/D.G. (Queen's Bays), 5/D.G., 11/Hsrs.; I Bty., R.H.A.; 1st Cav. M.G. Sqdn.; 1st Signal Troop.	VII, & VII Bde. Ammn. Coln.	...	...	1st	1st	1st	1st	771st	27 (H.T.)	57 (M.T.)33	574	...
	2nd Cav.	4/D.G., 9/R. Lcrs., 18/Hsrs.; H Bty., R.H.A.; 2nd Cav. M.G. Sqdn.; 2nd Signal Troop.						3rd	10th					
	9th Cav.	8/Hsrs.,32 15/Hsrs., 19/Hsrs.; Y Bty., R.H.A.; 9th Cav. M.G. Sqdn.; 9th Signal Troop.						9th	39th					

NOTES ON ORDER OF BATTLE

1 In August, 1914, it was styled "The Cavalry Division." It became 1st Cavalry Division on 16/9/14. (A.R.O. No. 93 of 15/9/14.)

2 Transferred on 13/9/14 to the 2nd Cav. Div. (on its formation). The 3rd and 5th Cav. Bdes. had been placed under Br.-Gen. H. Gough on 6/9/14.

3 Transferred to 2nd Cav. Div. on 14/10/14.

4 The 3 Sqdns. of the Comp. Regt. were transferred on 11/11/14 to the 3 Household Regts. (1/L.G. and 2/L.G., 7th Cav. Bde., and R.H.G., 8th Cav. Bde.) in the 3rd Cav. Div. The place of the Comp. Regt. in the 4th Cav. Bde. was taken on 11/11/14 by 1/Q.O.O. Hsrs. from 1st Cav. Div.

5 Transferred on 17/9/14 to 2nd Cav. Div. (on formation), D Bty. joining 3rd Cav. Bde., and E Bty. the 5th Cav. Bde. J, R.H.A., joined 4th Cav. Bde., 17/9/14.

6 (Tempy.) Z, R.H.A., was formed on 1/9/14 of Centre and Left Secs. of I, R.H.A., to replace L. On 3/9/14 the Left Sec. of I was replaced by a sec. of D. On 15/9/14 the sec. of D left to rejoin its own Bty.; and on 17/9/14 a sec. of J joined (tempy.) Z. On 27/9/14 the secs. rejoined I and J, and (tempy.) Z ceased to exist. Its place was taken by H (see note 7).

7 After Néry, L Bty. was sent back on 6/9/14 to Le Mans, and on 19/10/14 it returned to England. L was replaced on 1/9/14 by (tempy.) Z, and on 28/9/14 by H Bty., R.H.A.

8 Transferred on 13/9/14 to 2nd Cav. Div. (on formation).

9 Transferred on 16/10/14 to 2nd Cav. Div.

10 Transferred on 16/9/14 to 2nd Cav. Div. (on formation).

11 Transferred on 15/10/14 to 2nd Cav. Div.

12 Formed 14/4/15, and joined 1st Cav. Div.

13 I Battery attached on 17/9/14 to 1st Cav. Bde.

14 H Battery attached to 2nd Cav. Bde. on 28/9/14.

15 Regt. reassembled (from divnl. sqdns.) on 14/4/15, and joined 9th Cav. Bde.

16 Regt. reassembled (from divnl. sqdns.) on 14/4/15, and joined 9th Cav. Bde.

17 Joined 9th Cav. Bde. from England on 12/6/15.

18 Joined 9th Cav. Bde. from 2nd Cav. Div. on 14/4/15.

19 Joined from England on 23/5/15.

20 Joined from England on 23/8/15.

21 Formed in France on 26/9/15.

22 Attached to First Army Artillery School, 7/12/15–19/4/16.

23 Cav. Bde. M.G. Sqdns. were formed on 28/2/16.

24 Transferred on 21/11/16 to XV, R.H.A. (29th Div.).

25 Joined 18/3/16.

26 Absorbed by 57 (M.T.) Coy. on 10/10/16.

27 Left on 10/3/18 to join the Longpré Group and form in it a Cav. Corps Cyclist Regt. During the German Offensive in March, 1918, the 1/Bedf. Yeo. was used to reinforce the 1st Cav. Div. (as well as the 1/Essex Yeo.).

28 Joined on 1/12/16 from XV, R.H.A. (29th Div.).

29 Left for G.H.Q. on 23/10/17.

30 Formed 16/9/17.

31 Left on 14/2/18.

32 Joined on 10/3/18 from Ambala Cav. Bde. (5th Cav. Div.). Came on British W.E. on 11/3/18 (absorbing the 4th Sqdn.).

35 On 13/3/18 the 2nd Echelon of Supply was taken away; it was re-formed on 5/4/18. On 13/3/18 the designation of the Supply Column was changed to 1st Cav. Divnl. M.T. Coy. On 11/10/18, No. 3 (Ammn.) Sec. of 1st C.D.M.T. Coy. amalgamated with that of 3rd C.D.M.T. Coy. and became Cav. Corps Ammn. Park.

THE CAVALRY DIVISION

then

1st CAVALRY DIVISION

FORMATION, BATTLES, AND ENGAGEMENTS

The Cavalry Division had no permanent existence before the outbreak of War. The units of which it was composed on mobilization were quartered at various stations in England and Ireland, viz. :—the 1st Cav. Bde., VII. Bde., R.H.A., 1st Field Sqdn., R.E., 1st Signal Squadron, and No. 1 Signal Troop, at Aldershot ; the 2nd Cav. Bde. and No. 2 Signal Troop, at Tidworth ; the 3rd Cav. Bde., III. Bde., R.H.A., 4th Field Troop, and No. 3 Signal Troop, in Ireland (at the Curragh, Newbridge, and Dublin) ; and the 4th Cav. Bde., and No. 4 Signal Troop, were stationed at Canterbury, Shorncliffe, and London. The division crossed to France between the 15th and 18th August, concentrated to the East and South-east of Maubeuge between the 18th and 20th August, and began to move forward on the 21st.

Throughout the War the 1st Cavalry Division served on the Western Front in France and Belgium, and was engaged in the following operations :—

1914

23 and 24 Aug. ...	...**Battle of Mons.**
24 Aug.–5 Sept. ...	...**RETREAT FROM MONS.**
24 Aug.	...**Elouges.**
25 Aug.	...**Solesmes.**
26 Aug.	...**Battle of le Cateau** [under II. Corps].
1 Sept.	...**Néry.**
6–9 Sept. ...	...**Battle of the Marne.**
12–15 Sept. ...	...**BATTLE OF THE AISNE.**
12 Oct.–2 Nov. ...	...**Battle of Messines** [Cav. Corps].

1915

BATTLES OF YPRES

9 –13 May ...	...**Battle of Frezenberg Ridge** [Cav. Corps, until 12/5 ; then Cav. Force, Second Army].
24 May	...**Battle of Bellewaarde Ridge** [Cav. Corps, Second Army].

1916

BATTLES OF THE SOMME

15 Sept.	...**Battle of Flers-Courcelette** [in reserve to XIV. Corps, Fourth Army].

6

1917

BATTLES OF ARRAS

9–12 April ... ...**First Battle of the Scarpe** [Cav. Corps, G.H.Q. Reserve. Reinforced First and Third Armies].

BATTLE OF CAMBRAI

20 and 21 Nov. ...**The Tank Attack** [Cav. Corps.; placed under IV. Corps, on 20/11, Third Army].

23–26 Nov. ... ...**Capture of Bourlon Wood** [IV. Corps, Third Army].

30 Nov.–3 Dec. ... ...**German Counter-Attacks** [VII. Corps; then, on 1/12, Cav. Corps, Third Army].

1918

FIRST BATTLES OF THE SOMME

21–23 March ... ...**Battle of St. Quentin** [XIX. Corps, Fifth Army].

24 and 25 March ...**Battle of Bapaume** ["Dismounted Div." (24–26/3/18), under Br.-Gen. Legard; with VII. Corps, Fifth Army].

26 and 27 March ...**Battle of Rosières** [Cav. Corps, Fifth Army].

THE ADVANCE TO VICTORY

8–10 Aug. ... ...**Battle of Amiens** [Cav. Corps, Fourth Army].

SECOND BATTLES OF THE SOMME

21 Aug. ... ...**Battle of Albert** [Third Army].

BATTLES OF THE HINDENBURG LINE

8 Oct. ... ...**Battle of Cambrai** [Cav. Corps; but working with XIII. Corps and II. Am. Corps, Fourth Army].

9–12 Oct. ... ...**Pursuit to the Selle** [Cav. Corps, Fourth Army].

THE FINAL ADVANCE

17 Oct.–6 Nov. ... ...**In Picardy** [Cav. Corps, Fourth Army].

7–11 Nov. ... ...**In Artois** [I. Corps, until 10/11, then Cav. Corps, Fifth Army].

On the 11th November, the 1st Cavalry Division was on the Fifth Army front, and its leading troops reached a line north of Mons and about nine miles east of Ath. The division was withdrawn on the 12th, and concentrated near Peruwelz (north of Condé). On the 16th November, orders were issued that the division would lead and cover the advance of the Second Army into Germany, and the forward march was begun the next day. Moving through Namur (22nd), the division crossed the German frontier on the 1st December, the 1st Cav. Bde. covering the advance of the Canadian Corps and the rest of the division leading the march of the II. Corps. On the 6th December, the 2nd Cav. Bde. pushed on, reached Cologne, and secured the bridges over the Rhine, and on the next day the 1st and 9th Cav. Bdes. also reached the Rhine, south and north of Cologne respectively. On the 12th December the division (less 1st Cav. Bde.) crossed the Rhine by the Hohenzollern Bridge, whilst the 1st Cav. Bde. crossed at Bonn; and on the 13th December the brigades moved forward to their final positions on the perimeter of the bridgehead. The advance into Germany was over.

2ND CAVALRY DIVISION

G.O.C.

Formation	Major-General H. DE LA P. GOUGH.
19 April, 1915	Major-General C. T. McM. KAVANAGH.
15 July, 1915	Major-General Sir P. W. CHETWODE, Bt.
6 November, 1916	Br.-Gen. T. T. PITMAN (acting).
16 November, 1916	Major-General W. H. GREENLY
	(tempy. to 14th Div. on 22/3/18).
22 March, 1918	Br.-Gen. T. T. PITMAN (acting).
27 March, 1918	Major-General W. H. GREENLY
	(sick, 28/3/18).
28 March, 1918	Br.-Gen. T. T. PITMAN (acting).
16 April, 1918	Major-General T. T. PITMAN.

G.S.O. 1.

Formation ...Lt.-Col. W. H. GREENLY.
16 April, 1915...Lt.-Col. A. A. KENNEDY.
8 May, 1915...Lt.-Col. P. D. FITZGERALD.
7 Aug., 1916...Lt.-Col. N. R. DAVIDSON.
22 June, 1917...Lt.-Col. E. DE BURGH
    (tempy. to 14th Div. on 22/3/18).
22 Mar., 1918...Major F. W. BULLOCK-
    MARSHAM (acting).
27 Mar., 1918...Lt.-Col. E. DE BURGH.
13 May, 1918...Lt.-Col. M. GRAHAM.

A.-A. & Q.-M.-G.

Formation ...Major C. D. CHRISTOPHER
    (missing and captured, 12/9/14).
18 Sept., 1914...Lt.-Col. E. C. THRING.
21 Nov., 1914...Lt.-Col. G. McK. FRANKS.
6 Mar., 1915...Lt.-Col. E. L. ELLINGTON.
26 July, 1915...Lt.-Col. O. K. CHANCE.
9 Nov., 1915...Lt.-Col. A. J. McCULLOCH.
31 Oct., 1917...Lt.-Col. the Hon. G. V. A.
    MONCKTON-ARUNDELL.

C.R.H.A.
(and Officer Commdg. III, R.H.A.)

23 Sept., 1914...Lt.-Col. R. W. BREEKS
    (acted as liaison officer).
19 Mar., 1915...Lt.-Col. G. GILLSON.
14 Sept., 1915...Lt.-Col. J. S. OLLIVANT.
25 July, 1916...Lt.-Col. T. M. ARCHDALE.
27 Dec., 1916...Lt.-Col. A. MELLOR.

C.R.E.

(The division had no C.R.E.)

3rd CAVALRY BRIGADE

(Transferred on 13/9/14 from 1st Cav. Div.)

[Mobilization] Br.-Gen. H. DE LA P. GOUGH.
16 Sept., '14...Br.-Gen. J. VAUGHAN.
16 Oct., '15...Br.-Gen. J. A. BELL-SMYTH.

4th CAVALRY BRIGADE

(Transferred on 14/10/14 to 2nd Cav. Div. from 1st Cav. Div.)

[Mobilization] Br.-Gen. Hon. C. E. BINGHAM.
30 May, '15...Br.-Gen. T. T. PITMAN (Sick, 8–16/12/16, leave 17–29/12/16).
8 Dec., '16...Lt.-Col. S. R. KIRBY (acting).
17 Dec., '16...Lt.-Col. A. DUGDALE (acting).
30 Dec., '16...Br.-Gen. T. T. PITMAN.
24 Mar., '18...Lt.-Col. S. R. KIRBY (acting).
9 April, '18...Br.-Gen. C. H. RANKIN.

5th CAVALRY BRIGADE

(Originally independent, the Bde. was transferred to 2nd Cav. Div. on 13/9/14.)*

[Mobilization] Br.-Gen. Sir P. W. CHETWODE, Bt.
15 July, '15...Br.-Gen. F. WORMALD (killed, 3/10/15).
4 Oct., '15...Br.-Gen. T. T. PITMAN (tempy.).

5 Oct., '15...Br.-Gen. C. L. K. CAMPBELL (died, 31/3/18).
21 Mar., '18...Lt.-Col. W. F. COLLINS (acting)
8 April, '18...Br.-Gen. N. W. HAIG.
4 Nov., '18...Lt.-Col. A. C. LITTLE (acting).
10 Nov., '18...Br.-Gen. N. W. HAIG.

*The 5th Cavalry Brigade (Br.-Gen. Sir P. W. Chetwode, Bt.) went to France in August, 1914, as an independent cavalry brigade. The brigade was then composed of the following units :—2nd Dgns. (R. Scots Greys), 12th R. Lcrs., 20th Hussars, J Battery, R.H.A., and Ammn. Coln., 4th Field Troop, 5th Signal Troop, and 5th Cav. Field Ambce. Before its incorporation in the 2nd Cavalry Division, the 5th Cavalry Bde. had been engaged in the Battle of Mons (23rd and 24th August), at Cérizy (28th August), in the Retreat from Mons (23rd August–5th September), and in the Battle of the Marne (6th–9th September, 1914).

GENERAL NOTES

On many occasions the 2nd Cavalry Division formed dismounted units for service in the trenches—each cavalry brigade forming a regiment under the command of the brigadier.

The following units also served with the 2nd Cavalry Division :—

YEOMANRY :—**1/Leic. Yeo.** (from 8th Cav. Bde., 3rd Cav. Div.), joined the Longpré Group on 14/3/18, and was absorbed on 4/4/18 by the regiments of the 3rd Cav. Bde.

ARTILLERY :—**1/Warwickshire R.H.A. Battery** (landed in France on 1/11/14), was attached to the 2nd Cav. Div. from 4/12/14 to 14/4/15, when it was transferred to the 9th Cav. Bde. (1st Cav. Div.).

OTHER UNITS :—**No. 4 Sanitary Section** from 12/1/1915–December, 1915 ; then as (renumbered) **No. 4A Sanitary Section** from January, 1916–Armistice.

2nd Cav. Div. Field Amb. Workshop joined the division by 26/2/15 ; and served with the division until 16/4/16, when the Workshop unit was absorbed by the Supply Column.

2ND CAVALRY DIVISION¹   ORDER OF BATTLE, 1914 - 1918

Dates	Brigades	CAVALRY — Regiments and attached Units	ARTILLERY — R.H.A. Brigades and Ammn. Colns.	R.H.A. Batteries	Light Armoured Cars	Engineers — Field Squadron	Signal Service — Signal Squadron	Cavalry Field Ambces.	Mobile Veterinary Sections	Divisional Employment Company	ARMY SERVICE CORPS — H.Q. 2nd Divnl. A.S.C.	2nd Cav. Supply Column	2nd Cav. Divnl. Aux. (Horse) Coy.	2nd Cav. Ammn. Park
											Company	Companies	Company	Company
1914 Sept.	3rd	4/Hsrs., 5/R. Ir. Lcrs., 16/Lcrs.; D Bty., R.H.A.;⁴ 3rd Signal Troop.	III⁴ & III Bde. Ammn. Coln.	...	...	2nd5	2nd6	2nd7 5th8	7th9 8th10	...	424 (H.T.)11	46 (M.T.)12 413 (M.T.)13	...	56 (M.T.)14
	5th	2/Dgns. (R. Scots Greys), 12/R.Lcrs., 20/Hsrs.; E Bty, R.H.A.;⁴ 5th Signal Troop.												
1916 Sept.	3rd	4/Hsrs., 5/R. Ir. Lcrs., 16/Lcrs.; D Bty., R.H.A.; 3rd Signal Troop.	III & III Bde. Ammn. Coln.	...	...	2nd	2nd	2nd 4th18 5th	7th 8th 9th19	...	424 (H.T.)	46 (M.T.) 413 (M.T.)	57520	56 (M.T.)
	4th15	6/D.G. (Carabiniers), 3/Hsrs., 1/Q.O.O. Hsrs.;16 J Bty., R.H.A.;17 4th Signal Troop.												
	5th	2/Dgns. (R. Scots Greys), 12/R. Lcrs., 20/Hsrs.; E Bty., R.H.A.; 5th Signal Troop.												
1916 June	3rd	4/Hsrs., 5/R. Ir. Lcrs., 16/Lcrs.; 3rd Cav. Bde. M.G. Sqdn.;21 3rd Signal Troop.	III & III Bde. Ammn. Coln.	...	...	2nd	2nd	2nd 4th 5th	7th 8th 9th	...	424 (H.T.)	46 (M.T.) 413 (M.T.)22	575	56 (M.T.)
	4th	6/D.G. (Carabiniers), 3/Hsrs., 1/Q.O.O. Hsrs.; J Bty., R.H.A.; 4th Cav. Bde. M.G. Sqdn.;21 4th Signal Troop.												
	5th	2/Dgns. (R. Scots Greys), 12/R. Lcrs., 20/Hsrs.; E Bty., R.H.A.; 5th Cav. Bde. M.G. Sqdn.;21 5th Signal Troop.												
1917 June	3rd	4/Hsrs., 5/R. Ir. Lcrs., 16/Lcrs.; 3rd Cav. M.G. Sqdn.; 3rd Signal Troop.	III & III Bde. Ammn. Coln.	...	...	2nd	2nd	2nd 4th 5th	7th 8th 9th	772nd25	424 (H.T.)	46 (M.T.)	575	56 (M.T.)24
	4th	6/D.G. (Carabiniers), 3/Hsrs., 1/Q.O.O. Hsrs.; J Bty. R.H.A.; 4th Cav. M.G. Sqdn.; 4th Signal Troop.												
	5th	2/Dgns. (R. Scots Greys), 12/R. Lcrs., 20/Hsrs.; E Bty. R.H.A.; 5th Cav. M.G. Sqdn.; 5th Signal Troop.												
1918 March	3rd	4/Hsrs., 5/R. Lcrs., 16/Lcrs.; 3rd Cav. M.G. Sqdn.; 3rd Signal Troop.	III & III Bde. Ammn. Coln.						2nd 4th 5th	7th 8th 9th	772nd	424 (H.T.)	46 (M.T.)25	575	...
	4th	6/D.G. (Carabiniers), 3/Hsrs., 1/Q.O.O. Hsrs.; J Bty., R.H.A.; 4th Cav. Bde. M.G. Sqdn.; 4th Signal Troop.												
	5th	2/Dgns. (R. Scots Greys), 12/R. Lcrs., 20/Hsrs.; E Bty., R.H.A.; 5th Cav. M.G. Sqdn.; 5th Signal Troop.												

NOTES ON ORDER OF BATTLE

1 Formed in the Field (on arrival on the Aisne) on 13/9/14.

2 Bde. transferred complete from The (or 1st) Cavalry Div. on 13/9/14.

3 Bde. (originally independent) was transferred complete on 13/9/14.

4 III, R.H.A., was transferred complete from the 1st Cav. Div. on 17/9/14; and the 2 Batteries were then posted to the 2 Cav. Bdes., viz.: D to 3rd, and E to 5th. Bde. H.Q. was then broken up, and was not re-formed until March, 1915.

5 Landed at Havre on 11/10/14, and on 15/10/14 absorbed 4th Field Trp. (then in France). Joined 2nd Cav. Div. on 16/10/14.

6 Formed in France about 28/9/14.

7 Transferred with 3rd Cav. Bde. from 1st Cav. Div. on 13/9/14.

8 Transferred to 2nd Cav. Div. with 5th Cav. Bde. on 13/9/14.

9 Joined 2nd Cav. Div. on 16/9/14.

10 Transferred with 3rd Cav. Bde. from 1st Cav. Div. on 16/9/14.

11 Formed in France on 10/10/14, and allotted as H.Q. Coy. to 2nd Cav. Div.

12 Formed on 3/8/14 in England, and crossed to France on 12/8/14.

13 Formed in France on 16/9/14, and allotted to 2nd Cav. Div. Supply Coln.

14 Formed on 3/8/14 in England, and crossed to France on 16/8/14.

15 Bde. transferred from 1st to 2nd Cav. Div. on 14/10/14.

16 Joined 1st Cav. Div. on 31/10/14; and posted to 4th Cav. Bde. on 11/11/14, to replace the Comp. Regt. of Household Cav. (squadrons returned to the Household Cav. Regts. in the 7th and 8th Cav. Bdes., 3rd Cav. Div.).

17 Left 5th Cav. Bde. on 16/9/14 to join 1st Cav. Div., and was posted to 4th Cav. Bde. and transferred with it to 2nd Cav. Div. on 14/10/14.

18 Joined from 1st Cav. Div. on 16/10/14.

19 Joined from 1st Cav. Div. on 15/10/14.

20 Formed in France on 25/9/15.

21 Bde. M.G. Sqdns. formed : 3rd on 29/2/16 ; 4th on 28/2/16 ; and 5th on 26/2/16.

22 Absorbed by 46 (M.T) Coy. on 10/10/16.

23 Formed on 16/9/17.

24 Left division in Dec., 1917.

25 On 12/3/18 the 2nd Echelon of Supply was taken away; it was re-formed on 5/4/18. On 12/3/18 the designation of the Supply Column was changed to 2nd Cav. Div. M.T. Coy.

2ND CAVALRY DIVISION

FORMATION, BATTLES, AND ENGAGEMENTS

On the 6th September, 1914, at the beginning of the Advance to the Aisne, the 3rd Cavalry Bde. (1st Cav. Div.), and the 5th Cavalry Bde. (until then independent), were placed under the orders of Br.-Gen. H. Gough. On the 13th September, on arrival on the Aisne, the two cavalry brigades (3rd and 5th) were formed into the 2nd Cavalry Division, the divisional troops (R.H.A., R.E., etc.) being added as they became available (see Order of Battle Table).

Throughout the War the 2nd Cavalry Division served on the Western Front in France and Belgium, and was engaged in the following operations :—

1914

12–15 Sept. ...	...**BATTLE OF THE AISNE**
12 Oct.–2 Nov. ...	...**Battle of Messines** [Cav. Corps].
13–17 Oct. ...	...**Battle of Armentières** (3rd and 4th Cav. Bdes.) [Cav. Corps].

BATTLES OF YPRES

30 and 31 Oct. ...	...**Battle of Gheluvelt** (3rd Cav. Bde. and part of 4th and 5th Cav. Bdes.) [I. Corps].

1915

10–12 March ...	...**Battle of Neuve Chapelle** (5th Cav. Bde.) [In Reserve to First Army].

BATTLES OF YPRES

26 April–3 May ...	...**Battle of St. Julien** [Plumer's Force, Second Army].
24 and 25 May ...	...**Battle of Bellewaarde Ridge** [V. Corps, Second Army].

1916

1917

BATTLES OF ARRAS

9–11 April ...	...**First Battle of the Scarpe** [Cav. Corps, Third Army].

BATTLE OF CAMBRAI

20 and 21 Nov.	...**The Tank Attack** [Cav. Corps, Third Army].
24–28 Nov. ...	...**Capture of Bourlon Wood** [Cav. Corps, Third Army].
30 Nov.–3 Dec. ...	...**The German Counter-Attacks** [Cav. Corps, Third Army].

1918

21 March–1 April	...**FIRST BATTLES OF THE SOMME.**
21–23 March ...	...**Battle of St. Quentin** [III. Corps, Fifth Army].

BATTLES OF THE LYS

14 and 15 April	...**Battle of Hazebrouck** [Cav. Corps, with Second Army].

THE ADVANCE TO VICTORY

8–11 Aug. ...	...**Battle of Amiens** [Cav. Corps, Fourth Army].

SECOND BATTLES OF THE SOMME

21–23 Aug. ...	...**Battle of Albert** [Third Army].
31 Aug.–3 Sept.	...**Second Battle of Bapaume** (4th Cav. Bde. and part 5th Cav. Bde.) [With Third Army].

BATTLES OF THE HINDENBURG LINE

27 Sept.–1 Oct. ...	...**Battle of the Canal du Nord** (3rd and 4th Cav. Bdes.) [With Third Army].
29 Sept.–2 Oct. ...	...**Battle of the St. Quentin Canal** (5th Cav. Bde.) [With Fourth Army].
3–5 Oct. ...	...**Battle of the Beaurevoir Line** (5th Cav. Bde.) [With Fourth Army].
8 and 9 Oct. ...	...**Battle of Cambrai** (5th Cav. Bde.) [With Fourth Army].
9–12 Oct. ...	...**Pursuit to the Selle** (3rd Cav. Bde.) [With First Army] ; (4th Cav. Bde.) [With Third Army] ; (5th Cav. Bde.) [With Fourth Army].

THE FINAL ADVANCE

17 Oct.–11 Nov.	...**In Picardy** [With First, Third, and Fourth Armies].
4 Nov.	...**Battle of the Sambre** (4th Cav. Bde.) [With Third Army] ; (5th Cav. Bde.) [With Fourth Army].
11 Nov.	...**Capture of Mons** (5/R. Lcrs. and 1 Sec. "D" R.H.A. (3rd Cav. Bde.)) [With 3rd Cdn. Div., Cdn. Corps, First Army].

On the 11th November the brigades of the 2nd Cavalry Division reached the following line :—5th Bde. (Fourth Army), Clairfayts (eight miles east of Avesnes) ; 4th Bde. (Third Army), Erquelinnes (eight miles east of Maubeuge) ; and 3rd Bde. (First Army), Havré and St. Denis (four miles east and north-east of Mons).

On the 15th November the 2nd Cavalry Division was re-formed near Maubeuge, and on the 16th orders were issued for the 2nd Cavalry Division to cover the front of the Fourth Army during the march into Germany. The advance was begun on the 17th November ; Ciney and Rochefort were reached on the 22nd, and on the 1st December the 5th Bde. crossed the German Frontier (south of St. Vith). Between the 17th and 20th December the division moved to the area (south and south-east of Liége) which had been allotted to it for winter quarters. Here it remained until the 30th January, 1919, when orders were received for the exchange of certain regiments with the 1st and 3rd Cavalry Divisions. The reconstituted 2nd Cavalry Division was to be sent back gradually to England, to be available for eventual service overseas. Finally at midnight, 31st March/1st April, the 2nd Cavalry Division ceased to exist.

3rd CAVALRY DIVISION

G.O.C.

29 Sept., 1914 (Formation)	Major-General the Hon. J. H. G. BYNG (to Cav. Corps, 19/4–4/5/15).
19 April, 1915	Br.-Gen. D. G. M. CAMPBELL (acting).
4 May, 1915	Major-General the Hon. J. H. G. BYNG.
7 May, 1915	Major-General C. J. BRIGGS.
12 October, 1915	Br.-Gen. C. B. BULKELEY-JOHNSON (acting).
15 October, 1915	Major-General J. VAUGHAN.
17 October, 1917	Br.-Gen. A. E. W. HARMAN (acting).
8 December, 1917	Major-General J., VAUGHAN.
14 March, 1918	Br.-Gen. A. E. W. HARMAN (acting).
5 May, 1918	Major-General A. E. W. HARMAN.

G.S.O. 1.

3 Oct., 1914...Lt.-Col. M. F. GAGE.
13 May, 1916...Major A. E. S. L. PAGET (acting).
22 May, 1916...Lt.-Col. R. G. HOWARD-VYSE.
25 May, 1916...Lt.-Col. A. E. S. L. PAGET (sick, 21/4/17).
21 April, 1917...Major E. DE BURGH (acting).
6 June, 1917...Lt.-Col. J. A. MUIRHEAD.
24 July, 1918...Lt.-Col. G. P. L. COSENS.

A.-A. & Q.-M.-G.

24 Sept., 1914...Lt.-Col. Hon. H. S. DAVEY.
25 Dec., 1914...Lt.-Col. R. O. BURNE (tempy.).
5 Jan., 1915...Lt.-Col. C. C. NEWNHAM.
19 Mar., 1916...Lt.-Col. W. A. FETHERSTONHAUGH.
2 Aug., 1917...Lt.-Col. G. P. L. COSENS.
24 July, 1918...Lt.-Col. T. W. PRAGNELL.

C.R.H.A.
(and Officer Commdg. XV., R.H.A.— renumbered IV., R.H.A., in May, 1915.)

1 Oct., 1914...Lt.-Col. C. H. DE ROUGEMONT.
21 Dec., 1914...Major E. O. LEWIN (acting).
19 Mar., 1915...Lt.-Col. J. G. ROTTON.
27 July, 1915...Lt.-Col. W. H. KAY.
14 April, 1916...Lt.-Col. P. WHEATLEY.
24 Aug., 1916...Lt.-Col. A. R. WAINEWRIGHT.
8 April, 1918...Lt.-Col. R. H. LASCELLES.

C.R.E.

(The division had no C.R.E.)

6th CAVALRY BRIGADE

(Formed in England on 19/9/14.)

21 Sept., '14...Br.-Gen. E. MAKINS
(sick, 7/11/14).
7 Nov., '14...Lt.-Col. O. B. B. SMITH-
BINGHAM (acting).
9 Nov., '14...Br.-Gen. D. G. M.
CAMPBELL.
19 April, '15...Lt.-Col. O. B. B. SMITH-
BINGHAM (acting).
4 May, '15...Br.-Gen. D. G. M.
CAMPBELL.
23 May, '16...Br.-Gen. A. E. W. HARMAN.
17 Oct., '17...Lt.-Col. A. BURT (acting).
8 Dec., '17...Br.-Gen. A. E. W. HARMAN.
14 Mar., '18...Br.-Gen. A. G. SEYMOUR
(sick, 8/8/18).
8 Aug., '18...Lt.-Col. F. H. D. C.
WHITMORE (acting).
15 Aug., '18...Lt.-Col. E. PATERSON
(acting).
2 Sept., '18...Br.-Gen. E. PATERSON.

7th CAVALRY BRIGADE

(Formed in England on 1/9/14.)

10 Sept., '14...Br.-Gen. C. T. McM.
KAVANAGH.
19 April, '15...Col. A. F. H. FERGUSON
(acting).
4 May, '15...Br.-Gen. A. A. KENNEDY.
9 Nov., '16...Lt.-Col. E. H. BRASSEY
(acting).
11 Nov., '16...Br.-Gen. B. P. PORTAL.
17 April, '18...Br.-Gen. A. BURT
(sick, 16/7/18).
16 July, '18...Lt.-Col. E. PATERSON
(acting).
15 Aug., '18...Lt.-Col. R. SPARROW
(acting).
17 Aug., '18...Br.-Gen. A. BURT.

8th CAVALRY BRIGADE

(Formed in Belgium on 20/11/14.)

23 Nov., '14...Br.-Gen. C. B. BULKELEY-
JOHNSON
(killed, 11/4/17).
11 April, '17...Lt.-Col. LORD
TWEEDMOUTH (acting).
14 April, '17...Br.-Gen. A. G. SEYMOUR.
(The 8th Cav. Bde. left the 3rd Cav.
Div. on 14/3/18.)

CANADIAN CAVALRY BRIGADE

(Transferred on 13/3/18 from the 5th
Cav. Div.)

[28 Jan., '15]...Br.-Gen. J. E. B. SEELY.
20 May, '18...Br.-Gen. R. W. PATERSON
(late Fort Garry Horse).

18

GENERAL NOTES

From March 22nd–25th (inclusive), 1918, the 3rd Cavalry Division provided the 3rd Dismounted Division, organized in three dismounted brigades.

Harman's Detachment (2nd Cav. Div. Mtd. Detnt. (Bonham's and Cook's Detnts.), 3rd Cav. Div. Mtd. Detnt. (Paterson), Reynolds's Detnt. of Northumberland Hsrs. (Corps Cav., III. Corps), " O " Battery, R.H.A., Theobald's Inf. Detnt., Detnt. of No. 13 Balloon Coy. (with eight Lewis guns), and Light Sec., 7th Cav. Fd. Ambce.) was formed on 23/3/18, and operated with 14th Div., III. Corps, Fifth Army, during the Battles of the Somme, until 27/3/18, when Harman's Detnt. was broken up, and **Reynolds's Force** (6th Cav. Bde. Detnt., 7th Cav. Bde. Detnt., North'd Hsrs., and two Vickers Guns— total strength about 300) was formed on the same day. Reynolds's Force was placed under III. Corps Heavy Artillery for reconnaissance duties. Reynolds's Force was broken up on 29/3/18, and the units rejoined their own formations.

On many occasions during the Great War, the 3rd Cavalry Division formed dismounted units for service in the trenches—each cavalry brigade forming a regiment under the command of the brigadier.

The following units also served with the 3rd Cavalry Division :—

CANADIAN CAVALRY BRIGADE—attached from 10/4/16–17/6/16. (Bde. transferred on 17/6/16 to 2nd Indian Cav. Div.)

OTHER UNITS :—**12th Sanitary Section** from 9/1/15 until the Armistice.

3rd Cav. Div. Field Amb. Workshop from 14/5/15–1/4/16, when it was absorbed into the 3rd Cav. Supply Column.

3RD CAVALRY DIVISION[1] ORDER OF BATTLE, 1914-1918

Dates	CAVALRY		ARTILLERY			Engineers	Signal Service	Cavalry Field Ambces.	Mobile Veterinary Sections	Divisional Employment Company	ARMY SERVICE CORPS			
	Brigades	Regiments and attached Units	R.H.A. Brigades and Ammn. Colns.	R.H.A. Batteries	Light Armoured Cars	Field Squadron	Signal Squadron				H.Q. 3rd Cav. Divnl. A.S.C. Company	3rd Cav. Supply Column Companies	3rd Cav. Divnl. Aux. (Horse) Coy. Company	3rd Cav. Ammn. Park Company
1914 October	6th[2]	3/D.G.,[3] 1/Royal Dgns.,[4] 10/Hsrs.;[5] C Bty., R.H.A.;[6] 6th Signal Troop.	XV[10] & XV Bde. Ammn. Coln.	...	...	3rd[11]	3rd[12]	6th[13] 7th[14]	13th[15] 14th[15]	...	81 (H.T.)[16]	73 (M.T.)[17] 414 (M.T.)[18]	...	78 (M.T.)[19]
	7th[7]	1/L.G., 2/L.G., R.H.G. 8 K Bty., R.H.A.;[9] 7th Signal Troop.												
1915 Sept.	6th	3/D.G., 1/Royal Dgns., 1/N. Som. Yeo.;[21] C Bty., R.H.A.; 6th Signal Troop.	IV[10] & IV Bde. Ammn. Coln.	...	...	3rd	3rd	6th 7th 8th[25]	13th 14th 20th[26]	...	81 (H.T.)	73 (M.T.) 414 (M.T.)	576[27]	76 (M.T.)
	7th	1/L.G., 2/L.G., 1/Leic. Yeo.;[22] K Bty., R.H.A.; 7th Signal Troop.												
	8th[20]	R.H.G., 10/Hsrs. 1/Essex Yeo.;[23] G Bty., R.H.A.;[24] 8th Signal Troop.												
1916 June	6th	3/D.G., 1/Royal Dgns., 1/N. Som. Yeo.; C Bty., R.H.A.; 6th Cav. Bde. M.G. Sqdn.;[28] 6th Signal Troop.	IV & IV Bde. Ammn. Coln.	...	No. 7 Bty.[29]	3rd	3rd	6th 7th 8th	18th 14th 20th	...	81 (H.T.)	73 (M.T.) 414 (M.T.)[30]	576	76 (M.T.)
	7th	1/L.G., 2/L.G., 1/Leic. Yeo.; K Bty., R.H.A.; 7th Cav. Bde. M.G. Sqdn.[28] 7th Signal Troop.												
	8th	R.H.G. 10/Hsrs. 1/Essex Yeo.; G Bty., R.H.A.; 8th Cav. Bde. M.G. Sqdn.;[28] 8th Signal Troop.												
1917 June	6th	3/D.G., 1/Royal Dgns., 1/N. Som. Yeo.;[33] C Bty., R.H.A.; 6th Cav. M.G. Sqdn.; 6th Signal Troop.	IV & IV Bde. Ammn. Coln.	...	No. 7 Bty.[43]	3rd	3rd	6th 7th 8th[44]	13th 14th 20th[45]	773rd[46]	81 (H.T.)	73 (M.T.)	576	78 (M.T.)[47]
	7th[31]	1/L.G.,[34] 2/L.G.,[35] 1/Leic. Yeo.;[36] K Bty., R.H.A.; 7th Cav. M.G. Sqdn.;[37] 7th Signal Troop.												
	8th[32]	R.H.G.,[38] 10/Hsrs.,[39] 1/Essex Yeo.;[40] G Bty., R.H.A.,[41] 8th Cav. M.G. Sqdn.;[42] 8th Signal Troop.												
1918 March	6th	3/D.G., 1/RoyalDgns. 10/Hsrs.,[49] C Bty., R.H.A.; 6th Cav. M.G. Sqdn.; 6th Signal Troop.	IV & IV Bde. Ammn. Coln.	...	...	3rd	3rd	6th 7th 7th Cdn.[48]	13th 14th "A" Cdn[48]	773rd	81 (H.T.)	73 (M.T.)[52]	576	...
	7th	7/D.G.,[50] 6/(Inniskilling) Dgns.,[50] 17/Lrs.,[50] K Bty., R.H.A.; 7th Cav. M.G. Sqdn.; 7th Signal Troop.												
	Canadian[48]	R. Cdn. Dgns., Lord Strathcona's Horse, Fort Garry Horse; R. Cdn. H.A. Bde.;[51] Cdn. Cav. M.G. Sqdn.; Cdn. Signal Troop.												

NOTES ON ORDER OF BATTLE

1 3rd Cav. Div. began formation at Windmill Hill Camp, near Salisbury, in September, 1914.

2 Began formation at Windmill Hill on 19/9/14.

3 Joined Bde. in Belgium on 4/11/14.

4 Joined on 19/9/14.

5 Joined at Windmill Hill. Transferred to 8th Bde. on 20/11/14.

6 Joined in Belgium on 19/10/14, and attached to 6th Bde.

7 Formed on 1/9/14 of the 3 Household Cav. Regts. The sqdns. of the Comp. Regt. of Household Cavy. (4th Cav. Bde.) rejoined their respective regts. in Belgium on 11/11/14.

8 Transferred to 8th Bde. on 21/11/14.

9 Joined 1/10/14; and attached to 7th Bde. on 16/10/14.

10 Formed 1/10/14. Renumbered IV, R.H.A., in May, 1915.

11 Formed 16/9/14. Joined 3rd Cav. Div. in Belgium on 19/10/14.

12 Formed 12/9/14.

13 Formed 14/9/14.

14 Formed 8/10/14.

15 Formed and went out with the division.

16 Formed, in England, 14/9/14.

17 Formed, in England, 4/9/14.

18 Formed, in France, 16/9/14.

19 Formed, in England, 4/9/14.

20 Formed, in Belgium, on 20/11/14.

21 Joined from England on 13/11/14.

22 Joined from England on 12/11/14.

23 Joined from England on 11/12/14.

24 Joined from V, R.H.A. (8th Division), on 25/11/14; and attached to 8th Bde.

25 Joined from England, and took over duty from 20th Fd. Amb. on 23/12/14.

26 Joined from England on 9/3/1915.

27 Formed in France on 23/9/15.

28 The 3 Bde. M.G. Sqdns. were all formed on 29/2/16.

29 Joined 30/8/16.

30 On 10/10/16, 414 Coy. was absorbed by 73 Coy.

31 Bde. reconstituted on 10/8/18.

32 Bde. left the division on 14/3/18.

33 Transferred to 8th Cav. Bde. on 13/3/18.

34 Left the division on 10/3/18.

35 Left the division on 10/3/18.

36 Transferred to 8th Cav. Bde. (in exchange with R.H.G.) on 7/11/17. 1/Leic. Yeo. left the division on 14/3/18.

37 Broken up on 14/4/18. The offrs. and men rejoined the Household Cav. Regts.

38 Transferred to 7th Cav. Bde. on 7/11/17 (see note 36). R.H.G. left the division on 10/3/18.

39 Transferred to 6th Cav. Bde. on 12/3/18.

40 Left division with the 8th Cav. Bde. on 14/3/18.

41 Transferred to XVII Bde. R.H.A. (5th Cav. Div.) on 13/3/18. G. & N. (of XVII) and XVII B.A.C. were transferred to V Army Bde., R.H.A., on 9/4/18; and 402 was then transferred to XIV A.F.A. Bde.

42 Transferred to the reconstituted 7th Cav. Bde. on 11/3/18 (instead of 11th Cav. M.G. Sqdn.). 8th was renumbered 7th on 4/5/18.

43 Left the division on 18/7/17.

44 Left the division on 14/3/18.

45 Left the division on 14/3/18.

46 Formed on 16/9/17.

47 Left the division on 23/12/17.

48 The Bde. was transferred complete from the 5th Cav. Div. on 13/3/18.

49 Transferred from 8th Cav. Bde. on 12/3/18.

50 These 3 Cav. Regts. were transferred on 1/3/18 to the Longpré Group (7/D.G. from the 5th Cav. Div. and the 6/Dgns. and 17/Lcrs. from 4th Cav. Div.). On 10/3/18 these 3 Cav. Regts joined the 7th Cav. Bde.; and on 11/3/18 the 3 Regts. came on the British War Estbmt. of 3 Sqdns. each (each Regt. absorbed its surplus squadron).

51 2 Btles., each 4, 13-pdr., guns. The Bde. rejoined the Cdn. Cav. Bde. on 14/4/18. It had been detached since Nov., 1917.

52 On 18/3/18 the 2nd Echelon of Supply was taken away; it was re-formed on 6/4/18. On 18/8/18 the designation of the Supply Coln. was changed to 3rd C.D.M.T. Coy. On 11/10/18 No.3 (Ammn.) Sec. of 3rd C.D.M.T. Coy. amalgamated with that of 1st C.D.M.T. Coy. and became Cav. Corps Ammn. Park.

3RD CAVALRY DIVISION

FORMATION, BATTLES, AND ENGAGEMENTS

The division had no existence before the outbreak of War. Only two brigades (and divisional troops) were allotted to it on its formation, in September, 1914, at Windmill Hill Camp, Ludgershall. The three Household Cav. Regts., which formed the 7th Bde., were quartered in peace time in London (2) and Windsor (1). The Bde. assembled at Ludgershall in the beginning of September, though the three Sqdns. of the Composite Household Regt. (already serving in France with the 4th Cav. Bde.) did not rejoin their respective regiments until 11th November. The two regiments (1/R. Dgns. and 10/Hsrs.) of the 6th Bde., which came from S. Africa, reached Ludgershall on the 19th and 22nd September, but the remaining regiment (3/D.G., from Cairo) did not join the Bde. until the 4th November. The third brigade (the 8th) was formed on the 20th November in Belgium (see Order of Battle Table). XV., R.H.A., was formed on the 1st October, and K Battery (from Christchurch) joined on the same day. C Battery (from Canterbury) joined in Belgium on the 19th October. The 3rd Field Sqdn., formed on the 16th September, at Ludgershall, embarked on the 12th October, disembarked at Boulogne on the 14th, and joined the division in front of Ypres on the 19th October. The 3rd Signal Sdqn, was formed at Ludgershall on the 12th September, and accompanied the division to Belgium.

The 3rd Cavalry Division left Ludgershall on the 5th October ; on the 6th embarkation began at Southampton ; on the 8th the division disembarked at Ostend ; and on the 9th it moved forward to Bruges.

Throughout the War the 3rd Cavalry Division served on the Western Front in France and Belgium, and was engaged in the following operations :—

1914

9 and 10 Oct. ...	...Antwerp Operations [IV. Corps].
19 Oct.–20 Nov.	...**BATTLES OF YPRES**
21–24 Oct. ...	...**Battle of Langemarck** [IV. Corps].
29–31 Oct. ...	...**Battle of Gheluvelt** [I. Corps].
11 Nov.	...**Battle of Nonne Bosschen** [I. Corps].

1915

BATTLES OF YPRES

11–13 May ...	...**Battle of Frezenberg Ridge** [Cav. Corps, until 12/5, then Cav. Force, Second Army].
26–28 Sept. ...	...**Battle of Loos (Defence of Loos)** [IV. Corps, First Army].

1916

1917

BATTLES OF ARRAS

9–12 April ...	...**First Battle of the Scarpe** [Cav. Corps, Third Army].
10 and 11 April	...**Attack of Monchy le Preux.**

1918

21–27 March and 1–5 April }	...BATTLES OF THE SOMME
21–23 March ...	...Battle of St. Quentin [III. Corps, Fifth Army].
24 and 25 March	...Actions at the Somme Crossings [XVIII. Corps, Fifth Army].
4 and 5 April ...	...Battle of the Avre [XIX. Corps, Fourth Army].

THE ADVANCE TO VICTORY

8–11 Aug. ...	...Battle of Amiens [Cav. Corps, Fourth Army].

BATTLES OF THE HINDENBURG LINE

8 and 9 Oct. ...	...Battle of Cambrai [Cav. Corps, Fourth Army].
9–12 Oct. ...	...The Pursuit to the Selle [Cav. Corps, Third and Fourth Armies].
9–11 Nov. ...	...THE FINAL ADVANCE IN FLANDERS [Cav. Corps, Second Army].

On the 11th November, the leading troops of the 3rd Cavalry Division had reached the line of the Dendre at Leuze and Lessines. That night the division was withdrawn to the east of the Schelde near Tournai. Instructions were received on the 15th that the 3rd Cavalry Division (moving on the left of the front allotted to the Cavalry Corps) would cover the advance of the Second Army. On the 17th, the division moved forward, on the 21st its headquarters were established at Waterloo, and the 6th Brigade (in which was the 1/Royal Dragoons) marched across the old battlefield. Transport difficulties prevented more than one cavalry division accompanying the Second Army, so the 3rd Cavalry Division remained to pass the winter in Belgium.

Beginning in December, demobilization was gradually carried out. On the 31st March, 1919, the 3rd Cavalry Division ceased to exist, and its place was taken (for administrative purposes) by the 3rd Cavalry Division Cadre Brigade.

GUARDS DIVISION

G.O.C.

15 August, 1915... ... ... Br.-Gen. F. J. HEYWORTH (tempy.).
18 August, 1915... ... ... Major-General EARL OF CAVAN.
3 January, 1916 ... ... Major-General G. P. T. FEILDING.
11 September, 1918 ... ... Major-General T. G. MATHESON.

G.S.O. 1.

25 Aug., 1915...Lt.-Col. Hon. W. P. HORE-
RUTHVEN.
21 Mar., 1916...Lt.-Col. C. P. HEYWOOD.
5 Sept., 1917...Lt.-Col. Hon. A. G. A.
HORE-RUTHVEN, V.C.
24 Dec., 1917...Lt.-Col. R. S. McCLINTOCK.
30 Mar., 1918...Lt.-Col. E. W. M. GRIGG.

A.-A. & Q.-M.-G.

16 Aug., 1915...Lt.-Col. W. H. V. DARELL.
24 Dec., 1916...Lt.-Col. F. G. ALSTON.
[6 Dec., 1918...Lt.-Col. H. L. AUBREY-
FLETCHER.]

B.-G., R.A.

30 Aug., 1915...Br.-Gen. C. E. GOULBURN.
12 Sept., 1915...Br.-Gen. A. E. WARDROP.
1 Mar., 1916...Br.-Gen. W. EVANS.
12 June, 1917...Br.-Gen. F. A. WILSON.

C.R.E.

26 Aug., 1915...Lt.-Col. J. E. VANRENEN
(sick, 1/10/15).
1 Oct., 1915...Major A. BROUGH (acting).
1 Nov., 1915...Lt.-Col. A. BROUGH.
10 July, 1917...Lt.-Col. E. F. W. LEES.

1st GUARDS BRIGADE*

[29 June, '15] Br.-Gen. G. P. T. FEILDING*
(wounded, 8/12/15).
8 Dec., '15...Lt.-Col. G. D. JEFFREYS
(acting).
13 Dec., '15...Br.-Gen. G. P. T. FEILDING
(invalided for treatment, 15/12/15).
15 Dec., '15...Lt.-Col. G. D. JEFFREYS
(acting).
9 Jan., '16...Br.-Gen. C. E. PEREIRA.
31 Dec., '16...Br.-Gen. G. D. JEFFREYS.
22 Sept., '17...Br.-Gen. C. R. CHAMPION
DE CRESPIGNY.

2nd GUARDS BRIGADE

26 Aug., '15...Br.-Gen. J. PONSONBY.
19 Nov., '16...Br.-Gen. Lord H. C.
SEYMOUR.
21 Mar., '17...Br.-Gen. J. PONSONBY.
22 Aug., '17...Br.-Gen. B. N. SERGISON-
BROOKE
(wounded, 23/3/18).
23 Mar., '18...Lt.-Col. G. B. S. FOLLETT
(acting).
25 Mar., '18...Br.-Gen. G. B. S. FOLLETT.
22 April, '18...Lt.-Col. A. F. A. N.
THORNE (acting).
25 April, '18...Br.-Gen. B. N. SERGISON-
BROOKE.

3rd GUARDS BRIGADE

15 Aug., '15...Lt.-Col. A. B. E. CATOR
(acting).
18 Aug., '15...Br.-Gen. F. J. HEYWORTH
(killed, 9/5/16).
9 May, '16...Lt.-Col. Lord H. C.
SEYMOUR (acting).
13 May, '16...Lt.-Col. W. MURRAY-
THREIPLAND (acting).
19 May, '16...Br.-Gen. C. E. CORKRAN.
21 Mar., '17...Br.-Gen. Lord H. C.
SEYMOUR.
2 April, '18...Lt.-Col. N. A. ORR-EWING
(acting).

22 April, '18...Br.-Gen. G. B. S. FOLLETT
(killed, 27/9/18).
28 Sept., '18...Lt.-Col. J. C. BRAND
(acting).
29 Sept., '18...Br.-Gen. C. P. HEYWOOD
(wounded, 5/11/18).
Night 5/6 Nov., '18 Lt.-Col. J. A.
STIRLING (acting).
11 Nov., '18...Br.-Gen. J. V. CAMPBELL,
V.C.

*The 4th Guards Bde. (Br.-Gen. Feilding) was transferred complete from the 2nd Div. to the Guards Div. On arrival, the Bde. was renumbered 1st Guards Bde. (see note 1, Order of Battle Table).

GENERAL NOTES

The following units also served with the Guards Division :—

45th Sanitary Section, from the formation of the division in August, 1915, until 9th April, 1917 (transferred to XVII. Corps).

Guards Divnl. Amb. Workshop, joined from England on 23rd August, 1915, and served with the division until 9th April, 1916 (transferred to the Divnl. Supply Coln.).

On the 17th November, 1918, the **4th Guards Bde.** (from G.H.Q. Reserve) rejoined the Guards Division at Maubeuge. The three battalions then returned to their original brigades, and the 4th Guards Bde. H.Q. and T.M.B. were disbanded.

On 2/2/18, the reorganization of the division on a 9-battalion basis was completed and by 25/2/18 the pioneer battalion was reorganized on a 3-company basis.

GUARDS DIVISION ORDER OF BATTLE, 1915 - 1918

Dates	Brigades	Battalions and attached Units	Mounted Troops	Field Artillery Brigades	Batteries	Bde. Ammn. Columns	Trench Mortar Medium	Trench Mortar Heavy	Divnl. Ammn. Col.	Engineers Field Cos.	Signal Service Divnl. Signal Coy.	Pioneers	M.G. Units	Field Ambulances	Mobile Vety. Secn.	Divnl. Emplnt. Coy.	Divnl. Train
1915 Aug. Sept.	1st Gds.1	2/G.G., 2/C.G., 3/C.G., 1/I.G. ; 1st Gds. Bde. M.G. Coy.2	Household Cavy. Divnl. Sqdn.11	LXXIV13	A, B, C, D	LXXIV B.A.C.	...	...	Gds. D.A.C.17	55th18	Gds.20	4/C.G. (P.)21	...	3rd22	46th25	...	Gds.26
	2nd Gds.5	3/G.G., 4 1/C.G.,5 1/S.G.,5 2/I.G.,4 2nd Gds. Bde. M.G. Coy.2		LXXV14	A, B, C, D	LXXV B.A.C.				76th19				4th23			
	3rd Gds.6	1/G.G.,7 4/G.G.,8 2/S.G.,9 1/W.G. ;10 3rd Gds. Bde. M.G. Coy.2	Household Cavy. Cyclist Coy.12	LXXVI14	A, B, C, D	LXXVI B.A.C.				76th19				9th24			
				LXI (H.)15	A (H.), B (H.), C (H.), D (H.)16	LXI B.A.C.											
1916 June	1st Gds.	2/G.G., 2/C.G., 3/C.G., 1/I.G. ; 1st Gds. Bde. M.G. Coy. ; 1st Gds. T.M. Bty.27	...	LXI28	A,31 B,32 C35	...37	X. Gds.38, Y. Gds.38, Z. Gds.38	V. Gds.39	Gds. D.A.C.57	55th	Gds.	4/C.G. (P.)	...	3rd	46th	...	Gds.
	2nd Gds.	3/G.G., 1/C.G., 1/S.G., 2/I.G. ; 2nd Gds. Bde. M.G. Coy. ; 2nd Gds. T.M. Bty.27		LXXIV29	A, B, C, D (H.)34					75th				4th			
	3rd Gds.	1/G.G., 4/G.G., 2/S.G., 1/W.G. ; 3rd Gds. Bde. M.G. Coy. ; 3rd Gds. T.M. Bty.27		LXXV29	A, B, C, D(H.)35					76th				9th			
				LXXVI30	A, B, C, D (H.)36												
1917 June	1st Gds.	2/G.G., 2/C.G.,40 1/I.G. ; 1st Gds. Bde. M.G. Coy. ; 1st Gds. T.M. Bty.	...	LXXIV...	A, B, C; D (H.)	...	X. Gds., Y. Gds., Z. Gds.41	V. Gds.41	Gds. D.A.C.	55th	Gds.	4/C.G. (P.)	4th Gds.42 M.G. Coy.	3rd	46th	Gds.43	Gds.
	2nd Gds.	3/G.G., 1/C.G., 1/S.G., 2/I.G. ;40 2nd Gds. Bde. M.G. Coy. ; 2nd Gds. T.M. Bty.		LXXV...	A, B, C; D (H.)					75th				4th			
	3rd Gds.	1/G.G., 4/G.G.,40 2/S.G., 1/W.G. ; 3rd Gds. Bde. M.G. Coy. ; 3rd Gds. T.M. Bty.								76th				9th			
1918 March	1st Gds.	2/G.G., 2/C.G., 1/I.G. ; 1st Gds. T.M. Bty.	...	LXXIV...	A, B, C; D (H.)	...	X. Gds., Y. Gds.	...	Gds. D.A.C.	55th	Gds.	4/C.G. (P.)	4th Bn.44 Guards M.G. Regt.	3rd	46th	Gds.	Gds.
	2nd Gds.	3/G.G., 1/C.G., 1/S.G. ; 2nd Gds. T.M. Bty.		LXXV...	A, B, C; D (H.)					75th				4th			
	3rd Gds.	1/G.G., 2/S.G., 1/W.G. ; 3rd Gds. T.M. Bty.								76th				9th			

NOTES ON ORDER OF BATTLE

1 4th Gds. Bde. joined complete from 2nd Div. (19/8/15), and renumbered 1st Gds. Bde. (20/8/15). The 2 Gds. Bns. of the old 1st Gds. Bde., 1st Div., joined the 2nd Gds. Bde. (see note 5).

2 Bde. M.G. Cos. were formed between 1/9–19/9/15.

Formed between 10–25/8/15.

4 Joined from England, 19/8/15.

5 Transferred from 1st Gds. Bde., 1st Div. (23/8/15); and arrived, 25/8/15.

6 Formed 15/8/15.

7 Transferred from 20th Bde., 7th Div. (4/8/16); and arrived, 5/8/16.

8 Joined from England, 18/8/15.

9 Transferred from 20th Bde., 7th Div. (8/8/15); and arrived, 9/8/15.

10 Joined from England, 20/8/15.

11 Arrived in France, 5/8/15. Broken up, 20/6/16, and held as reinforcements for 1st Life Gds.

12 Arrived in France, 13/8/15. Broken up, 27/5/16, and held as reinforcements for 2nd L.G. and R.H.G. (The Blues).

13 Joined 30/8/15, from 16th Divnl. Artillery (Ireland).

14 Joined 4/9/15, from 16th Divnl. Artillery (Ireland).

15 Joined from England, 24/8/15, from 11th Divnl. Artillery (left behind when 11th Div. went to Gallipoli in July, 1915).

16 D/LXI was transferred to 50th Div., 21/2/16.

17 Joined from England, 3/9/15.

18 Joined 1/9/15, from 7th Div.

19 Joined on 25 and 26/8/16, from 16th Div. (Ireland).

20 Joined 18/8/15, from 16th Div. (Ireland).

21 Joined from England, 18/8/15.

22 Joined from 1st Div. on 25/8/15.

23 Joined, with 1st Gds. Bde., from 2nd Div. (note 1).

24 Joined from 3rd Div. on 28/8/15.

25 Joined from England on 17/8/15.

26 Joined on 24/8/15. 11, 124, 188, and 436 Cos., A.S.C.

27 Bde. T.M. Bties. formed : 1st between 2–18/5/16 ; 2nd in April, 1916 ; and 3rd by 24/3/16.

28 Reorganized 14/11/16 into 2, 6-gun bties. Bde. then broken up, and A became C/LXXIV, and B became B/LXXV.

29 18-pdrs. reorganized 14/11/16 into 6-gun bties. In LXXIV, C was split between A and B ; and in LXXV, B between A and C.

30 18-pdrs. reorganized 14/11/16 into 6-gun bties. Bde. became A.F.A. Bde. 19/1/17. D (H.) split up between D/LXXIV and D/LXXV. B/LXXXI joined 19/1/17 and became C ; and 503 (H.) joined (from England) 7/4/17, and became D (H.). A/LXXXVI was split up on 13/11/16 between B and C.

31 Until 15/5/16, D/LXXIV.

32 Until 15/5/16, D/LXXV.

33 Until 15/5/16, D/LXXVI. C/LXI was split up on 13/11/16 between A and B/LXI.

34 Until 15/5/16, A/LXI (H.).

35 Until 15/5/16 B/LXI (H.).

36 Until 15/5/16, C/LXI (H.).

37 D.A.C. reorganized, and B.A.C.'s abolished, 13/5/16.

38 Formed March, 1916.

39 Formed May, 1916.

40 On 8/2/18 4/G.G., 3/C.G., and 2/I.G., were formed into 4th Gds. Bde. (Br.-Gen. Lord Ardee). The Bde. joined 31st Div. at noon on 8/2/18.

On 12/2/18, 94th M.G. Coy. and 94th T.M. Bty. joined the Bde. (temporarily). The 4th Gds. T.M. Bty. was formed on 16/3/18.

41 On the reorganization of the T.M.B.'s on 8/2/18, Z was distributed between X and Y ; and V left the division.

42 Joined on 27/3/17, from England.

43 Formed by 30/6/17.

44 On 1/3/18 the Bn. (consisting of 1st, 2nd, 3rd, and 4th Gds. M.G. Cos.) was formed as 4th Bn. M.G. Guards. In May, the designation of the Bn. became 4th Bn. Guards M.G. Regt. (authy. R.W. d/d. 10/5/18).

GUARDS DIVISION

FORMATION, BATTLES, AND ENGAGEMENTS

In July, 1915, His Majesty approved the formation of a Guards Division, and in August, 1915, the Guards Division was formed in France, the units, on arrival, being concentrated around Lumbres (near St. Omer).

Throughout the War the Guards Division served on the Western Front in France and Belgium, and it was engaged in the following operations :—

1915

26 Sept.-8 Oct. ...	...**Battle of Loos** [XI. Corps, First Army].
16–19 Oct. ...	...**Hohenzollern Redoubt** [XI. Corps, First Army].

1916

BATTLES OF THE SOMME

15–16 Sept. 20–22 Sept. }...	...**Battle of Flers-Courcelette** [XIV. Corps, Fourth Army].
25–28 Sept. ...	...**Battle of Morval** [XIV. Corps, Fourth Army].
25 Sept.	...**Capture of Lesboeufs.**

1917

14–24 March ...	...**German Retreat to the Hindenburg Line** [XIV. Corps, Fourth Army].

BATTLES OF YPRES

31 July–2 Aug. ...	...**Battle of Pilckem Ridge** [XIV. Corps, Fifth Army].
9 Oct.	...**Battle of Poelcappelle** [XIV. Corps, Fifth Army].
12 Oct.	...**First Battle of Passchendaele** [XIV. Corps, Fifth Army].

BATTLE OF CAMBRAI

24–28 Nov. ...	...**Capture of Bourlon Wood** [IV. Corps, Third Army].
30 Nov.–3 Dec. ...	...**German Counter-Attacks** [III. Corps, Third Army].
30 Nov.	...**Recapture of Gouzeaucourt.**

1918

FIRST BATTLES OF THE SOMME

21–23 March ...	...**Battle of St. Quentin** [VI. Corps, Third Army].
24 and 25 March	...**First Battle of Bapaume** [VI. Corps, Third Army].
28 March ...	...**First Battle of Arras** [VI. Corps, Third Army].

THE ADVANCE TO VICTORY
SECOND BATTLES OF THE SOMME

21–23 Aug. ...	...**Battle of Albert** [VI. Corps, Third Army].

SECOND BATTLES OF ARRAS

26–30 Aug. ...	...**Battle of the Scarpe** [VI. Corps, Third Army].
2 and 3 Sept. ...	...**Battle of the Drocourt-Quéant Line** [VI. Corps, Third Army].

BATTLES OF THE HINDENBURG LINE

12 Sept.	...**Battle of Havrincourt** [VI. Corps, Third Army].
27 Sept.	...**Battle of the Canal du Nord** [VI. Corps, Third Army].
8 and 9 Oct. ...	...**Battle of Cambrai** [VI. Corps, Third Army].
9–12 Oct. ...	...**Pursuit to the Selle** [VI. Corps, Third Army].

THE FINAL ADVANCE IN PICARDY

17–22 Oct. ...	...**Battle of the Selle** [VI. Corps, Third Army].
4 Nov.	...**Battle of the Sambre** [VI. Corps, Third Army].
9 Nov.	...**Occupation of Maubeuge.**

On the 11th November the Guards Division was in and around Maubeuge. On the 17th November, the 4th Guards Brigade rejoined the division (see note on p. 27). Ordered to the Rhine, the Guards Division began its march on the 18th November, and crossed the frontier into Germany on the 11th December. On the 14th December the 2nd Guards Brigade was sent on by train to Cologne and detrained there on the same day. Divisional H.Q. opened at Cologne on the 18th December, and the remainder of the Guards Division reached its final area on the 19th. Battalions began to return to England on the 20th February, 1919, and the moves of the last units of the division were completed by the 29th April, 1919.

1st DIVISION

G.O.C.

Mobilization... ... ... Major-General S. H. LOMAX
(wounded, 31/10/14).
31 October, 1914... ... ... Major-General H. J. S. LANDON (tempy.).
22 November, 1914 ... ... Major-General Sir D. HENDERSON.
19 December, 1914 ... ... Major-General R. C. B. HAKING.
11 September, 1915 ... ... Major-General A. E. A. HOLLAND.
12 June, 1916 ... ... Major-General E. P. STRICKLAND.

G.S.O. 1

Mobilization ...Col. R. FANSHAWE.
22 Sept., 1914...Col. F. W. KERR
(killed, 31/10/14).
3 Nov., 1914...Col. H. S. JEUDWINE.
3 Jan., 1915...Lt.-Col. E. S. H. NAIRNE.
26 July, 1915...Lt.-Col. J. A. LONGRIDGE
(killed, 18/8/16).
18 Aug., 1916...Lt.-Col. W. G. S. DOBBIE.
10 Jan., 1918...Lt.-Col. E. N. TANDY.
[25 Nov., 1918...Lt.-Col. D. J. C. K.
BERNARD.]

A.-A. & Q.-M.-G.

Mobilization ...Lt.-Col. N. J. G. CAMERON.
18 Sept., 1914...Lt.-Col. A. F. GORDON.
10 Apl., 1915...Lt.-Col. H. S. L.
RAVENSHAW.
19 May, 1915...Lt.-Col. J. B. G. TULLOCH.
17 Mar., 1917...Lt.-Col. A. E. HOLBROOK.
26 July, 1917...Lt.-Col. H. H. SPENDER-
CLAY.
8 Nov., 1918...Lt.-Col. S. A. THOMPSON.

B.-G., R.A.

Mobilization ...Br.-Gen. N. D. FINDLAY
(killed, 10/9/14).
10 Sept., 1914...Br.-Gen. H. S. HORNE
(tempy.).
18 Sept., 1914...Br.-Gen. E. A. FANSHAWE.
8 July, 1915...Br.-Gen. C. E. D. BUDWORTH.
19 Oct., 1915...Br.-Gen. G. N. CARTWRIGHT.
19 Oct., 1917...Br.-Gen. H. F. E. LEWIN.

C.R.E.

Mobilization ...Lt.-Col. A. L. SCHREIBER.
30 Apl., 1915...Major C. RUSSELL-BROWN
(acting).
10 May, 1915...Lt.-Col. H. F. THUILLIER.
2 Oct., 1915...Lt.-Col. C. RUSSELL-
BROWN.
22 Feb., 1918...Lt.-Col. C. E. P. SANKEY.

1st (GUARDS) BRIGADE

Mobilization...Br.-Gen. F. I. MAXSE.
26 Sept., '14...Br.-Gen. C. FITZCLARENCE
(killed, 12/11/14).
12 Nov., '14...Col. D. L. MacEwen
(acting).
23 Nov., '14...Br.-Gen. H. C. LOWTHER.

[On 23/8/15 the 2 Guards Bns. were transferred to the Guards Div. and the 1st (Guards) Bde. became 1st Bde.]

1st BRIGADE

23 Aug., '15...Br.-Gen. A. J. REDDIE.
18 Oct., '17...Br.-Gen. J. R. M.
MINSHULL-FORD.
21 Oct., '17...Br.-Gen. C. J. C. GRANT.
29 Mar., '18...Lt.-Col. Sir T. W. H. J.
ERSKINE, Bt. (acting).
3 April, '18...Br.-Gen. W. B. THORNTON.
22 Sept., '18...Br.-Gen. L. L. WHEATLEY.

2nd BRIGADE

Mobilization...Br.-Gen. E. S. BULFIN
(wounded, 1/11/14).
10 Nov., '14...Col. C. CUNLIFFE-OWEN
(acting).
23 Nov., '14...Br.-Gen. C. B. WESTMACOTT.
5 May, '15...Br.-Gen. G. H. THESIGER.
22 Aug., '15...Br.-Gen. J. H. W. POLLARD
(wounded, 1/10/15).
5 Oct., '15...Br.-Gen. H. F. THUILLIER.
10 Mar., '16...Br.-Gen. A. B. HUBBACK
(wounded, 1/7/17).
6 July, '17...Br.-Gen. G. C. KEMP
(wounded, 2/3/18).
2 Mar., '18...Lt.-Col. R. BELLAMY
(acting).
5 Mar., '18...Br.-Gen. Sir W. A. I. KAY,
Bt.
(wounded, 17/3/18).
17 Mar., '18...Lt.-Col. R. BELLAMY
(acting)
(wounded, 21/3/18).
21 Mar., '18...Lt.-Col. G. St. G. ROBINSON
(acting).
23 Mar., '18...Br.-Gen. G. C. KELLY
(wounded, 26/9/18).
26 Sept., '18...Lt.-Col. D. S. JOHNSON
(acting).
[21 Nov., '18...Br.-Gen. G. C. KELLY
(returned).]

3rd BRIGADE

Mobilization...Br.-Gen. H. J. S. LANDON
(in tempy. cd., 1st Div., 31/10/14).
1 Nov., '14...Col. A. C. LOVETT (acting).
22 Nov., '14...Br.-Gen. R. H. K. BUTLER.
21 Feb., '15...Br.-Gen. H. R. DAVIES.
19 Nov., '16...Br.-Gen. G. S. G.
CRAUFURD.
3 Mar., '17...Br.-Gen. R. C. A.
McCALMONT.
15 Mar., '17...Br.-Gen. J. L. CLARKE.
21 Mar., '17...Br.-Gen. R. C. A.
McCALMONT.
18 Nov., '17...Br.-Gen. R. B. BARKER.
23 Jan., '18...Br.-Gen. H. H. S. MORANT
(wounded, 21/5/18).
23 May, 18...Br.-Gen. Sir W. A. I. KAY,
Bt.
(killed, 4/10/18).
4 Oct., '18...Br.-Gen. J. V. CAMPBELL,
V.C.

(Of 137th Bde. (46th Div.),
remained in tempy. command for 24 hours).
6 Oct., '18...Br.-Gen. E. ST. G. AUBYN.

GENERAL NOTES

In 1917 the following units were attached to the 1st Division for the projected Belgian coastal operation :—

> 11th M.M.G. Bty.,
> 12th M.M.G. Bty.,
> 14th M.M.G. Bty.
> and
> 13th Cyclist Bn.
> 17th Cyclist Bn.
>
> from 19/7–17/10/1917.

The following Units also served with the 1st Division :—

INFANTRY (T.F.) :—**5/R. Suss.** joined 2nd Bde., 21/2/15, and was transferred to 48th Div., as Pioneers, 20/8/15.

5/King's Own joined 2nd Bde., from 28th Div., 21/10/15, and was transferred to the 55th Div., 7/1/16.

4/R.W.F. joined 3rd Bde., 7/12/14, and was transferred to the 47th Div., as Pioneers, 1/9/15.

6/Welsh joined 3rd Bde., from 28th Div., on 23/10/15, and became Divisional Pioneers on 15/5/16.

ARTILLERY :—**No. 3 Pom-Pom Section (A.-A.)**, 22/9–16/12/1914.

7th Mountain Battery, from 24/12/14–4/2/15 (transferred to 2nd Division).

OTHER UNITS :—**13th Sanitary Section**, joined by 30/1/15, and served with the division until 2/4/16 (transferred to a Fourth Army Area).

1st Divnl. Ambulance Workshop, joined by 30/1/15, and served until 7/4/16 (transferred to Divnl. Supply Coln.).

On 8/2/18 the reorganization of the division on a 9-battalion basis was completed ; and by 26/2/18 the pioneer battalion was reorganized on a 3-company basis.

1st DIVISION ORDER OF BATTLE, 1914 - 1918

Dates	INFANTRY Brigades	Battalions and attached Units	Mounted Troops	ARTILLERY Field Artillery Brigades	Batteries	Bde. Ammn. Columns	Heavy Battery	T.M.B. Medium	T.M.B. Heavy	Divnl. Ammn. Col.	Engineers Field Cos.	Signal Service Divnl. Signal Coy.	Pioneers	M.G. Units	Field Ambulances	Mobile Vety. Sectn.	Divnl. Emplnt. Coy.	Divnl. Train
1914 August	1st (G'ds.) 2nd 3rd	1/C.G.,[1] 1/S.G.,[1] 1/B.W., 2/R.M.F.[2] 2/R. Suss., 1/L.N.I., 1/North'n., 2/K.R.R.C. 1/Queen's,[3] 1/S.W.B., 1/Glouc., 2/Welsh.	C. Sqdn., 15/Hsrs.[4]	XXV. XXVI. XXXIX XLIII (H.)	113, 114, 115 116, 117, 118[5] 46, 51, 54 30 (H.), 40 (H.), 57 (H.)[6]	XXV B.A.C. XXVI B.A.C. XXXIX B.A.C. XLIII (H.) B.A.C.	26 H.B.[7] & Hy. Bty. A.C.	…		1st D.A.C.	23rd 26th	1st	…	…	1st 2nd 3rd[17]	2nd	…	1st[8]
1915 Sept.	1st 2nd 3rd	1/B.W., 1/Cam. H., 10/Glouc.,[9] 8/R. Berks,[10] 14/Lond. (L.S.)[11] 2/R. Suss., 1/L.N.I., 1/North'n., 2/K.R.R.C., 9/King's,[12] 1/S.W.B., 1/Glouc., 2/Welsh, 2/R.M.F.; [3]	B Sqdn., 1/N'berland Hsrs.,[4] [13]; 1st Cyclist Coy.[14]	XXV. XXVI. XXXIX XLIII (H.)[15]	113, 114, 115 116, 117 46, 51, 54 30 (H.), 40 (H.)	XXV B.A.C. XXVI XXXIX XLIII (H.) B.A.C.	…	…		1st D.A.C.	23rd 26th 1/Lowland[16]	1st	…	…	1st 2nd 141st[17]	2nd	…	1st
1916 June	1st 2nd 3rd	1/B.W., 1/Cam. H., 10/Glouc., 8/R. Berks.; 1st Bde. M.G. Coy.;[18] 1st T.M. Bty.[19] 2/R. Suss., 1/L.N.I., 1/North'n., 2/K.R.R.C.; 2nd Bde. M.G. Coy.;[18] 2nd T.M. Bty.[19] 1/S.W.B., 1/Glouc., 2/Welsh, 2/R.M.F.; 3rd Bde. M.G. Coy.;[18] 3rd T.M. Bty.[19]	…	XXV. XXVI[20] XXXIX	113, 114, 115; D. (H.)[21] 116, 117; 40 (H.)[15] 46, 51, 54; 30 (H.)[15]	[22]	…	X.125 Y.123 Z.123	V.1[24]	1st D.A.C.[22]	23rd 26th 1/Lowland	1st	6/Welsh (P.)[25]	…	1st 2nd 141st	2nd	…	1st
1917 June	1st 2nd 3rd	1/B.W., 1/Cam. H., 10/Glouc.,[26] 8/R. Berks.[27] 1st M.G. Coy.; 1st T.M. Bty. 2/R. Suss., 1/L.N.I., 1/North'n., 2/K.R.R.C.; 2nd M.G. Coy.; 2nd T.M. Bty. 1/S.W.B., 1/Glouc., 2/Welsh, 2/R.M.F.;[29] 3rd M.G. Coy.; 3rd T.M. Bty.	…	XXV. XXXIX	113, 114, 115; 40 (H.)[20]; 21 46, 51, 54; 30 (H.)[21]	…	…	X.1 Y.1 Z.130	V.130	1st D.A.C.	23rd 26th 409th (Lowland)	1st	6/Welsh (P.)	216th M.G. Coy.[32]	1st 2nd 141st	2nd	204th[31]	1st
1918 March	1st 2nd 3rd	1/B.W., 1/L.N.I.,[28] 1/Cam. H.; 1st T.M. Bty. 2/R. Suss., 1/North'n., 2nd T.M. Bty. 1/S.W.B., 1/Glouc., 2/Welsh; 3rd T.M. Bty.	…	XXV. XXXIX	113, 114, 115; & 40 (H.) 46, 51, 54; & 30 (H.)	…	…	X.1 Y.1	…	1st D.A.C.	23rd 26th 409th	1st	6/Welsh (P.)	No. 1 Battn. M.G.C.[32]	1st 2nd 141st	2nd	204th	1st

NOTES ON ORDER OF BATTLE

1 Transferred, on 23/8/15, to 2nd Guards Bde., on formation of Guards Div.

2 Transferred to A.H.Q., 4/9/14; replaced on 5/9/14 by 1/Cam. H.

3 Transferred to I Corps H.Q., 8/11/14; replaced on 9/11/14 by 2/R.M.F.

4 Transferred to 9th Cav. Bde. on formation; and handed over to B Sqdn., Northumberland Hsrs., on 13/4/15 (from 7th Div.).

5 Transferred to 28th Div. on 4/2/15, and joined XXXI Bde. on 17/2/16.

6 Transferred to 8th Div. on 23/6/15, and joined CXXVIII (H.) Bde. on 5/8/15.

7 On the reorganization of the Artillery, in Feb., 1915, 26 H.B. was transferred in April to II Bde., No. 1 Group H.A.R. 26 H.B. was attached to 2nd Div. from 4/2/15—20/4/15.

8 7th, 18th, 16th and 36th Cos., A.S.C.

9 Joined 17/8/15.

10 Joined 16/8/15.

11 Joined 1st Bde., 7/11/14, and was transferred to 56th Div. on 8/2/16.

12 Joined 2nd Bde., 29/3/15, transferred to 3rd Bde., 12/11/15, and transferred to 55th Div. on 7/11/16.

13 Transferred to XIII Corps Cav., 18/4/16.

14 Transferred to I Corps Cyclist Bn., 15/6/16.

15 How. Bde. broken up, 22/5/16; 30 (less 1 sec.) transferred to XXXIX, and 40 (less 1 sec.) to XXXVI. 1 sec. 30 and 1 sec. 40 formed D/XXV.

16 Joined on 28/12/14.

17 3rd Fd. Amb. was transferred on 24/8/15 to Gds. Div. (on its formation); and 141st Fd. Amb. joined on 24/8/15.

18 Formed on 26/1/16.

19 T.M. Bties. joined the Bdes. by 27/11/15.

20 Became an A.F.A. Bde. on 14/1/17. 40 (H.) was transferred to XXV; and A/CLXV (from 33rd Div.) joined and became A/XXVI.

21 Joined 22/5/16. Formed from 1 sec. 30 and 1 sec. 40. On 16/1/17 D/XXV was broken up and the secs. returned to 30 (H.) and 40 (H.)

22 B.A.C.'s were abolished, and the D.A.C. was reorganized on 22/5/16.

23 X, Y and Z joined by 16/3/16.

24 V was formed on 13/1/17.

25 Joined 3rd Inf. Bde. on 23/10/15 from 28th Div. The Bn. was transferred and became Pioneers on 15/6/16.

26 Transferred to 19th Entrenching Bn. on 19/2/18.

27 Transferred to 53rd Bde., 18th Div., on 2/2/18.

28 Transferred to 1st Bde. on 7/2/18.

29 Transferred to 48th Bde., 16th Div., on 8/2/18.

30 On 9/2/18 Z was distributed between X and Y; and V (Heavy) T.M.B. was broken up.

31 6th Divnl. Emplynt. Coy. arrived on 19/5/17; and it was renumbered 204th on 14/8/17.

32 Formed on 28/2/18. The Bn. consisted of 1st, 2nd, 3rd, and 216th M.G. Cos. 216th M.G. Coy. joined the 1st Div. on 22/3/17.

1st DIVISION

MOBILIZATION, BATTLES, AND ENGAGEMENTS

On the outbreak of War the 1st Division was quartered at Aldershot, and it mobilized there. The division crossed to France between the 11th and 15th August, concentrated around le Nouvion, and began to move forward on the 21st August.

Throughout the War the 1st Division served on the Western Front in France and Belgium, and it was engaged in the following operations :

1914

23 and 24 Aug. ...	...**Battle of Mons** [I. Corps].
24 Aug.–5 Sept....	...**RETREAT FROM MONS** [I. Corps].
27 Aug.	...**Etreux** (1st Guards Bde.).
6–9 Sept. ...	...**Battle of the Marne** [I. Corps].
13–26 Sept. ...	...**BATTLE OF THE AISNE** [I. Corps].
13 Sept.	...**Passage of the Aisne.**
20 Sept.	...**Actions on the Aisne Heights.**
26 Sept.	...**Action of Chivy.**
19 Oct.–15 Nov.	...**BATTLES OF YPRES** [I. Corps].
21–24 Oct. ...	...**Battle of Langemarck** [I. Corps].
29–31 Oct. ...	...**Battle of Gheluvelt** [I. Corps].
11 Nov.	...**Battle of Nonne Bosschen** [I. Corps].
20–21 Dec. ...	...**Defence of Givenchy.**

1915

25 Jan.	...**Givenchy.**
29 Jan.	...**Cuinchy.**
9 May	...**BATTLE OF AUBERS RIDGE** [I. Corps, First Army]. **Attack at Rue du Bois.**
25 Sept.–1 Oct. and 5–8 Oct. ...	...**Battle of Loos** [IV. Corps, First Army].
13 Oct.	...**Hohenzollern Redoubt** [IV. Corps, First Army].

1916

BATTLES OF THE SOMME

14–17 July ...	...**Battle of Bazentin Ridge** [III. Corps, Fourth Army].
23–26 July and 15 Aug.–3 Sept.	...**Battle of Pozières Ridge** [III. Corps, Fourth Army].
15–22 Sept. ...	...**Battle of Flers-Courcelette** [III. Corps, Fourth Army].
25–28 Sept. ...	...**Battle of Morval** [III. Corps, Fourth Army].

1917

14-21 March ... ...**German Retreat to the Hindenburg Line** [III. Corps, Fourth Army].

21 June–20 Oct. ...**Operations on the Flanders Coast.**

10 July ... ...**Defence of Nieuport** [XV. Corps, Fourth Army].

BATTLES OF YPRES

5–10 Nov. ... ...**Second Battle of Passchendaele** [II. Corps, Second Army].

1918

BATTLES OF THE LYS

9–11 April ... ...**Battle of Estaires** [I. Corps, First Army].

15 April ... ...**Battle of Hazebrouck** (3rd Bde.) [under 55th Division, XI. Corps, First Army].

18 and 19 April ... ...**Battle of Bethune** [I. Corps, First Army].

THE ADVANCE TO VICTORY

SECOND BATTLES OF ARRAS

2 and 3 Sept. ... ...**Battle of the Drocourt-Quéant Line** [Cdn. Corps, First Army].

BATTLES OF THE HINDENBURG LINE

18 Sept. ... ...**Battle of Epéhy** [IX. Corps, Fourth Army].

29 Sept.–2 Oct. ... ...**Battle of the St. Quentin Canal** [IX. Corps, Fourth Army].

3–5 Oct. ... ...**Battle of the Beaurevoir Line** [IX. Corps, Fourth Army].

THE FINAL ADVANCE IN PICARDY

17–25 Oct. ... ...**Battle of the Selle** [IX. Corps, Fourth Army].

4 Nov. ... ...**Battle of the Sambre** [IX. Corps, Fourth Army].

4 Nov. ... ...**Passage of the Sambre-Oise Canal.**

On the 11th November the 1st Division was resting and training around Fresnoy le Grand and Wassigny. Ordered to the Rhine, the 1st Division began its advance on the 18th November, entered Germany on the 16th December, and on the 24th the division reached its destination, the vicinity of Bonn.

2ND DIVISION

G.O.C.

Mobilization...	Major-GENERAL C. C. MONRO.
(from 5 Aug., 1914)	
26 December, 1914	Br.-Gen. R. FANSHAWE (acting).
1 January, 1915	Major-General H. S. HORNE.
5 November, 1915	Major-General W. G. WALKER, V.C.
27 December, 1916	Major-General C. E. PEREIRA.

G.S.O. 1.

Mobilization ...Col. Hon. F. GORDON.
5 Sept., 1914...Lt.-Col. A. J. B. PERCIVAL.
18 Sept., 1914...Col. R. WHIGHAM.
26 Dec., 1914...Major L. R. VAUGHAN
(acting).
2 Jan., 1915...Lt.-Col. N. MALCOLM.
4 Jan., 1915...Lt.-Col. H. E. GOGARTY.
24 Feb., 1915...Lt.-Col. L. R. VAUGHAN.
14 April, 1916...Lt.-Col. C. P. DEEDES.
7 May, 1917...Lt.-Col. E. D. GILES.
5 Jan., 1918...Lt.-Col. E. R. CLAYTON.

A.-A. & Q.-M.-G.

Mobilization ...Lt.-Col. G. CONWAY-
GORDON.
7 Feb., 1915...Lt.-Col. G. D. JEBB.
15 July, 1915...Lt.-Col. S. W. ROBINSON.
28 Oct., 1916...Lt.-Col. J. P. VILLIERS-
STUART.
26 July, 1917...Lt.-Col. E. ARMSTRONG.

B.-G., R.A.

Mobilization ...Br.-Gen. E. M. PERCEVAL.
1 Feb., 1915...Br.-Gen. W. H. ONSLOW.
8 Sept., 1915...Br.-Gen. G. H. SANDERS.

C.R.E.

Mobilization ...Lt.-Col. R. H. H. BOYS
(wounded, 31/10/14).
31 Oct., 1914...Major C. N. NORTH
(killed, 1/11/14).
1 Nov., 1914...Captain A. J. DARLINGTON.
9 Nov., 1914...Major A. H. TYLER
(killed, 11/11/14).
10 Nov., 1914...Major G. H. FOULKES.
12 Nov., 1914...Lt.-Col. G. P. SCHOLFIELD.
20 June, 1916...Lt.-Col. C. M. BROWNE.
24 June, 1916...Lt.-Col. P. K. BETTY.

4th (GUARDS) BRIGADE

Mobilization...Br.-Gen. R. Scott-Kerr
(wounded, 1/9/14).
1 Sept., '14...Col. G. P. T. Feilding
(acting).
18 Sept., '14...Br.-Gen. F. R. Earl of
Cavan.
29 June, '15...Br.-Gen. G. P. T. Feilding.
(Bde. transferred to Guards Div., 19/8/15.)

6th BRIGADE

Mobilization...Br.-Gen. R. H. Davies.
23 Sept., '14...Br.-Gen. R. Fanshawe.
26 Dec., '14...Lt.-Col. C. S. Davidson.
(acting).
1 Jan., '15...Br.-Gen. R. Fanshawe.
30 May, '15...Br.-Gen. A. C. Daly.
21 Jan., '17...Br.-Gen. R. K. Walsh.
28 April, '18...Br.-Gen. A. H. S. Hart-
Synnot
(wounded, 11/5/18).
12 May, '18...Br.-Gen. F. G. Willan.

5th BRIGADE

Mobilization...Br.-Gen. R. C. B. Haking
(wounded, 16/9/14).
16 Sept., '14...Col. C. B. Westmacott
(acting).
20 Nov., '14...Br.-Gen. R. C. B. Haking.
20 Dec., '14...Lt.-Col. H. R. Davies
(acting).
31 Dec., '14...Br.-Gen. A. A. Chichester.
13 July, '15...Br.-Gen. C. E. Corkran.
15 May, '16...Br.-Gen. W. Bullen-Smith.
25 Mar., '18...Lt.-Col. R. H. Pipon
(acting).
5 April, '18...Br.-Gen. W. L. Osborn
(wounded, 5/10/18).
5 Oct., '18...Lt.-Col. R. H. Pipon
(acting).
12 Nov., '18...Br.-Gen. W. L. Osborn.

19th BRIGADE

(Joined 19/8/15, from 27th Div.)
[14 June, '15]...Br.-Gen. P. R. Robertson.
(Bde. transferred to 33rd Div., 25/11/15.)

99th BRIGADE

(Joined 25/11/15, from 33rd Div.
99th Bde. landed in France on 16/11/15).
[May, '15]...Br.-Gen. R. O. Kellett.
5 Jan., '18...Lt.-Col. G. P. S. Hunt
(acting).
24 Jan., '18...Br.-Gen. R. B. Barker
(killed, 24/3/18).
24 Mar., '18...Lt.-Col. E. A. Winter
(acting).
27 Mar., '18...Br.-Gen. W. E. Ironside.
6 Sept., '18...Br.-Gen. A. E. McNamara.

GENERAL NOTES

4th (GUARDS) BRIGADE—2/G.G., 2/C.G., 3/C.G., and 1/I.G. (with 4th Field Amb. and 11 Coy., A.S.C.)—was transferred on 19/8/15 to the Guards Div. (on formation), and became 1st Guards Brigade.

The following Units also served with the 2nd Division :—

INFANTRY :—2/R. Innis. Fus., joined 5th Bde. from G.H.Q. on 26/1/15 ; transferred to Third Army Troops on 22/7/15.

7/King's, joined 6th Bde. from England on 12/3/15 ; transferred to 5th Bde. on 4/9/15.

ARTILLERY :—No. 11 Pom-Pom Section (A.-A.), from 22/9/14–25/1/15.

7th Mountain Battery, from 4/2/15–9/12/15. The Bty. then went to Salonika, where it disembarked on 29/12/15.

26 Heavy Battery, from 4/2/15–20/4/15. The Bty. joined II. Bde., R.G.A.

1 Siege Battery, from 4/2/15–20/4/15. The Bty. joined XII. Bde., R.G.A.

OTHER UNITS :—11th Sanitary Section, from 9/1/15–27/12/16 (transferred to II. Corps).

2nd Divisional Ambulance Workshop, joined by 4/4/15 and served until 9/4/16. Then it was transferred to Divnl. Supply Coln.

On 9/2/18 the reorganization of the division on a 9-battalion basis was completed ; and by 27/2/18 the pioneer battalion was reorganized on a 3-company basis.

Dates	INFANTRY Brigades	Battalions and attached Units	Mounted Troops	ARTILLERY — Field Artillery: Brigades	Batteries	Bde. Ammn. Columns	Heavy Battery	Trench Mortar Batteries: Medium	Heavy	Divnl. Ammn. Col.	Engineers Field Cos.	Signal Service Divnl. Signal Coy.	Pioneers	M.G. Units	Field Ambulances	Mobile Vety. Secn.	Divnl. Emplnt. Coy.	Divnl. Train
1914 August	4th (Gds.)1 5th... 6th...	2/G.G., 2/C.G., 3/C.G., 1/I.G. 2/Worc., 2/O.&B.L.I., 2/H.L.I., 2/Conn. Rang.2 1/King's, 2/S. Staff, 1/R. Berks., 1/K.R.R.C.	B. Sqdn., 15/Hsrs.;3 2nd Cyclist Coy.	XXXIV... XXXVI... XLI... XLIV (H.)	22,4 50, 70 15, 48, 71 9, 16, 17 47 (H.) 56 (H.) 60 (H.)5	XXXIV B.A.C. XXXVI B.A.C. XLI B.A.C. XLIV (H.) B.A.C.	35 H.B.6 & Hy. Bty. A.C.	...	...	2nd D.A.C.	6th 11th	2nd	...	...	4th 5th 6th	3rd	...	2nd7
1915 Sept.	5th... 6th... 19th15	1/Queen's,8 2/Worc.,9 2/O.& B.L.I., 2/H.L.I., 7/King's,10 9/H.L.I.11 1/King's, 2/S. Staff, 1/R. Berks.,12 1/K.R.R.C.,12 5/King's,13 1/Herts.14 2/R.W.F., 1/Sco. Rif., 1/Midd'x., 2/A. & S.H., 5/Sco. Rif.16	B. Sqdn., S. Irish H.;17 2nd Cyclist Coy.18	XXXIV... XXXVI... XLI... XLIV (H.)19	50, 70 15, 48, 71 9, 16, 17 47 (H.) 56 (H.)	XXXIV B.A.C. XXXVI B.A.C. XLI B.A.C. XLIV (H.) B.A.C.	...	...	...	2nd D.A.C.	5th 11th20 1/E. Anglian21	2nd	...	...	5th 6th 19th15	3rd	...	2nd22
1916 June	5th... 6th... 99th28	2/O.&B.L.I., 2/H.L.I., 17/R.F.,23 24/R.F.,23 5th Bde. M.G. Coy.,24 5th T.M. Bty.25 1/King's, 2/S. Staff, 13/Essex,26 17/Midd'x.,27 6th Bde. M.G. Coy.,24 6th T.M. Bty.25 1/R. Berks.,12 1/K.R.R.C.,12 22/R.F., 23/R.F.; 99th Bde. M.G. Coy.,24 99th T.M. Bty.25	...	XXXIV29 XXXVI... XLI...	50, 70; 56 (H.),19 15, 48, 71; D (H.),19 9, 16, 17; 47 (H.),19	...30	...	X.2,31 Y.2,31 Z.2,31	V.2,32	2nd D.A.C.	5th 226th33 1/E. Anglian	2nd	10/ D.C.L.I (P.)35	...	5th 6th 100th28	3rd	...	2nd34
1917 June	5th... 6th... 99th...	2/O.&B.L.I., 2/H.L.I., 17/R.F.,35 24/R.F.; 5th M.G. Coy.; 5th T.M. Bty. 1/King's, 2/S. Staff, 13/Essex,36 17/Midd'x.,37 6th M.G. Coy.; 6th T.M. Bty. 1/R. Berks., 1/K.R.R.C., 22/R.F.,38 23/R.F.; 99th M.G. Coy.; 99th T.M. Bty.	...	XXXVI... XLI...	15, 48, 71; D (H.); 9, 16, 17; 47 (H.)	...	...	X.2 Y.2 Z.239	V.239	2nd D.A.C.	5th 226th 483rd (E. Anglian)	2nd	10/ D.C.L.I. (P.)	242nd M.G. Coy.41	5th 6th 100th	3rd	205th40	2nd
1918 March	5th... 6th... 99th...	2/O.&B.L.I., 2/H.L.I., 24/R.F.; 6th T.M. Bty. 1/King's, 2/S. Staff, 17/R.F.,35 6th T.M. Bty. 1/R. Berks., 1/K.R.R.C., 23/R.F.; 99th T.M. Bty.	...	XXXVI... XLI...	15, 48, 71; D (H.); 9, 16, 17; 47 (H.)	...	...	X.2 Y.2	...	2nd D.A.C.	5th 226th 483rd	2nd	10/ D.C.L.I. (P.)	No. 2 Battn.41 M.G.C.	5th 6th 100th	3rd	205th	2nd

NOTES ON THE ORDER OF BATTLE

1 Transferred (with 4th Fd. Amb.) to Guards Div. on 19/8/15, and renumbered 1st Gds. Bde.

2 Transferred on 26/11/14 to Ferozepore Bde., Lahore Div.

3 Transferred on 14/4/16 to 9th Cav. Bde. (on formation). Replaced on 2/5/15 by B Sqdn., S. Irish Horse.

4 Transferred to III (28th Div.), 4/2/15; and 'oined III on 20/2/15.

5 60 (H.) transferred to Lahore Div., 23/6/15.

6 On the reorganization of the Artillery (Feb., 1916), 36 H.B was transferred to II Bde., No. 1 Group, H.A.R., in April, 1915.

7 11, 28, 31, and 35 Cos., A.S.C.

8 Joined, 21/7/15, from I Corps Troops; transferred to 33rd Div., 15/12/15.

9 Transferred to 33rd Div., 15/12/15.

10 Joined, 4/9/15, from 6th Bde.; transferred to 7th Div., 11/11/15.

11 Joined, 23/11/14; transferred to G.H.Q., 30/1/16.

12 Transferred to 99th Bde., 18/12/15.

13 Joined, 24/2/15; transferred to 99th Bde., 15/12/15; then transferred to 55th Div., 7/1/16.

14 Joined, 4th (Gds.) Bde., 20/11/14; transferred to 6th Bde., 19/8/16; transferred to G.H.Q., 28/2/16.

15 Transferred from 27th Div., 19/8/16, to replace 4th (Gds.) Bde. 19th Bde. was transferred to the 33rd Div., 25/11/15 (with 19th Fd. Amb.).

16 Joined 19th Bde., 19/11/14.

17 Transferred to IV Corps Cavalry, 10/5/16.

18 Transferred to IV Corps Cyclist Bn., 10/5/16.

19 XLIV (H.) was broken up on 26/5/16. 47 (less 1 sec.) was transferred to XLI, and 56 (less 1 sec.) to XXXIV. 1 sec. 47, and 1 sec. 56 formed D/XXXVI.

20 Transferred to 33rd Div., on 2/12/15, in exchange with 226th Fd. Coy.

21 Joined on 5/1/15.

22 8, 28, 31, 35 Cos. A.S.C. No. 11 Coy. was transferred with 4th Gds. Bde. to Guards Div. (note 1).

23 Transferred from 99th Bde. on 13/12/15.

24 Bde. M.G. Cos. formed : 5th on 1/1/16 ; 6th on 4/1/16 ; and the 99th, formed in England, landed in France on 26/4/16, and joined on 28/4/16.

25 The Bde. T.M. Btles. were formed : 5th by 11/3/16 and the 6th and 99th by 18/3/16.

26 Transferred from 100th Bde., 33rd Div., on 22/12/15.

27 Transferred from 100th Bde., 33rd Div., on 8/12/15.

28 Transferred (with 100th Fd. Amb.) from 33rd Div. on 25/11/15.

29 Became an A.F.A. Bde. on 25/1/17. 521 (H.) had been posted to XXXIV on 16/11/16 and became D/XXXIV. On 25/1/17 D/XXXIV was broken up and secs. joined 47/XLI and D/XXXVI. At the same time A/LX joined from 11th Div. and became C/XXXIV ; and ⅓ of C (H.)/LX made 56 (H.) up to 6 hows.

30 B.A.C.'s abolished and D.A.C. reorganized on 26/5/16.

31 Formed in April, 1916.

32 Formed on 26/5/16.

33 Joined on 23/6/16.

34 28, 31, 35 and 172 Cos. A.S.C. No. 8 Coy. was transferred with 19th Inf. Bde. to 33rd Div. (note 15). No. 172 Coy. came with 99th Bde. on 25/11/15 from 33rd Div. (note 28).

35 Transferred to 6th Bde. on 8/2/18.

36 Disbanded on 10/2/18.

37 Disbanded on 10/2/18. Part went to 18/Middx., part to 21/Middx., and the remainder to No. 6 Entrenching Bn.

38 Disbanded on 2/2/18.

39 Z was distributed between X and Y by 24/2/18. V (Heavy) T.M.B. left the division by 3/1/18.

40 7th Divnl. Emplnt. Coy. arrived on 18/5/17 ; and it was renumbered 205th in June, 1917.

41 Formed on 4/8/18 ; it consisted of 6th, 6th, 99th and 242nd M.G. Cos. (242nd M.G. Coy. joined the division on 18/7/17).

2ND DIVISION

MOBILIZATION, BATTLES, AND ENGAGEMENTS

On the outbreak of War the 2nd Division (less the 4th (Guards) Brigade in the London District) was quartered at Aldershot, and mobilized there (4th (Guards) Brigade mobilizing at Windsor and in London).

The division crossed to France between the 11th and 16th August, concentrated around Wassigny, Etreux, etc., and began to move forward on the 21st August.

Throughout the War the 2nd Division served on the Western Front in France and Belgium, and it was engaged in the following operations :—

1914

23 and 24 Aug. ...	...Battle of Mons [I. Corps].
24 Aug.–5 Sept.	...RETREAT FROM MONS [I. Corps].
25 Aug.	...Landrecies (4th Guards Bde.).
1 Sept.	...Villers Cotterêts.

6–9 Sept. ...	...Battle of the Marne [I. Corps].
13–26 Sept. ...	...BATTLE OF THE AISNE [I. Corps].
13 Sept.	...Passage of the Aisne.
20 Sept.	...Actions on the Aisne Heights.

19 Oct.–20 Nov.	...BATTLES OF YPRES [I. Corps].
21–24 Oct. ...	...Battle of Langemarck [I. Corps].
29–31 Oct. ...	...Battle of Gheluvelt [I. Corps].
11 Nov.	...Battle of Nonne Bosschen [I. Corps].

1915

1 Feb.	...Cuinchy.
6 Feb.	...Cuinchy.
15–20 May ...	...Battle of Festubert [I. Corps, First Army].
25 Sept.–4 Oct. ...	...Battle of Loos [I. Corps, First Army].
13–19 Oct.	...Hohenzollern Redoubt [I. Corps, First Army].

1916

BATTLES OF THE SOMME

25 July–9 Aug. ...	...Battle of Delville Wood [XIII. Corps, Fourth Army].
27 and 28 July ...	...Capture and Consolidation of Delville Wood.
8 and 9 Aug. ...	...Attack of Waterlot Farm—Guillemont.
13–16 Nov. ...	...Battle of the Ancre [V. Corps, Fifth Army].

1917

11 Jan.–13 March	...**Operations on the Ancre** [II. Corps, Fifth Army].
17 and 18 Feb. ...	...**Actions of Miraumont.**
25 Feb.–2 March	...**Capture of the Thilloys.**
10 March... ...	...**Capture of Grevillers Trench (near Irles).**
14–19 March ...	...**German Retreat to the Hindenburg Line** [II. Corps, Fifth Army].

BATTLES OF ARRAS

12–14 April ...	...**Battle of Vimy Ridge** [XIII. Corps, First Army].
28 and 29 April...	...**Battle of Arleux** [XIII. Corps, First Army].
3 May	...**Third Battle of the Scarpe** [XIII. Corps, First Army].

BATTLE OF CAMBRAI

27 and 28 Nov. ...	...**Capture of Bourlon Wood** [IV. Corps, Third Army].
30 Nov.–3 Dec. ...	...**German Counter Attacks** [IV. Corps, handed over on 1/12 to V. Corps, Third Army].

1918

FIRST BATTLES OF THE SOMME

22 and 23 March	...**Battle of St. Quentin** [V. Corps, Third Army].
24 and 25 March	...**First Battle of Bapaume** [V. Corps, Third Army].
28 March ...	...**Battle of Arras** [V. Corps, Third Army].

THE ADVANCE TO VICTORY

SECOND BATTLES OF THE SOMME

21–23 Aug. ...	...**Battle of Albert** [VI. Corps, Third Army].
24 Aug.	...**Capture of Mory Copse** (99th Brigade).
25 Aug.	...**Capture of Behagnies and Sapignies** (5th Brigade).
3 Sept.	...**Second Battle of Bapaume.** **Assault of the Drocourt-Quéant Line** [VI. Corps, Third Army].

BATTLES OF THE HINDENBURG LINE

11 and 12 Sept....	...**Battle of Havrincourt** [VI. Corps, Third Army].
27 Sept.–1 Oct. ...	...**Battle of the Canal du Nord** [VI. Corps, Third Army].
1 Oct.	...**Capture of Mont sur l'Œuvre.**
8 Oct.	...**Battle of Cambrai** [VI. Corps, Third Army].
8 Oct.	...**Capture of Forenville.**

THE FINAL ADVANCE IN PICARDY

23–25 Oct. ...	...**Battle of the Selle** [VI. Corps, Third Army].

On the 11th November the 2nd Division was in VI. Corps reserve, and was billeted north of le Quesnoy. Ordered to the Rhine, the division began its advance on the 18th November, entered Germany on the 9th December, and on the 27th December reached its destination between Düren and Cologne.

3RD DIVISION

G.O.C.

Mobilization... ... ...Major-General H. I. W. HAMILTON
(killed, 14/10/14).
15 October, 1914... ... ...Major-General C. J. MACKENZIE
(invalided, 29/10/14).
29 October, 1914... ... ...Major-General F. D. V. WING (tempy.).
21 November, 1914 ... ...Major-General J. A. L. HALDANE.
7 August, 1916 ... ...Major-General C. J. DEVERELL.

G.S.O. 1.

Mobilization ...Col. F. R. F. BOILEAU
(died of wounds, 26/8/14).
27 Aug., 1914...Col. F. B. MAURICE.
11 Feb., 1915...Lt.-Col. C. EVANS.
12 Aug., 1915...Lt.-Col. H. S. DE BRETT.
17 Nov., 1916...Lt.-Col. W. H. TRAILL.

A.-A. & Q.-M.-G.

Mobilization ...Col. R. C. BOYLE.
31 Dec., 1914...Lt.-Col. F. C. DUNDAS.
26 Feb., 1915...Lt.-Col. A. F. SILLEM.
3 July, 1915...Lt.-Col. W. H. V. DARELL.
22 Aug., 1915...Lt.-Col. Hon. R. H.
COLLINS.
4 April, 1918...Lt.-Col. T. W. PRAGNELL.
24 July, 1918...Lt.-Col. G. H. GILL.

B.-G., R.A.

Mobilization ...Br.-Gen. F. D. V. WING.
29 Oct., 1914...Br.-Gen. A. H. SHORT
(tempy.).
24 Feb., 1915...Br.-Gen. H. G. SANDI-
LANDS.
18 Feb., 1916...Br.-Gen. E. W. M. POWELL.
24 July, 1916...Br.-Gen. J. S. OLLIVANT.

C.R.E.

Mobilization ...Lt.-Col. C. S. WILSON.
4 Mar., 1916...Lt.-Col. C. A. ELLIOTT.
13 Feb., 1918...Lt.-Col. W. C. COOPER.
24 June, 1918...Major P. DE H. HALL
(acting).
15 July, 1918...Lt.-Col. R. P. PAKENHAM-
WALSH.

7th BRIGADE

Mobilization...Br.-Gen. F. W. N.
                        McCracken.
23 Nov., '14...Br.-Gen. C. R. Ballard.
23 July, '15...Br.-Gen. C. Gosling.
(Bde. transferred to 25th Div. on 18/10/15.)

76th BRIGADE

(Transferred from 25th Div. on 15/10/15.)
[July, '15]...Br.-Gen. E. St. G. Pratt.
11 April, '16...Br.-Gen. R. J. Kentish.
1 Oct., '16...Br.-Gen. C. L. Porter.
4 Oct., '18...Br.-Gen. E. E. Metcalfe.

9th BRIGADE

Mobilization...Br.-Gen. F. C. Shaw
                        (wounded, 12/11/14).
12 Nov., '14...Br.-Gen. W. Douglas
                        Smith.
(Bde. transferred temporarily to 28th Div.
            on 17/2/15.)

85th BRIGADE

(Transferred temporarily from 28th Div.
            on 19/2/15.)
[24 Dec., '14] Br.-Gen. A. J. Chapman.
  (Bde. rejoined 28th Div. on 5/4/15.)

8th BRIGADE

Mobilization...Br.-Gen. B. J. C. Doran.
23 Oct., '14...Br.-Gen. W. H. Bowes.
25 Mar., '15...Br.-Gen. A. R. Hoskins.
3 Oct., '15...Br.-Gen. J. D. McLachlan.
13 Mar., '16...Br.-Gen. E. G. Williams.
3 Dec., '16...Br.-Gen. G. Bull
            (wounded 7/12/16, died 11/12/16).
11 Dec., '16...Br.-Gen. H. G. Holmes
                        (wounded, 30/4/17).
30 April, '17...Lt.-Col. A. F. Lumsden
                        (acting).
15 May, '17...Br.-Gen. H. G. Holmes.
20 Oct., '17...Br.-Gen. W. E. C. Tanner.
2 April, '18...Br.-Gen. W. J. Webb-
                        Bowen
            (wounded, 2/4/18).
3 April, '18...Br.-Gen. L. A. E. Price-
                        Davies, V.C.
12 April, '18...Br.-Gen. B. D. Fisher.

9th BRIGADE

(Rejoined from 28th Div. on 2/4/15.)
[12 Nov., '14] Br.-Gen. W. Douglas
                        Smith.
9 Mar., '16...Br.-Gen. H. C. Potter
            (wounded 23/7/16, evacd. 25/7/16).
26 July, '16...Br.-Gen. H. C. R. Green.
5 Aug., '16...Br.-Gen. H. C. Potter.

GENERAL NOTES

On 17/2/15 the **9th Infantry Brigade** was transferred temporarily to the 28th Division, and on 19/2/15 it was replaced by the **85th Infantry Brigade** (2/Buffs, 3/R.F., 2/E. Surrey, 3/Midd'x., 10/King's (until 2/3/15), 8/Midd'x. (from 11/3/15), and H.A.C.). The **9th Bde.** returned to the 3rd Division on 2/4/15, and the **85th Bde.** (less H.A.C., of 7th Inf. Bde., see note 10) rejoined the 28th Division between 2–6/4/15.

The following Units also served with the 3rd Division :—

CAVALRY :—B. Sqdn., Glasgow Yeo., from 10/5/16–1/6/16 (transferred to V. Corps, Cav. Regt.).

INFANTRY :—1/Devon joined 8th Inf. Bde. from L. of C. Defence Troops on 14/9/14, and was transferred to 14th Inf. Bde., 5th Division, on 30/9/14.

    1/L.R.B. joined 8th Inf. Bde. from G.H.Q. on 25/10/15, and was transferred to 169th Bde., 56th Division, on 10/2/16.

ARTILLERY :—No. 5 Pom-Pom Section (A.-A.), from 20/9/14, until December, 1914.

    5th Mountain Battery, from 14/12/14–3/3/15 (transferred to 8th Division).

OTHER UNITS :—No. 4 A (renumbered No. 5, in April, 1916) Sanitary Section, from 9/1/15 until 3/4/17 (transferred to Arras Area).

    3rd Divnl. Ambulance Workshop, joined by 18/4/15 and served until 9/4/16 (transferred to Divnl. Supply Coln.).

On 12/2/18 the reorganization of the division on a 9-battalion basis was completed, and by 27/2/18 the pioneer battalion was reorganized on a 3-company basis.

3RD DIVISION   ORDER OF BATTLE, 1914 - 1918

Dates	INFANTRY Brigades	Battalions and attached Units	Mounted Troops	ARTILLERY — Field Artillery Brigades	Batteries	Bde. Ammn. Columns	Heavy Battery	Trench Mortar Batteries Medium	Heavy	Divnl. Ammn. Col.	Engineers Field Cos.	Signal Service Divnl. Signal Coy.	Pioneers	M.G. Units	Field Ambulances	Mobile Vety. Secn.	Divnl. Emplnt. Coy.	Divnl. Train
1914 August	7th.. 8th.. 9th..	3/Worc., 2/S. Lanc., 1/Wilts., 2/R. Ir. Rif. 2/R. Scots., 2/R. Ir. Regt.,1 4/Midd'x, 1/Gord. H.2 1/N.F., 4/R.F., 1/Linc., 1/R.S.F.	A. Sqdn., 15/Hsrs.,3 3rd Cyclist Coy.	XXIII..... XI.......... XLII....... XXX (H.)	107, 108, 109 6, 23, 49 29, 41, 45 128 (H.),4 129 (H.), 130 (H.)	XXIII B.A.C. XI. B.A.C. XLII B.A.C. XXX (H.) B.A.C.	48 H.B.5 & Hy. Bty. A.C.	...	...	3rd D.A.C.	56th 57th6	3rd	...	...	7th 8th 9th7	11th	...	3rd8
1915 Sept.	7th9.. 8th.. 9th..	3/Worc., 2/S. Lanc., 1/Wilts., 2/R. Ir. Rif., H.A.C.,10 4/S. Lanc.11 2/R. Scots., 2/Suff.,12 4/Midd'x,13 1/Gord. H.,14 4/Gord. H.15 1/N.F., 4/R.F., 1/Linc.,16 1/R.S.F., 10/King's.17	C. Sqdn., N. Irish H.18 3rd Cyclist Coy.19	XXIII..... XI.......... XLII....... XXX (H.)20	107, 108, 10921 6, 23, 49 29, 41, 45 129 (H.), 130 (H.)	XXIII B.A.C. XI. B.A.C. XLII B.A.C. XXX (H.) B.A.C.	...	...	...	3rd D.A.C.	56th 1/Cheshire 22 1/E. Riding23	3rd	...	...	7th 8th 142nd7	11th	...	3rd
1916 June	8th.. 9th.. 76thAl	2/R. Scots, 1/R.S.F.,24 8/E. York.,25 7/K.S.L.I.,26 8th Bde. M.G. Coy.,27 8th T. M. Bty 28 1/N.F., 4/R.F., 13/King's,29 12/W. York.,30 9th Bde. M.G. Coy.,31 9th T.M. Bty.32 2/Suff.,33 1/Gord. H.,34 8/King's Own, 10/R.W.F.; 76th Bde. M.G. Coy.,37 76th T.M. Bty.38	...	XXIII34.. XI............ XLII.......	107, 108 · D (H.),35 130 (H.),20 29, 41, 45 · 129 (H.),20	...56	...	X.357 Y.357 Z.357	V.358	3rd D.A.C.56	56th 1/Cheshire 1/E. Riding	3rd	20/ K.R.R.C. (P.)39	...	7th 8th 142nd	11th	...	3rd
1917 June	8th.. 9th.. 76th..	2/R. Scots, 1/R.S.F., 8/E. York.,40 7/K.S.L.I.; 8th M.G. Coy.; 8th T.M. Bty. 1/N.F., 4/R.F., 13/King's, 12/W. York.,40 9th M.G. Coy.; 9th T.M. Bty. 2/Suff., 1/Gord. H., 8/King's Own, 10/R.W.F.,41 76th M.G. Coy.; 76th T.M. Bty.	...	XL.......... XLII.......	6, 23, 49 ; 130 (H.) 29, 41, 45 ; 129 (H.)	...	...	X.3 Y.3 Z.342	V.342	3rd D.A.C.	56th 488th (Cheshire) 529th (E. Riding)	3rd	20/ K.R.R.C. (P.)	233rd M.G. Coy.44	7th 8th 142nd	11th	206th45	3rd
1918 March	8th.. 9th.. 76th..	2/R. Scots, 1/R.S.F., 7/K.S.L.I., 8th T.M. Bty. 1/N.F., 4/R.F., 13/King's; 9th T.M. Bty. 2/Suff., 1/Gord. H., 8/King's Own ; 76th T.M. Bty.	...	XL.......... XLII.......	6, 23, 49 ; 130 (H.) 29, 41, 45 ; 129 (H.)	...	...	X.3 Y.3	...	3rd D.A.C.	56th 488th 529th	3rd	20/ K.R.R.C. (P.)	No. 3 Bn., M.G.C.44	7th 8th 142nd	11th	206th	3rd

NOTES ON ORDER OF BATTLE

1 Transferred to Army Troops, at St. Omer, on 24/10/14, and replaced in 8th Bde. on 25/10/14 by 2/Suff.

2 Transferred to Army Troops, at Fère en Tardenois, on 12/9/14, and replaced by 1/Devon. 1/Devon was transferred to 14th Bde., 5th Div., on 30/9/14, and 1/Gord. H. returned to 8th Bde.

3 Transferred on 14/4/15 to 9th Cav. Bde. (on formation). Replaced by C. Sqdn., N. Irish Horse.

4 Transferred to 4th Div., 25/8/15.

5 On the reorganization of the Artillery in Feb., 1916, 48 Hy. Bty. was transferred on 19/4/15, to IV Hy. Bde., No. 1 Group, H.A.R.

6 Transferred to 46th (N. Midland) Div., 7/4/15.

7 Transferred, on 28/8/15, to Guards Div. (on formation); replaced by 142nd Fd. Amb.

8 15th, 21st, 22nd, and 29th Cos., A.S.C.

9 7th Bde. (less H.A.C. and 4/S. Lanc.) was transferred to 25th Div. on 18/10/15; it was replaced by 76th Bde. from the 25th Div. on 15/10/15.

10 Joined 8th Bde., 10/11/14; transferred to 7th Bde., 9/12/14; and left on 14/10/15, on transfer to G.H.Q.

11 Joined, 24/2/16; became Pioneers 12/10/15; and transferred on 9/1/16 to 55th Div.

12 Transferred to 76th Bde., 22/10/15.

13 Transferred to 21st Div., 18/11/15.

14 Transferred to 76th Bde., 19/10/15.

15 Joined, 27/2/15; attached 76th Bde., 19/10/15—4/2/16; and transferred to 51st Div., 23/2/16.

16 Transferred to 21st Div., 18/11/15.

17 Joined, 2/8/15; transferred to 55th Div., 6/1/16.

18 Transferred to X Corps Cavalry, 11/5/16.

19 Transferred. on 31/5/16 to Reserve Army Cyclist Bn. (formed 18/6/16).

20 Bde. broken up, 14/5/16. 129 (less 1 sec.) joined XLII, and 130 (less 1 sec.) joined XL. 1 sec. 129 and 1 sec. 130 formed D/XXIII on 11/5/16.

21 109 was transferred on 10/2/16 to CCLXXXIII (56th Div.).

22 Joined on 22/12/14.

23 Joined on 20/9/15.

24 Transferred from 9th Bde. on 5/4/16.

25 Transferred from 62nd Bde., 21st Div., on 16/11/15.

26 Transferred from 76th Bde., on 19/10/15.

27 Bde. M.G. Coes. were formed : 8th on 22/1/16 ; 9th by 8/2/16 ; and 76th by 18/4/16.

28 Bde. T.M. Bties. were formed : 8th by 18/4/16 ; 9th on 1/5/16 ; and 76th on 1/4/16 (43 T.M. Bty. was transferred and renamed 76th Lt. T.M.B.).

29 Transferred from 76th Bde. to 8th Bde. on 23/10/15; and from 8th Bde. to 9th Bde. on 4/4/16.

30 Transferred from 63rd Bde., 21st Div., on 16/11/15.

31 76th Bde. (8/King's Own, 13/King's, 10/R.W.F., and 7/K.S.L.I.) was transferred from 25th Div. on 15/10/15.

32 Transferred from 8th Bde. on 22/10/15.

33 Transferred from 8th Bde. on 19/10/15.

34 Became an A.F.A. Bde. on 21/1/17. On 24/1/17 A/CLXIX of the 31st Div. joined, and became C/XXIII on 29/1/17. On 24/1/17, 1 sec. C(H.)/XXIII (31st Div.) joined and made C(H.)/CLXIX (31st Div.) up to 6 hows. C(H.)/XXIII then became D(H.)/XXIII on 29/1/17 (see note 35).

35 D(H.)/XXIII, from 11/5/16—21/1/17, was formed of 1 sec. 129, and 1 sec. 130. On 21/1/17 D was broken up and sec. rejoined 129 and 130. On 23/11/16, 534(H.) joined XXIII and became C(H.)/XXIII. C/XXIII was relettered D/XXIII on 29/1/17 (see note 34 above).

36 B.A.C.'s were abolished and D.A.C. was reorganized 9–16/5/16.

37 Formed in February, 1916.

38 Formed by July, 1916.

39 Joined on 19/5/16.

40 8/E. York. and 12/W. York. were amalgamated on 17/2/18, and formed 10/Entrenching Bn.

41 10/R.W.F. amalgamated on 15/2/18 with 19/R.W.F. (40th Div.) and formed 8/Entrenching Bn.

42 Z was distributed between X. and Y. in Febry., 1918. V. was transferred on 6/3/18 to VI Corps, and became V./VI.

43 8th D.E. Coy. joined on 31/5/17 ; and 8th was renumbered 206th in June, 1917.

44 Formed on 6/3/18. It consisted of 8, 9, 76, and 238 M.G. Cos. 238 M.G. Coy. joined the 3rd Div. on 18/7/17.

3RD DIVISION

MOBILIZATION, BATTLES, AND ENGAGEMENTS

On the outbreak of War the 3rd Division was quartered in the Southern Command (with its Heavy Battery at Woolwich). The units mobilized at their peace stations, and the division crossed to France between the 11th and 16th August, concentrated around Aulnoye and Avesnes, and began to move forward on the 21st August.

Throughout the War the 3rd Division served on the Western Front in France and Belgium, and it was engaged in the following operations :—

1914

23 and 24 Aug. ...	...**Battle of Mons** [II. Corps].
24 Aug.–5 Sept....	...**RETREAT FROM MONS** [II. Corps].
25 Aug.	...**Solesmes** (7th Infantry Brigade).
26 Aug.	...**Battle of le Cateau** [II. Corps].

6–9 Sept. ...	...**Battle of the Marne** [II. Corps].
13–20 Sept. ...	...**BATTLE OF THE AISNE** [II. Corps].
13 Sept.	...**Passage of the Aisne.**
20 Sept.	...**Actions on the Aisne Heights.**

10 Oct.–2 Nov. ...	...**Battle of La Bassée** [II. Corps].

(3rd Div. (less 8th Bde., left under Indian Corps) was relieved on 29/10.)

31 Oct.–2 Nov. ...	...**Battle of Messines** (parts of 7th and 9th Bdes.) [Cav. Corps].
1 and 2 Nov. ...	...**Battle of Armentières** (3/Worc., 7th Bde.) [III. Corps].
5–21 Nov. ...	...**BATTLES OF YPRES** [I. Corps].
11 Nov.	...**Battle of Nonne Bosschen** [I. Corps].

(In this battle the 3rd Div. was formed of 7th, 9th, and 15th Bdes.)

14 Dec.	...**Attack on Wytschæte.**

1915

16 June	...**First Attack on Bellewaarde** [V. Corps, Second Army].
19 July	...**Hooge** [V. Corps, Second Army].
25 Sept.	...**Second Attack on Bellewaarde** [V. Corps, Second Army].

1916

2 March	...**Recapture of The Bluff** (76th Bde.) [under 17th Div., V. Corps, Second Army].
27 March–4 April	...**Capture of St. Eloi Craters** [V. Corps, Second Army].
30 April	...**Wulverghem** (German Gas Attack) [V. Corps, Second Army].

BATTLES OF THE SOMME

14–25 July ...	...**Battle of Bazentin Ridge** [XIII. Corps, Fourth Army].
14–19 Aug. ...	...**Battle of Delville Wood** [XIII. Corps, until m/n. 16/17 Aug., then XIV. Corps, Fourth Army].
13–18 Nov. ...	...**Battle of the Ancre** [V. Corps, Fifth Army].

1917

BATTLES OF ARRAS

9–14 April ... ...**First Battle of the Scarpe** [VI. Corps, Third Army].

23 and 24 April ... ...**Second Battle of the Scarpe** [VI. Corps, Third Army].

28 and 29 April ... ...**Battle of Arleux** [VI. Corps, Third Army].

3 and 4 May ... ...**Third Battle of the Scarpe** [VI. Corps, Third Army].

13 and 14 May ... ...**Capture of Rœux** [VI. Corps, Third Army].

BATTLES OF YPRES

22–25 Sept. ... ...**Battle of the Menin Road Ridge** [V. Corps, Fifth Army].

26–30 Sept. ... ...**Battle of Polygon Wood** [V. Corps, Fifth Army, until 10 a.m., 28/9, then under II. Anzac Corps, Second Army].

1918

FIRST BATTLES OF THE SOMME

21–23 March ... ...**Battle of St. Quentin** [VI. Corps, Third Army].

24 and 25 March... ...**First Battle of Bapaume** [VI. Corps, Third Army].

28 March ... ...**Battle of Arras** [VI. Corps, Third Army].

BATTLES OF THE LYS

9–11 April ... ...**Battle of Estaires** [I. Corps, First Army ; transferred to XI. Corps on 11/4, less 9th Bde. attached to 55th Div. (XI.), from night of 9/10/4–15/4].

12–15 April ... ...**Battle of Hazebrouck, including Defence of Hinges Ridge** [I. Corps, First Army].

18 April ... ...**Battle of Bethune** [I. Corps, First Army].

THE ADVANCE TO VICTORY

SECOND BATTLES OF THE SOMME

21–23 Aug. ... ...**Battle of Albert** [VI. Corps, Third Army].

31 Aug.–2 Sept. ... ...**Second Battle of Bapaume** [VI. Corps, Third Army].

BATTLES OF THE HINDENBURG LINE

27 Sept.–1 Oct. ... ...**Battle of the Canal du Nord** [VI. Corps, Third Army].

8 Oct. ... ...**Battle of Cambrai** [VI. Corps, Third Army].

THE FINAL ADVANCE IN PICARDY

23–25 Oct. ... ...**Battle of the Selle** [VI. Corps, Third Army].

On the 11th November the 3rd Division was in VI. Corps Reserve and was billeted in the le Quesnoy-Bavai area. Ordered to the Rhine, the division began its march on the 20th November, entered Germany on the 11th December, and on the 20th December reached its destination between Düren and Cologne.

4TH DIVISION

G.O.C.

Mobilization...	Major-General T. D'O. Snow
	(incapacitated, 9/9/14).
9 September, 1914	Br.-Gen. H. F. M. Wilson (acting).
23 September, 1914	Major-General Sir H. Rawlinson, Bart.
4 October, 1914...	Major-General H. F. M. Wilson.
28 September, 1915	Major-General Hon. W. Lambton
	(incapacitated, 12/9/17).
12 September, 1917	Br.-Gen. R. A. Berners (acting).
21 September, 1917	Major-General T. G. Matheson.
14 September, 1918	Major-General L. J. Lipsett
	(killed, 14/10/18).
15 October, 1918...	Major-General C. H. T. Lucas.

G.S.O. 1.

Mobilization ...Colonel J. E. Edmonds.
4 Sept., 1914...Lt.-Col. A. A. Montgomery.
18 Aug., 1915...Lt.-Col. W. H. Bartholomew.
28 Dec., 1916...Lt.-Col. W. H. E. Segrave.
13 Mar., 1917...Lt.-Col. W. M. St. G. Kirke.
31 July, 1917...Lt.-Col. A. F. C. Williams.
16 Sept., 1917...Lt.-Col. H. Karslake.
5 Aug., 1918...Lt.-Col. R. H. Johnson
        (tempy.).
8 Aug., 1918...Lt.-Col. L. Carr.

A.-A. & Q.-M.-G.

Mobilization.....Lt.-Col. F. P. S. Taylor.
2 June, 1915...Lt.-Col. F. F. Ready.
19 May, 1916...Lt.-Col. W. P. H. Hill.
15 Oct., 1916...Lt.-Col. G. H. Martin.
21 Aug., 1918...Lt.-Col. H. Street.

B.-G., R.A.

Mobilization.....Br.-Gen. G. F. Milne.
29 Jan., 1915...Br.-Gen. R. F. Fox.
5 Sept., 1915...Br.-Gen. W. Strong.
27 April, 1916...Br.-Gen. C. Prescott-Decie
        (wounded, 24/1/17).
25 Jan., 1917...Lt.-Col. A. T. Butler (acting).
3 Feb., 1917...Br.-Gen. F. T. Ravenhill
        (invalided, 1/6/17).
1 June, 1917...Br.-Gen. C. A. Sykes
        (invalided, 17/12/17).
3 Dec., 1917...Br.-Gen. E. B. Macnaghten
        (tempy.).
26 Dec., 1917...Lt.-Col. W. B. Thompson
        (acting).
14 Feb., 1918...Br.-Gen. C. A. Sykes.

C.R.E.

Mobilization.....Lt.-Col. H. B. Jones.
13 May, 1916...Lt.-Col. S. Mildred.
24 Feb., 1917...Lt.-Col. C. R. Johnson.

10th BRIGADE

Mobilization. Br.-Gen. J. A. L. HALDANE.
18 Nov., '14...Br.-Gen. C. P. A. HULL.
5 Feb., '16...Br.-Gen. C. A. WILDING.
27 Dec., '16...Br.-Gen. C. GOSLING
(killed, 12/4/17).
12 April, '17...Lt.-Col. G. N. B. FORSTER
(acting).
14 April, '17...Br.-Gen. A. G. PRITCHARD.
27 Nov., '17...Br.-Gen. H. W. GREEN.
16 April, '18...Br.-Gen. J. GREENE.

11th BRIGADE

Mobilization. Br.-Gen. A. G.
HUNTER-WESTON.
26 Feb., '15...Br.-Gen. J. A. HASLER
(killed, 27/4/15).
27 April, '15...Lt.-Col. F. R. HICKS (acting).
29 April, '15...Br.-Gen. C. B. PROWSE
(killed, 1/7/16).
1 July, '16...Major W. A. T. B.
SOMERVILLE* (acting).
3 July, '16...Br.-Gen. H. C. REES.
7 Dec., '16...Br.-Gen. R. A. BERNERS.
15 Oct., '17...Lt.-Col. F. A. W. ARMITAGE
(acting).
21 Oct., '17...Br.-Gen. T. S. H. WADE.
19 Sept., '18...Br.-Gen. W. J. WEBB-
BOWEN.

12th BRIGADE

Mobilization. Br.-Gen. H. F. M. WILSON.
9 Sept., '14...Lt.-Col. F. G. ANLEY
(acting).
23 Sept., '14...Br.-Gen. H. F. M. WILSON.
4 Oct., '14...Br.-Gen. F. G. ANLEY.
(Bde. transferred to 36th Div., 4/11/15.)

107th Brigade

(Transferred temporarily from 36th Div.
on 3/11/15.)
[20 Oct., '15]...Br.-Gen. W. M.
WITHYCOMBE.
(Bde. rejoined 36th Div. on 7/2/16.)

12th BRIGADE

(Rejoined from 36th Div., 3/2/16.)
[4 Oct., '14]...Br.-Gen. F. G. ANLEY.
4 June, '16...Br.-Gen. J. D. CROSBIE.
11 Jan., '17...Br.-Gen. A. CARTON DE
WIART, V.C.
(wounded, 23/11/17).
23 Nov., '17...Lt.-Col. H. W. GLENN
(acting).
29 Nov., '17...Br.-Gen. E. A. FAGAN.
8 Oct., '18...Br.-Gen. E. B. MACNAGHTEN.

*On 1/7/16 the Br.-Gen. was killed and all the Bn. Cdrs. were killed or wounded.   The Bde. Major then assumed command, and, after relief, brought the Brigade out of action.

GENERAL NOTES

At le Cateau, on 26/8/14, the 4th Division fought without the following Units :—
B. Sqdn., 19/Hsrs. (15/9/14), 4th Cyclist Coy. (28/8/14), 31st Hy. Bty. and A.C. (9/9/14),
4th D.A.C. (30/8/14), 7th and 9th Field Cos. (28/8/14), 4th Signal Coy. (28/8/14), 10th
and 12th Field Ambs. (29/8/14), 11th Field Amb. (1/9/14), 4th Divisional Train (28/8/14).

N.B. : The date on which the particular Unit rejoined the 4th Division is shown
in brackets.

The 12th Inf. Bde. (less 2/Mon.) with the 10th Field Amb. was attached to the
36th Div. from 4/11/15–3/2/16, its place in the 4th being taken by the 107th Bde. (36th
Div.), and the 110th Field Amb. During this period 2/Mon. was attached to the 107th
Bde.

———————

The following Units also served with the 4th Division :—

INFANTRY :—1/L.R.B., joined 11th Bde. 17/11/14, transferred to G.H.Q. troops on
19/5/15.

9/A. & S.H., joined 10th Bde. on 21/5/15 (from 81st Bde., 27th Div.), and was
transferred to VI. Corps Troops on 22/7/15 (also see note 9, p. 61).

3/10/Middlesex, replaced 1/R. Ir. F. in 10th Bde., 2/8/17 ; and on 20/2/18 became
11th Entrenching Bn.

ARTILLERY :—No. 4 Pom-Pom Section (A.-A.), from 20/9/1914–January, 1915.

2nd Mountain Battery, from 14/12/14–21/4/15 (transferred to III. Corps).

OTHER UNITS :—3A Sanitary Section, from 20/2/1915–29/3/1917 (transferred to XIX.
Corps).

4th Divnl. Amb. Workshop, joined by 11/4/15, and served until 9/4/16 (transferred
to Divnl. Supply Coln.).

———————

On 14/2/18, the reorganization of the division on a 9-battalion basis was completed ;
and on 28/2/18 the pioneer battalion (21/W. York.) was reorganised on a 3-company
basis.

4TH DIVISION

ORDER OF BATTLE, 1914 - 1918

Dates	Bri-gades	Battalions and attached Units	Mounted Troops	Brigades	Batteries	Bde. Ammn. Columns	Heavy Battery	Medium	Heavy	Divnl. Ammn. Col.	Field Cos.	Divnl. Signal Coy.	Pioneers	M.G. Units	Field Ambu-lances	Mobile Vety. Secn.	Divnl. Emplnt. Coy.	Divnl. Train
		INFANTRY		ARTILLERY — Field Artillery				Trench Mortar Batteries			Engineers	Signal Service						
1914 August	10th	1/R. War., 2/Sea. H., 1/R. Ir. F., 2/R.D.F.	B. Sqdn., 19/Hsrs.2 ; 4th Cyclist Coy.	XIV......	39,3 68, 88	XIV B.A.C.	31 H.B.5 & Hy. Bty. A.C.	...	...	4th D.A.C.	7th6 9th	4th	...	...	10th 11th 12th	4th7	...	4th8
	11th	1/Som. L.I., 1/E. Lanc., 1/Hants., 1/R.B.		XXIX....	125, 126, 127	XXIX B.A.C.												
	12th	1/K.O., 2/L.F., 2/R. Innis. F.,1 2/Essex.		XXXII....	27, 134, 135	XXXII B.A.C.												
				XXXVII (H.)4	31 (H.), 35 (H.), 55 (H.)	XXXVII (H.) B.A.C.												
1915 Sept.	10th	1/R. War., 2/Sea. H., 1/R. Ir. P., 2/R.D.F., 7/A. & S.H.9	A. Sqdn., 1/Northants. Yeo.13 ; 4th Cyclist Coy.14	XIV....	68, 88	XIV B.A.C.	...	...	...	4th D.A.C.	9th 1/W. Lanc.16 1/Durham17	4th	...	...	10th 11th 12th	4th	...	4th
	11th	1/Som. L.I., 2/R. Ir. Regt.,10 1/E. Lanc., 1/Hants., 1/R.B.		XXIX....	125, 126, 127	XXIX B.A.C.												
	12th	1/K.O., 2/L.F., 2/Essex, 5/S. Lanc.,11 2/Mon.12		XXXII....	27, 134, 135	XXXII B.A.C.												
				CXXVII (H.)15	86 (H.), 128 (H.)	CXXVII (H.) B.A.C.												
1916 June	10th	1/R. War., 2/Sea. H., 1/R. Ir. F., 2/R.D.F.;18 10th Bde. M.G. Coy.;19 10th T.M. Bty.20	...	XIV22	68, 88; 86 (H.),23	...24	...	X.425 Y.425 Z.425	V.425	4th D.A.C.24	9th 1/Renfrew26 1/Durham	4th	21/W. York.27 (P.)	...	10th 11th 12th	4th	...	4th
	11th	1/Som. L.I.,1/E. Lanc.,1/Hants., 1/R.B.; 11th Bde. M.G. Coy.;19 11th T.M. Bty.20		XXIX....	125, 126, 127; 128 (H.)23													
	12th	1/K.O., 2/L.F., 2/Duke's,21 2/Essex; 12th Bde. M.G. Coy.;19 12th T.M. Bty.20		XXXII....	27, 134, 135; D. (H.)23													
1917 June	10th	Household Bn, 28 1/R. War., 2/Sea. H., 1/R. Ir. F.;29 10th M.G. Coy.; 10th T.M. Bty.	...	XXIX....	125, 126, 127; 128 (H.)	...	...	X.432 Y.432 Z.432	V.432	4th D.A.C.	9th 406th (Renfrew) 526th (Durham)	4th	21/W. York. (P.)	234th M.G. Coy.33	10th 11th 12th	4th	207th33	4th
	11th	1/Som. L.I., 1/E. Lanc.,30 1/Hants., 1/R.B.; 11th M.G. Coy.; 11th T.M. Bty.		XXXII....	27, 134, 135; 86 (H.)32													
	12th	1/K.O., 2/L.F., 2/Duke's,31 2/Essex; 12th M.G. Coy.; 12th T.M. Bty.																
1918 March	10th	1/R. War., 2/Duke's,31 2/Sea. H.; 10th T.M. Bty.	...	XXIX....	125, 126, 127; 128 (H.)	...	...	X.4 Y.4	...	4th D.A.C.	9th 406th 526th	4th	21/W. York.34 (P.)	No. 4 Battn. M.G.C.35	10th 11th 12th	4th	207th	4th
	11th	1/Som. L.I., 1/Hants., 1/R.B.; 11th T.M. Bty.		XXXII....	27, 134, 135; 86 (H.)													
	12th	1/K.O., 2/L.F., 2/Essex; 12th T.M. Bty.																

60

NOTES ON ORDER OF BATTLE

1 Became G.H.Q. Troops, 6/12/14.

2 Joined a composite Cav. Regt. on 29/8/14. B. Sqdn. rejoined 4th Div. on the Aisne on 15/9/14. Transferred on 14/4/15 to 9th Cav. Bde. (on formation), and replaced by A. Sqdn., 1/Northants Yeo., from 8th Div.

3 Transferred to XIX Bde., 27th Div., on 8/2/15.

4 XXXVII (H.) was transferred to IV Corps on 17/2/15; and XXXVII (H.) (31 and 35) joined 7th Divnl Arty. on 24/8/15. 55 (H.) was attached to 7th Divnl. Arty., 28/11/14–8/3/15; the battery joined 8th Divnl. Arty. on 10/5/15.

5 On the reorganization of the Artillery in Feb., 1916, 31 H.B. left the 4th Div. on 29/4/15, and joined II Group, H.A.R., in June, 1915.

6 Transferred to 48th Div., 29/4/15.

7 Reported to 4th Div. at Ligny on 25/8/14.

8 18, 25, 82, and 38 Coa. A.S.C.

9 Joined, 6/1/15. Amalgamated with 9/A. & S.H. (from 81st Bde., 27th Div.) on 21/5/15. Resumed independent formation (9/A. & S.H. was transferred to Corps Troops, VI Corps), and on 1/3/16, 7/A. & S.H. was transferred to 154th Bde., 51st Div.

10 Joined 12th Bde. (from G.H.Q. Troops), 14/3/15; transferred to 11th Bde., 26/7/15 and transferred to 22nd Bde., 7th Div., on 22/5/16.

11 Joined 16/2/15, transferred for training under 36th Div., 7/11/15; and transferred to 166th Bde., 55th Div., on 6/1/16.

12 Joined 20/11/14. Amalgamated with 1st and 3rd Bns., 27/5/15, and attached to 84th Bde., 28th Div., 29/5/15; resumed independent formation, 24/7/15; rejoined 12th Bde., 25/7/15; and transferred to L. of C., 30/1/16. (Became Pioneers, 29th Div., on 1/5/16.)

13 Joined 13/4/15; transferred to VI Corps Cav., 11/5/16.

14 Transferred to VII Corps Cyclist Bn., 11/5/16.

15 86 (H.) joined from 6th Div. on 18/5/16 and 128 (H.) from 3rd Div. on 25/5/15. The Bde. was formed on 6/8/15. The Bde. was broken up on 21/5/16, and 86 (H.) joined XIV and 128 (H.) joined XXIX.

16 Joined from G.H.Q. Troops, 14/2/15; transferred to 55th Div., 28/2/16. (Attached to 48th Div., 18/4/15–28/4/15.)

17 Joined, 20/9/15.

18 Transferred to 48th Bde., 16th Div., 15/11/16.

19 10th formed on 22/12/15, 11th on 23/12/15, and 12th on 24/1/16.

20 Formed June, 1916 (12th was formed on 11/6/16).

21 Joined 4th Div. (from 13th Bde., 5th Div.) on 15/1/16; transferred to 12th Bde., 8/2/16.

22 Became an A.F.A. Bde. on 14/1/17. B/CLXXXVIII joined from 40th Div. and became A/XIV. 86 (H.) was transferred to XXXII.

23 D/XXXII was formed of one sec. each from 86 and 128. On 14/1/17 D/XXXII was broken up and the two seca. rejoined 86 and 128.

24 D.A.C. reorganized, and B.A.C.'s abolished, 11/5/16.

25 From June, 1916.

26 Joined 2/5/16.

27 Joined 21/5/16.

28 Joined (from England) 17/11/16. Broken up 10/2/18 (drafts sent to Household Cav. and Foot Guards).

29 Transferred on 2/8/17 to 36th Div. Replaced in 10th Bde. by 8/10/Midd x. (became 11th Entrenching Bn. on 20/2/18).

30 Transferred on 1/2/18 to 103rd Bde., 34th Div.

31 Transferred from 12th to 10th Bde. on 10/2/18.

32 On 8/2/18 Z.4 was distributed amongst X.4 and Y.4; and V.4 formed XVII Corps H.T.M.B.

33 4th D.E. Coy. arrived 17/5/17, and in June, 1917, it was renumbered 207th.

34 Reorganized on a 3-company basis, 28/2/18.

35 Formed 26/2/18. Consisted of 10th, 11th, 12th, and 234th M.G. Cos. (234th joined the div. on 16/7/17).

4TH DIVISION

On the outbreak of War the 4th Division was quartered in the Eastern Command (at Woolwich, Shorncliffe, Dover, and Colchester), and mobilized there. The division concentrated at Harrow on the 18th and 19th August, began entraining at Harrow on the 21st August, crossed to France on the 22nd August, entrained for the front on the 23rd, and on the 24th detrained at Bohain, Busigny, le Cateau, and Bertry. On the 25th the 4th Division advanced to cover the withdrawal of the 3rd Division (II. Corps) and 19th Infantry Brigade.

Throughout the War the 4th Division served on the Western Front in France and Belgium, and was engaged in the following operations :

1914

25 Aug.–5 Sept....	...**RETREAT FROM MONS** [II. Corps, 26–30/8/14, and III. Corps, from 31/8/14.]
26 Aug.	...**Battle of le Cateau** [under II. Corps].
1 Sept.	...**Néry** (1/R. War. R. and 2/R.D.F., 10th Bde.).

6–9 Sept. ...	...**Battle of the Marne** [III. Corps].
12 Sept.	...**Crossing of the Aisne** (11th Bde.).
13–20 Sept. ...	...**BATTLE OF THE AISNE** [III. Corps].
13 Oct.–2 Nov. ...	...**Battle of Armentières** [III. Corps].
13 Oct.	...**Capture of Meteren.**
21 Oct. & 30 & 31 Oct.	...**Battle of Messines** (2/Essex, 21/10, and 2/R. Innis. F., 30 and 31/10).

1915

25 April–25 May	...**BATTLES OF YPRES** [V. Corps, Second Army].
25 April–4 May ...	...**Battle of St. Julien** [V. Corps, Second Army, and from 28/4–7/5 in Plumer's Force].
8–13 May... ...	...**Battle of Frezenberg Ridge** [V. Corps, Second Army].
24 and 25 May ...	...**Battle of Bellewaarde Ridge** [V. Corps, Second Army].

1916

BATTLES OF THE SOMME

⎧ 1–21 July ...	...[VIII. Corps, Fourth Army ; then from 3/7 VIII. Corps, Reserve Army].
⎩ 10–25 Oct. ...	...[XIV. Corps, Fourth Army].
1 and 2 July ...	...**Battle of Albert** [VIII. Corps, Fourth Army].
10–18 Oct. ...	...**Battle of the Transloy Ridges** [XIV. Corps, Fourth Army].

1917

BATTLES OF ARRAS

9–14 April ...	...**First Battle of the Scarpe** [XVII. Corps, Third Army].
3 and 4 May ...	...**Third Battle of the Scarpe** [XVII. Corps, Third Army].

BATTLES OF YPRES

28 Sept.–3 Oct. ...	...**Battle of Polygon Wood** [XIV. Corps, Fifth Army].
4 Oct.	...**Battle of Broodseinde** [XIV. Corps, Fifth Army].
9 Oct.	...**Battle of Poelcappelle** [XIV. Corps, Fifth Army].
12 Oct.	...**First Battle of Passchendaele** [XIV. Corps, Fifth Army].

1918

FIRST BATTLES OF THE SOMME

28 March ...	...**First Battle of Arras** [XVII. Corps, Third Army].

BATTLES OF THE LYS

13–15 April ...	...**Battle of Hazebrouck** [I. Corps, First Army]. (Including Defence of Hinges Ridge.)
18 April	...**Battle of Bethune** [I. Corps, First Army].

THE ADVANCE TO VICTORY

SECOND BATTLES OF ARRAS

29 and 30 Aug. ...	...**Battle of the Scarpe** [Cdn. Corps, First Army].
2 and 3 Sept. ...	...**Battle of the Drocourt-Quéant Line** [Cdn. Corps, First Army].

BATTLES OF THE HINDENBURG LINE

27 Sept.–1 Oct. ...	...**Battle of the Canal du Nord** [XXII. Corps, First Army].

THE FINAL ADVANCE IN PICARDY

17–25 Oct. ...	...**Battle of the Selle** [XXII. Corps, First Army].
1 and 2 Nov. ...	...**Battle of Valenciennes** [XXII. Corps, First Army].

On the 11th November the 4th Division, in XXII. Corps Reserve, was concentrated to the south-east of Valenciennes. The division did not proceed to the Rhine as part of the Army of Occupation, but it moved to Valenciennes, and here, on the 4th December, it was visited by H.M. the King. On the 6th January, 1919, the division moved to the Binche–la Louvière area, and demobilization was carried out.

5TH DIVISION

G.O.C.

Mobilization... ... ... Major-General Sir C. Fergusson, Bt.
18 October, 1914... ... ... Major-General T. L. N. Morland.
15 July, 1915 ... ... Major-General C. T. McM. Kavanagh.
1 April, 1916 ... ... Major-General R. B. Stephens.
4 July, 1918 ... ... Major-General J. Ponsonby.

G.S.O. 1.

Mobilization ...Lt.-Col. C. F. Romer.
24 Feb., 1915...Col. E. S. Heard.
22 Mar., 1915...Lt.-Col. A. R. Cameron.
21 Oct., 1915...Lt.-Col. R. A. M. Currie.
 3 Oct., 1916...Lt.-Col. G. C. W. Gordon-
Hall.
11 May, 1918...Major W. P. Buckley
(acting).
20 May, 1918...Lt.-Col. G. C. W. Gordon-
Hall.
25 June, 1918...Major A. Anderson
(acting).
 2 July, 1918...Lt.-Col. G. C. W. Gordon-
Hall.

A.-A. & Q.-M.-G.

Mobilization ...Col. J. S. Moore
(missing, 26/8/14).
27 Aug., 1914...Lt.-Col. N. G. Anderson.
17 July, 1915...Lt.-Col. R. F. A. Hobbs.
25 Feb., 1918...Capt. H. Courtenay
(acting).
 8 Mar., 1918...Lt.-Col. O. W. White.

B.-G., R.A.

Mobilization ...Br.-Gen. J. E. W.
Headlam.
21 Feb., 1915...Br.-Gen. A. H. Short
(tempy.).
26 Feb., 1915...Br.-Gen. J. G. Geddes.
10 Oct., 1915...Br.-Gen. A. H. Hussey.

C.R.E.

Mobilization ...Lt.-Col. J. A. S. Tulloch.
14 July, 1915...Lt.-Col. J. R. White
(acting).
20 July, 1915...Lt.-Col. C. E. G. Vesey.
 6 April, 1916...Lt.-Col. J. R. White.
21 May, 1918...Lt.-Col. E. E. F. Homer.

13th BRIGADE

Mobilization...Br.-Gen. G. J. CUTHBERT.
1 Oct., '14...Br.-Gen. W. B. HICKIE
(invalided, 13/10/14).
13 Oct., '14...Col. A. MARTYN (acting)
(wounded, 7/11/14).
7 Nov., '14...Lt.-Col. W. M. WITHY-
COMBE (acting).
3 Dec., '14...Br.-Gen. F. J. COOPER
(invalided, 1/2/15).
1 Feb., '15...Lt.-Col. L. J. BOLS (acting).
8 Feb., '15...Br.-Gen. R. WANLESS
O'GOWAN.
(Bde. transferred temporarily to 28th Div.
on 19/2/15.)

84th Brigade

(Bde. transferred temporarily from 28th
Div. on 23/2/15.)
[25 Dec., '14] Br.-Gen. F. WINTOUR
(sick, 23/2/15).
24 Feb., '15...Br.-Gen. L. J. BOLS.
(Bde. returned to 28th Div. 7/4/15.)

13th BRIGADE

(Bde. returned from 28th Div. 7/4/15.)
[8 Feb., '15]...Br.-Gen. R. WANLESS
O'GOWAN.
21 Aug., '15...Br.-Gen. C. C. M. MAYNARD
(sick, 31/8/15).
31 Aug., '15...Col. P. M. ROBINSON
(acting).
18 Sept., '15...Br.-Gen. C. C. M. MAYNARD
(sick, 20/10/15).
23 Oct., '15...Lt.-Col. E. S. D'E. COKE
(acting).
2 Nov., '15...Br.-Gen. L. O. W. JONES
(injured, 16/11–18/12/17).
16 Nov., '17...Lt.-Col. L. MURRAY
(acting).
18 Dec., '17...Br.-Gen. L. O. W. JONES
(sick, 8/9/18, died, 14/9/18).
8 Sept., '18...Lt.-Col. C. T. FURBER
(acting).
15 Sept., '18...Lt.-Col. J. W. C. KIRK
(acting).
21 Sept., '18...Br.-Gen. A. T. BECKWITH.

14th BRIGADE

Mobilization...Br.-Gen. S. P. ROLT
(sick, 20/10/14).
20 Oct., '14...Lt.-Col. J. R. LONGLEY
(acting).
23 Oct., '14...Br.-Gen. F. S. MAUDE
(wounded, 12/4/15).
12 April, '15...Lt.-Col. E. G. WILLIAMS
(acting).
17 April, '15...Br.-Gen. G. H. THESIGER
(tempy.).
4 May, '15...Br.-Gen. F. S. MAUDE.
10 Sept., '15...Br.-Gen. C. W. CROMPTON.
26 Dec., '15...Br.-Gen. C. R. BALLARD.
On 12/1/16 the Bde. was redesignated

95th BRIGADE

[26 Dec., '15] Br.-Gen. C. R. BALLARD
(wounded, 20/7/16).
20 July, '16...Lt.-Col. M. ARCHER-SHEE
(acting).
21 July, '16...Br.-Gen. LORD E. C.
GORDON-LENNOX
(wounded, 14/4/18).
15 April, '18...Br.-Gen. C. B. NORTON.

15th BRIGADE

Mobilization...Br.-Gen. COUNT GLEICHEN.
2 Mar., '15...Br.-Gen. E. NORTHEY.
(Bde. transferred temporarily to 28th Div.
on 3/3/15.)

83rd Brigade

(Bde. transferred temporarily from 28th
Div. on 3/3/15.)
[26 Dec., '14] Br.-Gen. R. C. BOYLE.
(Bde. returned to 28th Div. 7/4/15.)

15th BRIGADE

(Bde. returned from 28th Div. 7/4/15.)
[2 Mar., '15] Br.-Gen. E. NORTHEY
(wounded, 22/6/15).
22 June, '15...Lt.-Col. C. R. J. GRIFFITH
(acting).
28 June, '15...Br.-Gen. M. N. TURNER.
6 Nov., '17...Br.-Gen. R. D. F. OLDMAN
(wounded, 11/5/18).
11 May, '18...Lt.-Col. G. C. W. GORDON-
HALL (acting).
20 May, '18...Br.-Gen. R. D. F. OLDMAN
(gassed, 25/6/18).
25 June, '18...Lt.-Col. G. C. W. GORDON-
HALL (acting).
7 July, '18...Lt.-Col. E. L. RODDY
(acting).
25 July, '18...Br.-Gen. R. D. F. OLDMAN.

GENERAL NOTES

The **13th Inf. Bde.** (2/K.O.S.B., 2/Duke's, 1/R.W.K., 2/K.O.Y.L.I.) was transferred temporarily to the 28th Division from 19/2/15–7/4/15, and was replaced from 23/2/15–7/4/15, by the 84th Bde., 28th Division (2/N.F., 1/Suff., 2/Ches., 1/Welsh, with 1/Mon. (from 27/2/15), and 9/Lond. attached).

The **15th Inf. Bde.** (1/Norf., 1/Bedf., 1/Ches., 1/Dorset, with 6/King's) was transferred temporarily to the 28th Division from 3/3/15–7/4/15, and was replaced from 3/3/15–7/4/15, by the 83rd Bde. 28th Division (2/K.O., 2/E. Yorks., 1/K.O.Y.L.I., 1/Y. and L., with 5/K.O. and 3/Mon. attached).

The following Units also served with the 5th Division :—

INFANTRY :—6/Ches. joined 15th Bde. on 17/12/14, and was transferred to G.H.Q. Troops on 1/3/15.

2/R. Innis. F. joined 14th Bde. from Third Army Troops on 18/11/15, and was transferred to 96th Bde., 32nd Div., on 30/12/15.

9/R. Scots. joined 14th Bde. on 27/11/15, and was transferred to Third Army Troops on 25/1/16.

ARTILLERY :—No. 6 Pom-Pom Section (A.-A.), from 12/9/14–December, 1914.

ENGINEERS :—1/S. Midland Field Coy. joined on 24/3/15 (from 27th Div.) ; transferred on 10/4/15 to 6th Div. It rejoined 48th (S.M.) Div. on 1/5/15.

2/1/N. Midland Field Coy. joined on 23/4/15 (from G.H.Q.) ; transferred on 19/6/15 to 28th Div.

OTHER UNITS :—No. 6 Sanitary Section, from 9/1/15–2/4/17 (transferred to XI. Corps).

5th Divnl. Ambulance Workshop joined by 13/6/15, and served until 16/4/16 (transferred to Divnl. Supply Coln.).

On 4/10/18 the division was reorganized on a 9-battalion basis ; and on 8/10/18 the pioneer battalion (14/R. War.) was reorganized on a 3-company basis.

Dates	Brigades	Battalions and attached Units	Mounted Troops	Art. Brigades	Art. Batteries	Bde. Ammn. Columns	Heavy Battery	T.M. Medium	T.M. Heavy	Divnl. Ammn. Col.	Engineers Field Cos.	Divnl. Signal Coy.	Pioneers	M.G. Units	Field Ambulances	Mobile Vety. Secn.	Divnl. Emplnt. Coy.	Divnl. Train
1914 (August) (France)	18th	2/K.O.S.B., 2/Duke's, 1/R.W.K., 2/K.O.Y.L.I.	A. Sqdn., 19/Hsrs.2	XV...... XXVII... VIII (H.)	11,3 52, 80 / 119, 120, 121 / 122, 123, 124 / 61 (H.)4 65 (H.)	XV B.A.C. XXVII B.A.C. XXVIII B.A.C. VIII (H.) B.A.C.	108 H.B5 & Hy. Bty. A.C.	...	...	5th D.A.C.	17th6 59th	5th	...	...	13th 14th 15th	5th7	...	5th8
	14th	2/Suff.,1 1/E. Surr., 1/D.C.L.I., 2/Manch.	5th Cyclist Coy.															
	15th	1/Norf., 1/Bedf., 1/Ches., 1/Dorset																
1915 Sept. (France)	13th	2/K.O.S.B. 2/Duke's,10 1/R.W.K. 2/K.O.Y.L.I.,11 9/Lond.12	C. Sqdn.,18 1/Northants. Yeo.;	XV...... XXVII... XXVIII... VIII (H.)20	52, 80 / 119, 120, 121 / 122, 123, 124 / 37 (H.) 65 (H.)	XV B.A.C. XXVII B.A.C. XXVIII B.A.C. VIII (H.) B.A.C.	...	...	...	5th D.A.C.	59th 2/Home Counties21 2/Durham22	5th	...	...	13th 14th 15th	5th	...	5th
	14th9	1/Devon,13 1/E.Surr., 1/D.C.L.I., 2/Manch,14 5/Ches.15	5th Cyclist Coy.19															
	15th	1/Norf., 1/Bedf., 1/Ches., 1/Dorset,16 6/King's17																
1916 June (France)	13th	2/K.O.S.B., 1/R.W.K., 14/R. War.,23 15/R.War.;24 13th Bde. M.G.Coy.;25 13th T.M. Bty.26	...	XV...... XXVII... XXVIII29	52, 80; D(H.) / 119, 120, 121; 37 (H.) / 122, 123, 124; 65 (H.)29	...30	...	X.531 Y.531 Z.531	V.532	5th D.A.C. 30	59th 2/Home Counties 2/Durham	5th	6/A. & S.H.33 (P.)	...	13th 14th 15th	5th	...	5th
	16th	1/Norf., 1/Bedf., 1/Ches., 16/R. War.;27 16th Bde. M.G. Coy.; 25 16th T.M. Bty.26																
	95th9	1/Devon, 1/E. Surr., 1/D.C.L.I., 12/Glouc.;28 95th Bde. M.G. Coy.;25 95th T.M. Bty.26																
1917 June (France)	13th	2/K.O.S.B., 14/R. War., 15/R. War.; 13th M.G. Coy.; 13th T.M. Bty.	...	XV...... XXVII...	52, 80, A.;29 D (H.)34 / 119, 120, 121; 37 (H.)34	...	...	X.535 Y.535 Z.535	V.535	5th D.A.C.	59th 491st (Home Counties) 527th (Durham)	5th	6/A. & S.H. (P.)	205th M.G. Coy.42	13th 14th 15th	5th	208th36	5th
	16th	1/Norf., 1/Bedf., 1/Ches., 16/R. War.; 15th M.G. Coy.; 15th T.M. Bty.																
	95th	1/Devon, 1/E. Surr., 1/D.C.L.I., 12/Glouc.; 95th M.G. Coy.; 95th T.M. Bty.																
1918 May (after return from Italy)	18th	2/K.O.S.B., 1/R.W.K., 14/R. War.,37 15/R. War.;38 13th T.M. Bty.	...	XV...... XXVII...	52, 80, A; D (H.)34 / 119, 120, 121; 37	...	...	X.5 Y.5	...	5th D.A.C.	59th 491st 527th	5th	6/A. & S.H.41 (P.)	No. 5 Battn., M.G.C.42	13th 14th 15th	5th	208th	5th
	15th	1/Norf., 1/Bedf., 1/Ches., 16/R. War.;39 15th T.M. Bty.																
	96th	1/Devon, 1/E. Surr., 1/D.C.L.I., 12/Glouc.;40 96th T.M. Bty.																
1918 Nov. (France)	13th	2/K.O.S.B., 1/R.W.K., 16/R. War.; 13th T.M. Bty.	...	XV...... XXVII...	52, 80, A; D (H.) / 119, 120, 121; 37 (H.)	...	...	X.5 Y.5	...	5th D.A.C.	59th 491st 527th	5th	14/R. War.87 (P.)	No. 5 Battn., M.G.C.	13th 14th 15th	5th	208th	5th
	16th	1/Norf., 1/Bedf., 1/Ches.; 16th T.M. Bty.																
	95th	1/Devon, 1/E. Surr., 1/D.C.L.I.; 95th T.M. Bty.																

NOTES ON ORDER OF BATTLE

1 Transferred on 30/9/14 to G.H.Q. at Fère en Tardenois. Replaced by 1/Devon.

2 Joined 2nd Cav. Bde. on 25/8/14, transferred to 5th Cav. Bde., 11/9/14; rejoined 5th Div. 15/9/14. Rejoined 5th Div. on 14/4/15, and transferred to 9th Cav. Bde. (on formation). Replaced by C, 1/Northants. Yeo., from 8th Div.

3 Transferred on 9/2/15 to I Bde., 27th Div.

4 Transferred to 27th Div., 21/2/15.

5 Following the reorganization of the Artillery in Feb., 1915, 108 H.B. left the division on 9/4/15; and was attached to XIII Hy. Bde. on 27/4/15.

6 Transferred on 26/3/15 to 27th Div.; replaced on 24/3/15 by 1/S.M Fd. Coy., transferred on 1/5/15 to 48th (S.M.) Div.; replaced on 23/4/15 by 2/1/N.M. Fd. Coy., transferred to 28th Div. on 19/6/15; and replaced by 2/Durham Fd. Coy. on 20/9/15.

7 Joined in France on 20/8/14.

8 4, 6, 33, and 37 Cos., A.S.C.

9 Redesignated 95th Inf. Bde. on 12/1/16.

10 Transferred to 12th Bde., 4th Div., 14/1/16.

11 Transferred to 97th Bde., 32nd Div., 28/12/15.

12 Joined 27/11/14; attached 83rd Bde. 3/3–7/4/15; and transferred to 169th Bde., 56th Div., 10/2/16.

13 Joined from 8th Bde., 3rd Div., on 30/9/14.

14 Transferred to 95th Bde., 32nd Div., 30/12/15.

15 Joined 19/2/15; became divnl. pioneer bn. on 29/11/15; transferred on 13/2/16 to 56th Div. as pioneers.

16 Transferred to 95th Bde. 32nd Div., 31/12/15.

17 Joined 27/2/16; transferred to Third Army Troops, 18/11/15.

18 Joined 12/4/15; transferred to VI Corps Cav., 11/5/16.

19 Transferred to VI Corps Cyclist Bn., 11/5/16.

20 Bde. broken up 21/5/16. 37 (H.) (less 1 sec.) to XXVII; 65 (H.) (less 1 sec.) to XXVIII; and 1 sec., 37, and 1 sec., 65 formed D (H.) of XV.

21 Joined 2/2/15.

22 Joined 20/9/15.

23 Joined on 28/12/15, from 95th Bde., 32nd Div.

24 Joined 14th Bde. on 26/12/15 from 95th Bde., 32nd Div.; transferred to 13th Bde. on 14/1/16.

25 13th formed 24/12/15; 15th on 27/12/15; and 14th (redesignated 95th on 12/1/16) on 20/12/15.

26 Formed April, 1916.

27 Joined on 28/12/15, from 95th Bde., 32nd Div.

28 Joined on 28/12/15, from 95th Bde., 32nd Div.

29 Became an A.F.A. Bde., 21/1/17. 65 (H.) was made up by 1 sec. from D/CXXVI; and A/CCC became A/XV. on 21/1/17.

30 D.A.C. reorganized, and B.A.C.'s abolished, 21/5/16.

31 Formed April, 1916.

32 Formed on 18/10/16.

33 Transferred from 152nd Bde., 51st Div., on 18/8/16.

34 526 (H.) joined XV on 14/10/16; and by 11/12/16 became C/XV. On 21/1/17 C/XV was broken up, and 1 sec. joined D/XV and 1 sec. 37/XXVII.

35 On 15/3/18 Z.5 was distributed between X.5 and Y.5. V.5 left in Nov., 1917, when the division moved to Italy.

36 No. 10 D.E. Coy. arrived on 22/5/17; and it was renumbered 208 D.E. Coy. in June.

37 Became Pioneers of 6th Div., 5/10/18.

38 Disbanded, 6/10/18.

39 Transferred to 18th Bde., 4/10/18.

40 Disbanded, 19/10/18.

41 Transferred to 153rd Bde., 51st Div., 5/10/18; and replaced as Pioneers by 14/R. War., from 13th Bde. (see note 37).

42 Formed 28/4/18 and consisted of 13th, 15th, 95th, and 205th M.G. Cos. (205th joined the div. on 19/3/17).

F

5TH DIVISION

MOBILIZATION, BATTLES, AND ENGAGEMENTS

On the outbreak of War, the 5th Division was quartered in Ireland, at Dublin, the Curragh, Kildare, Belfast, Londonderry, etc. ; and it mobilized in Ireland. The advance party left the Curragh on the 7th August, and landed at Havre on the 13th. The division began to move on the 13th August, and reached Havre on the 17th. Concentration around Landrécies took place between the 16th and 20th August, and the division moved forward on the 21st.

In the War the 5th Division served on the Western Front in France and Belgium, between August, 1914, and 27th November, 1917, when it began to move to the Italian Front. The 5th Division returned to France on the 1st April, 1918, and concentrated around Doullens on the 9th April. For the remainder of the War the division served on the Western Front in France and Belgium.

The 5th Division was engaged in the following operations :—

1914

23 and 24 Aug. ...	...Battle of Mons [II. Corps].
23 Aug.–5 Sept. ...	...RETREAT FROM MONS [II. Corps].
24 Aug.	...Elouges (1/Norf. and 1/Ches., and 119 R.F.A.).
26 Aug.	...Battle of le Cateau [II. Corps].
1 Sept.	...Crépy en Valois.
6–9 Sept. ...	...Battle of the Marne [II. Corps].
13–20 Sept. ...	...BATTLE OF THE AISNE [II. Corps].
13 Sept.	...Passage of the Aisne.
20 Sept.	...Actions on the Aisne Heights.
10 Oct.–2 Nov. ...	...Battle of la Bassée [II. Corps].
31 Oct.–2 Nov. ...	...Battle of Messines (2/K.O.S.B., 2/K.O.Y.L.I.) [Cav. Corps].
1 and 2 Nov. ...	...Battle of Armentières (1/Dorset) [III. Corps].
5–19 Nov. ...	...BATTLES OF YPRES [I. Corps].
11 Nov.	...Battle of Nonne Bosschen (2/K.O.S.B., 2/Duke's (13th Bde.), and 1/Bedf., 1/Ches. (15th Bde.)) [I. Corps].

1915

17–22 April ...	...Capture of Hill 60 [II. Corps, Second Army].
23 April–1 May ...	...BATTLES OF YPRES [V. Corps, Second Army].
23 April	...Battle of Gravenstafel Ridge (13th Bde.) [V. Corps].
24 April–1 May ...	...Battle of St. Julien (13th Bde.) [V. Corps, from 27/4, in Plumer's Force].

1916

BATTLES OF THE SOMME

20–25 July ...	...Attacks on High Wood [XV. Corps, Fourth Army].
3–6 Sept. ...	...Battle of Guillemont [XIV. Corps, Fourth Army].
18–22 Sept. ...	...Battle of Flers-Courcelette [XIV. Corps, Fourth Army].
25 and 26 Sept. ...	...Battle of Morval [XIV. Corps, Fourth Army].

1917

BATTLES OF ARRAS

9–14 April	...	...Battle of Vimy Ridge [Cdn. Corps, First Army].
23 April ...	...	...Attack on la Coulotte [Cdn. Corps, First Army].
3 and 4 May	...	...Third Battle of the Scarpe [Cdn. Corps, First Army].
28 June ...	...	...Capture of Oppy Wood [XIII. Corps, First Army].

BATTLES OF YPRES

1–3 Oct. ...	...	...Battle of Polygon Wood [X. Corps, Second Army].
4 Oct. ...	...	...Battle of Broodseinde [X. Corps, Second Army].
9 Oct. ...	...	...Battle of Poelcappelle [X. Corps, Second Army].
26 Oct.–10 Nov. ...		...Second Battle of Passchendaele [X. Corps, Second Army].

On the 23rd November the division was warned that it would be moved to Italy. Entrainment began on the 27th November, and concentration was completed by the 20th December to the east of the R. Brenta and not far from Padua. The division formed part of the XI. Corps.

1918

The 5th Division took over part of the line along the Piave on the 27th January, and held it until relieved on the 18th March. On the 24th, the division was warned that it would return to France. Entrainment began on the 1st April, and concentration was completed on the 9th April between Doullens and Frévent.

BATTLES OF THE LYS

12–15 April	...	...Battle of Hazebrouck, including Defence of Nieppe Forest [XI. Corps, First Army].

28 June ...	...	...La Becque.

THE ADVANCE TO VICTORY

SECOND BATTLES OF THE SOMME

21–23 Aug.	...	...Battle of Albert [IV. Corps, Third Army].
31 Aug.–3 Sept. ...		...Second Battle of Bapaume [IV. Corps, Third Army].

BATTLES OF THE HINDENBURG LINE

18 Sept. ...	...	...Battle of Epéhy [IV. Corps, Third Army].
27–30 Sept.	...	...Battle of the Canal du Nord [IV. Corps, Third Army].
9–12 Oct.	...	...The Pursuit to the Selle [IV. Corps, Third Army].

THE FINAL ADVANCE IN PICARDY

17–23 Oct.	...	...Battle of the Selle [IV. Corps, Third Army].
5–10 Nov.	...	...The division gradually fought its way forward through the northern portion of the Forest of Mormal, crossed the Sambre (near Pont sur Sambre), and advanced across the Maubeuge–Avesnes Road on the 8th, and here it was relieved on the 10th November.

On the 11th November, the 5th Division was in IV. Corps Reserve, near le Quesnoy, and on the 3rd December it was visited by H.M. the King. Between the 13th–21st December the division moved into Belgium and was cantoned in the villages between Namur and Wavre, remaining in these billets until its demobilization began in February, 1919.

6TH DIVISION

G.O.C.

Mobilization...	Major-General J. L. KEIR.
27 May, 1915	Major-General W. N. CONGREVE, V.C.
14 November, 1915	Major-General C. ROSS.
21 August, 1917...	Major-General T. O. MARDEN.

G.S.O. 1.

Mobilization ...Col. W. T. FURSE.
29 Dec., 1914...Lt.-Col. J. S. M. SHEA.
7 July, 1915...Lt.-Col. G. F. BOYD.
22 June, 1916...Lt.-Col. L. F. RENNY.
24 Mar., 1917...Lt.-Col. T. T. GROVE.

A.-A. and Q.-M.-G.

Mobilization ...Col. W. CAMPBELL.
6 Oct., 1914...Major F. C. DUNDAS
(acting).
14 Oct., 1914...Col. R. WANLESS O'GOWAN.
15 Feb., 1915...Lt.-Col. R. S. MAY.
6 Feb., 1916...Lt. Col. M. R. WALSH.
30 Aug., 1917...Lt.-Col. M. B. SAVAGE
(sick, 16/12/17).
16 Dec., 1917...Major C. MACFIE (acting).
2 Jan., 1918...Lt.-Col. P. HUDSON.

B.-G., R.A.

Mobilization ...Br.-Gen. W. L. H. PAGET.
27 May, 1915...Br.-Gen. G. HUMPHREYS.
21 June, 1916...Br.-Gen. E. S. CLEEVE.
25 Oct., 1916...Br.-Gen. E. F. DELAFORCE.

C.R.E.

Mobilization ...Lt.-Col. G. C. KEMP.
15 Aug., 1915...Lt.-Col. A. G. STEVENSON.
20 Dec., 1915...Col. T. A. H. BIGGE
(invalided, 6/1/16).
6 Jan., 1916...Capt. R. H. MACKENZIE
(acting).
28 Jan., 1916...Lt.-Col. H. R. S. CHRISTIE.
10 Nov., 1916...Major A. C. HOWARD
(acting).
29 Nov., 1916...Capt. (Major, 14/12/16)
R. H. MACKENZIE (acting).
2 Jan., 1917...Lt.-Col. G. F. B. GOLDNEY.
23 Sept., 1918...Lt.-Col. H. A. L. HALL.

16th BRIGADE

Mobilization...Br.-Gen. E. C. INGOUVILLE-
WILLIAMS.
16 June, '15...Br.-Gen. C. L. NICHOLSON.
26 July, '16...Br.-Gen. W. L. OSBORN.
26 Oct., '17...Br.-Gen. H. A. WALKER
(wounded, 16/10/18).
16 Oct., '18...Br.-Gen. P. W. BROWN
(tempy.).
19 Oct., '18...Br.-Gen. W. G.
BRAITHWAITE.

17th BRIGADE

Mobilization...Br.-Gen. W. R. B. DORAN.
11 Feb., '15...Br.-Gen. G. M. HARPER.
24 Sept., '15...Br.-Gen. J. W. V. CARROLL.

On 14/10/15, the 17th Bde. was transferred to the 24th Div.; its place in the
6th Div. had been taken on 11/10/15 by
the

71st BRIGADE

(from the 24th Div.)
[31 Aug., '15] Br.-Gen. M. T. SHEWEN.
27 May, '16...Br.-Gen. J. F. EDWARDS
(sick, 4/10/16).
6 Oct., '16...Br.-Gen. E. FEETHAM.
19 Aug., '17...Br.-Gen. P. W. BROWN
(tempy., to 16th Bde., 16/10/18).
16 Oct., '18...Lt.-Col. F. LATHAM (acting).
19 Oct., '18...Br.-Gen. P. W. BROWN.

18th BRIGADE

Mobilization...Br.-Gen. W. N. CONGREVE,
V.C.
29 May, '15...Br.-Gen. H. S. AINSLIE
(sick, 5/8/15).
5 Aug., '15...Lt.-Col. F. W. TOWSEY
(acting).
14 Aug., '15...Br.-Gen. R. J. BRIDGFORD
(incapacitated, 19/4/16).
19 April, '16...Lt.-Col. C. J. HOBKIRK
(acting).
29 April, '16...Br.-Gen. W. K.
McCLINTOCK.
12 June, '16...Br.-Gen. H. S. TEW.
16 Aug., '16...Lt.-Col. A. E. IRVINE
(acting).
19 Aug., '16...Br.-Gen. R. J. BRIDGFORD.
14 Sept., '17...Br.-Gen. G. S. G.
CRAUFURD.

GENERAL NOTES

19th INFANTRY BRIGADE. The Brigade, formed on 22 and 23/8/14, at Valenciennes, from L. of C. Defence Troops, was composed as follows :—2/R.W.F., 1/Scottish Rif., 1/Midd'x., and 2/A. and S. H., with 19th Bde. Ammn. Col., Field Amb., and Train. (On 19/11/14, the 5/Scottish Rif. joined the 19th Bde.)

From 12/10/14–31/5/15 the 19th Bde. was attached to the 6th Division, and on the latter date it was transferred to the 27th Division.

Before attachment to the 6th Div., the 19th Bde. had taken part in the following operations :—Battle of Mons (23 and 24/8/14) ; Retreat from Mons (24/8–5/9) ; Solesmes (25/8) ; Battle of le Cateau (26/8, under II. Corps) ; Néry (1/9, under III. Corps) ; Battle of the Marne (6–9/9, under III. Corps) ; and Battle of the Aisne (12–15/9, under III. Corps). Until 31/5/15 the Bde. was commanded by :—

Formation (22/8/14), Major-Gen. L. G. Drummond (sick, 27/8/14).

27 Aug., 1914, Lt.-Col. B. E. Ward (acting).

5 Sept., 1914, Br.-Gen. Hon. F. Gordon (until 14/6/15).

The following Units also served with the 6th Division :—

INFANTRY :—5/L.N.L. joined the 16th Bde. (from England) on 15/2/15, and was transferred to 151st Bde., 50th Div., on 11/6/15.

2/Lond. joined G.H.Q. Troops (from Malta) on 28/1/15, and was transferred to the 17th Bde. on 21/2/15. The Battalion left the 6th Div. with the 17th Bde. on 14/10/15 (see note 7).

ARTILLERY :—**No. 2 Pom-Pom Section (A.-A.),** from 4/10–16/12/14.

OTHER UNITS :—**No. 8 Sanitary Section** joined from England on 9/1/15, and served with the division until transfer to No. 5 Sanitary Area, First Army, on 5/4/17.

6th Divnl. Amb. Workshop arrived from England on 10/6/15, and remained until 9/4/16 (transferred to Divnl. Supply Coln.).

On 9/2/18, the reorganization of the division on a 9-battalion basis was completed ; and by 26/2/18 the pioneer battalion was reorganized on a 3-company basis.

6TH DIVISION ORDER OF BATTLE, 1914 - 1918

Dates	Brigades	INFANTRY — Battalions and attached Units	Mounted Troops	Field Artillery — Brigades	Field Artillery — Batteries	Bde. Ammn. Columns	Heavy Battery	Trench Mortar Batteries — Medium	Trench Mortar Batteries — Heavy	Divnl. Ammn. Col.	Engineers — Field Cos.	Signal Service — Divnl. Signal Coy.	Pioneers	M.G. Units	Field Ambulances	Mobile Vety. Secn.	Divnl. Emplnt. Coy.	Divnl. Train
1914 Sept.	16th 17th 18th	1/Buffs, 1/Leic., 1/K.S.L.I., 2/Y. & L. 1/R.F., 1/N. Staff., 2/Leins., 3/R.B. 1/W. York., 1/E. York., 2/Sher. For., 2/D.L.I.	C. Sqdn., 19/Hsrs.;1 6th Cyclist Coy.	II XXIV XXXVIII XII (H.)	21, 42, 53 110, 111, 112 24, 34, 72 43 (H.), 86 (H.),2 87 (H.)	II B.A.C. XXIV B.A.C. XXXVIII B.A.C. XII (H.) B.A.C.	24 H.B.3 & Hy. Bty. A.C.	...		6th D.A.C.	12th 38th4	6th	...	...	16th 17th 18th	6th5	...	6th6
1915 Sept.	16th 17th7 18th	1/Buffs, 1/Leic.,8 1/K.S.L.I., 2/Y. & L. 1/R.F., 1/N. Staff., 2/Leins., 3/R.B., 2/Lond.9 1/W. York.,10 2/Sher. For.,11 2/D.L.I., 16/Lond. (Q.W.R.)12	B Sqdn., 1/Northants. Yeo.;13; 18 6th Cyclist Coy.14	II XXIV XXXVIII XII (H.)15	21, 42, 53 110, 111, 112 24, 34,16 72 43 (H.), 87 (H.)	II B.A.C. XXIV B.A.C. XXXVIII B.A.C. XII (H.) B.A.C.	...			6th D.A.C.	12th 1/London17	6th	...	...	16th 17th 18th	6th	...	6th
1916 June	16th 18th 71st18	1/Buffs, 1/K.S.L.I., 2/Y. & L., 8/Bedf.;19 16th Bde. M.G. Coy.;20 16th T.M. Bty.21 1/W. York., 2/D.L.I., 11/Essex.;22 14/D.L.I.;23 18th Bde. M.G. Coy.;20 18th T.M. Bty.21 1/Leic.,24 2/Sher. For.,25 9/Norf., 9/Suff.; 71st Bde. M.G. Coy.;20 71st T.M. Bty.21	...	II XXIV XXXVIII 26	21, 42, 53 ; 87 (H.) 110,111,112; 43 (H.) 24, 72, D (H.)27	...30	...	X.628 Y.628 Z.628	W.629	6th D.A.C.30	12th 2/2/W. Riding31 1/London	6th	11/Leic. (P.)32	...	16th 17th 18th	6th	...	6th
1917 June	16th 18th 71st	1/Buffs, 1/K.S.L.I., 2/Y. & L., 8/Bedf.;33 16th M.G. Coy.; 16th T.M. Bty. 1/W. York., 2/D.L.I., 11/Essex.; 14/D.L.I.;34 18th M.G. Coy.; 18th T.M. Bty. 1/Leic., 2/Sher. For., 9/Norf., 9/Suff.;35 71st M.G. Coy.; 71st T.M. Bty.	...	II XXIV	21, 42, 53 ; 87 (H.)26 110, 111, 112; 43 (H.)26	...	...	X.656 Y.656 Z.656	W.637	6th D.A.C.	12th 459th (W. Riding) 509th (London)	6th	11/Leic. (P.)	192nd M.G. Coy.39	16th 17th 18th	6th	209th38	6th
1918 March	16th 18th 71st	1/Buffs, 1/K.S.L.I., 2/Y. & L.; 16th T.M. Bty. 1/W. York., 2/D.L.I., 11/Essex; 18th T.M. Bty. 1/Leic., 2/Sher. For., 9/Norf.; 71st T.M. Bty.	...	II XXIV	21, 42, 53 ; 87 (H.) 110, 111, 112; 43 (H.)	...	...	X.6 Y.6	...	6th D.A.C.	12th 459th 509th	6th	11/Leic. (P.)	No. 6 Battn. M.G.C.39	16th 17th 18th	6th	209th	6th

NOTES ON ORDER OF BATTLE

1 Transferred on 14/4/15 to 9th Cav. Bde. (on formation). Replaced same day by B. Sqdn., 1/Northants. Yeo., from 8th Div.

2 Transferred to 4th Div. on 18/5/15.

3 Consequent on the reorganization of the Artillery, 24 H.B. left the 6th Div. on 17/4/15, and joined IV Bde., R.G.A. (No. 1 Group, H.A.R.).

4 Transferred to 28th Div. on 7/4/15.

5 Mobilized at the Curragh, crossed to France on 16/8/14, and joined 6th Div. at Harfleur on 17/9/14.

6 17th, 19th, 23rd, and 24th Cos., A.S.C.

7 Bde. transferred to 24th Div. on 14/10/15; it was replaced by the 71st Bde.

8 Transferred to 71st Bde. on 17/11/15.

9 Joined 21/2/15.

10 Transferred to 64th Bde., 21st Div., 28/11/15.

11 Transferred to 71st Bde. on 27/10/15.

12 Joined 12/11/14; transferred to 169th Bde., 56th Div., and left 6th Div. on 9/2/16.

13 Transferred to VI Corps Cav. on 9/5/16.

14 Transferred to XIV Corps Cyclist Bn., 26/5/16.

15 Bde. broken up 12/5/16 : 43 (H.) (less 1 sec.) to XXIV ; 87 (H.) (less 1 sec.) to II ; 1 sec. 43 and 1 sec. 87 formed D (H.) XXXVIII.

16 Transferred to 47th Div. on 16/2/16.

17 Joined from England on 23/12/14.

18 71st Bde. (9/Norf., 9/Suff., 8/Bedf., 11/Essex) was transferred from the 24th Div. on 11/10/15.

19 Transferred from 71st Bde. on 17/11/15.

20 16th Coy. formed in Feb., 1916 ; 18th Coy. in Jany., 1916 ; and 71st Coy. joined, from England, on 14/3/16.

21 16th T.M.B. formed on 3/4/16 ; 18th on 16/4/16 ; and 71st in April, 1916.

22 Transferred from 71st Bde. on 27/10/15.

23 Transferred from 64th Bde., 21st Div., on 28/11/15.

24 Transferred from 16th Bde. on 17/11/15.

25 Transferred from 18th Bde. on 27/10/15.

26 Became an A.F.A. Bde. on 14/1/17. 508 (H.) joined on 8/12/16 and became C/XXXVIII. C was broken up on 14/1/17, 1 sec. going to 43 (H.) and 1 sec. to 87 (H.).

27 D was made up to 6 hows. by 1 sec. from B/XCVI (from 21st Div.).

28 X, Y, and Z. were formed on 1/4/16 ; X from 26, Y from 88, and Z from 300 T.M.B.'s.

29 Formed on 20/7/16.

30 D.A.C. reorganized and B.A.C.'s abolished on 12/5/16.

31 Joined from England on 13/10/15.

32 Joined from England on 1/4/16.

33 Disbanded, 16/2/18.

34 Disbanded, 1/2/18.

35 Disbanded, 16/2/18. The surplus went to No. 5 Entrenching Bn.

36 Reorganized into X. and Y. in March, 1918.

37 W. became V., H.T.M.B., of VI Corps 6/3/18.

38 No. 11 Divnl. Emplynt. Coy. arrived on 20/5/17 ; and, in June, 1917, it was renumbered 209th.

39 Formed, 1/3/18. It consisted of 16th, 18th, 71st, and 192nd M.G. Cos. (192nd joined the division from England on 15/12/16).

6TH DIVISION

MOBILIZATION, BATTLES, AND ENGAGEMENTS

On the outbreak of War, the 6th Division was quartered partly in Ireland (Headquarters and 17th Bde. at Cork ; 16th Bde. at Fermoy ; Field Artillery at Mallow, Waterford, Fermoy, Ballincollig, Kilkenny, and Cahir ; and the Engineers at Fermoy, Cork, and Limerick), and partly in the Northern Command (18th Bde. at Lichfield, York, and Sheffield). The 24th Heavy Battery was in the Eastern Command (at Woolwich). Units mobilized at their peace stations, and between 15th–21st August those in Ireland embarked for England. The division concentrated in camps in the neighbourhood of Cambridge and Newmarket. Here, until 7th September, divisional training was carried out ; then, on the 7th the division began entraining for Southampton, and on the 9th September the first units began to disembark at St. Nazaire. After arrival, the division entrained for the Front, and by the 13th September it had concentrated at and north of Coulommiers (to the east of Paris) ; and on the 14th it began to advance towards the Aisne.

Throughout the War the 6th Division served on the Western Front in France and Belgium, and was engaged in the following operations :—

1914

19 and 20 Sept. ...	...**BATTLE OF THE AISNE** [I. Corps].
20 Sept.	...**Actions on the Aisne Heights.**

---

13 Oct.–2 Nov. ...	...**Battle of Armentières** [III. Corps].

1915

9 Aug.	...**Hooge** [VI. Corps, Second Army].

1916

BATTLES OF THE SOMME

15–18 Sept., and 21 and 22 Sept. ...	...**Battle of Flers-Courcelette** [XIV. Corps, Fourth Army].
25–28 Sept. ...	...**Battle of Morval** [XIV. Corps, Fourth Army].
25 Sept.	...**Capture of Lesbœufs.**
9 –18 Oct. ...	...**Battle of the Transloy Ridges** [XIV. Corps, Fourth Army].

1917

13–22 April ...	...**Fighting on Hill 70 (Lens)** [I. Corps, First Army].
20 Nov.–3 Dec. ...	...**BATTLE OF CAMBRAI.**
20 and 21 Nov. ...	...**The Tank Attack** [III. Corps, Third Army].
23–28 Nov. ...	...**Capture of Bourlon Wood** [III. Corps, Third Army].
30 Nov.–3 Dec. ...	...**The German Counter-Attacks** [III. Corps, Third Army].

1918

FIRST BATTLES OF THE SOMME

21–22 March ... ...Battle of St. Quentin [IV. Corps, Third Army].

BATTLES OF THE LYS

13–15 April ... ...Battle of Bailleul (71st Bde.) [under 25th Div. on 13/4, then 49th Div., IX. Corps, Second Army].

17–19 April ... ...First Battle of Kemmel Ridge (71st Bde.) [under 49th Div., IX. Corps, Second Army].

25 and 26 April ... ...Second Battle of Kemmel Ridge [XXII. Corps, Second Army].

29 April ... ...Battle of the Scherpenberg [XXII. Corps, Second Army].

THE ADVANCE TO VICTORY

BATTLES OF THE HINDENBURG LINE

18 Sept. ... ...Battle of Epéhy [IX. Corps, Fourth Army].

29 and 30 Sept. ... ...Battle of the St. Quentin Canal [IX. Corps, Fourth Army].

8–9 Oct.... ... ...Battle of Cambrai [IX. Corps, Fourth Army].

THE FINAL ADVANCE IN PICARDY

17 and 20–25 Oct. ...Battle of the Selle [IX. Corps, Fourth Army].

On the 11th November the 6th Division (less the Artillery, left to cover the 32nd Division) was in IX. Corps Reserve, and was billeted in and around Bohain (south of le Cateau). Between the 14th and 18th November the 6th Division moved forward to Solre le Château (south-east of Maubeuge), where it assembled for the march to the Rhine, forming part of the IX. Corps (transferred on 28th November to the Second Army). The advance began on the 18th November, the division crossed the German Frontier on the 13th December, and on the 23rd it reached its destination around Brühl (between Cologne and Bonn) after a 220-mile march.

7TH DIVISION

G.O.C.

27 August, 1914	Major-General T. CAPPER (wounded 1/4/15 ; invalided, 6/4/15).
6 April, 1915	Br.-Gen. S. T. B. LAWFORD (acting).
19 April, 1915	Major-General H. DE LA P. GOUGH.
14 July, 1915	Br.-Gen. S. T. B. LAWFORD (acting).
19 July, 1915	Major-General Sir T. CAPPER (died of wounds, 27/9/15).
26 September, 1915	Br.-Gen. (Major-Gen. 27/9) H. E. WATTS.
7 January, 1917	Major-General G. DE S. BARROW.
1 April, 1917	Major-General T. H. SHOUBRIDGE (sick, 9/2/18).
9 February, 1918	Br.-Gen. J. McC. STEELE (acting).
22 March, 1918	Major-General T. H. SHOUBRIDGE.

G.S.O. 1.

27 Aug., 1914...Col. H. M. DE F. MONTGOMERY.
12 Nov., 1914...Col. A. R. HOSKINS.
25 Mar., 1915...Lt.-Col. Hon. J. F. GATHORNE-HARDY.
1 Jan., 1916...Lt.-Col. C. BONHAM-CARTER.
14 Oct., 1916...Lt.-Col. G. W. HOWARD.
23 Oct., 1918...Lt.-Col. W. B. G. BARNE.

A.-A. & Q.-M.-G.

5 Sept., 1914...Lt.-Col. J. L. J. CLARKE.
5 Oct., 1914...Lt.-Col. C. J. PERCEVAL (wounded, 22/10/14).
22 Oct., 1914...Major W. H. V. DARELL (acting).
8 Nov., 1914...Lt.-Col. C. M. RYAN.
11 Nov., 1914...Lt. Col. A. C. DALY.
30 May, 1915...Major W. H. V. DARELL (acting).
12 June, 1915...Lt.-Col. R. S. GORTON.
12 Sept., 1915...Major R. H. D. TOMPSON (acting).
22 Sept., 1915...Lt.-Col. Hon. M. A. WINGFIELD.
26 July, 1917...Lt.-Col. B. J. LANG.

B.-G., R.A.

3 Sept., 1914...Br.-Gen. H. K. JACKSON.
14 Mar., 1915...Br.-Gen. J. F. N. BIRCH. (to B.-G., R.A., I. Corps, on 19/7/15.)
26 July, 1915...Br.-Gen. J. G. ROTTON.
20 Aug., 1916...Br.-Gen. H. S. SELIGMAN.
10 Oct., 1916...Lt.-Col. H. C. STANLEY-CLARKE (acting).
9 Nov., 1916...Br.-Gen. H. C. STANLEY-CLARKE.

C.R.E.

Sept., 1914...Lt.-Col. A. T. MOORE.
6 Jan., 1915...Lt.-Col. R. P. LEE.
18 Sept., 1915...Lt.-Col. G. H. BOILEAU.
15 Nov., 1917...Lt.-Col. A. W. REID.
9 Feb., 1918...Major E. CREWDSON (acting).
13 Mar., 1918...Lt.-Col. E. BARNARDISTON.
16 Oct., 1918...Lt.-Col. W. A. FITZG. KERRICH.

20th BRIGADE

15 Sept., '14...Br.-Gen. H. RUGGLES-
BRISE
(wounded, 2/11/14).
2 Nov., '14...Major A. B. E. CATOR
(acting).
14 Nov., '14...Br.-Gen. F. J. HEYWORTH.
16 Aug., '15...Br.-Gen. Hon. J. F. H. F. S.
TREFUSIS
(killed, 24/10/15).
24 Oct., '15...Lt.-Col. J. D. INGLES
(acting).
26 Oct., '15...Lt.-Col. L. B. BOYD-MOSS
(acting).
29 Oct., '15...Br.-Gen. C. J. DEVERELL.
7 Aug., '16...Br.-Gen. H. C. R. GREEN.

22nd BRIGADE

7 Sept., '14...Br.-Gen. S. T. B. LAWFORD.
27 Aug., '15...Br.-Gen. J. McC. STEELE.
9 Feb., '18...Lt.-Col. B. BEAUMAN
(acting).
16 Feb., '18...Lt.-Col. C. S. BURT
(acting).
18 Feb., '18...Lt.-Col. R. N. O'CONNOR
(acting).
16 Mar., '18...Br.-Gen. J. McC. STEELE.

21st BRIGADE

31 Aug., '14...Br.-Gen. H. E. WATTS.
27 Sept., '15...Br.-Gen. R. A. BERNERS.
3 Dec., '15...Br.-Gen. Hon. C. J.
SACKVILLE-WEST.
(Bde. transferred to 30th Div. on 19/12/15.)

91st BRIGADE

(Joined from 30th Div. on 20/12/15.)
[1 Jan., '15] ...Br.-Gen. F. J. KEMPSTER.
3 Feb., '16...Br.-Gen. J. R. M.
MINSHULL-FORD.
20 Nov., '16...Br.-Gen. H. R. CUMMING.
12 May, '17...Col. W. W. NORMAN
(acting).
16 May, '17...Br.-Gen. R. T. PELLY.

GENERAL NOTES

The following Units also served with the 7th Division :—

INFANTRY :—**6/Ches.** joined the 20th Bde. from G.H.Q. Troops on 9/1/16 ; transferred to 118th Bde., 39th Div., on 25/2/16 (and joined 118th Bde. on 29/2/16).

8/R. Scots. (consisting of 6 Coys. 8/R. Scots, 1 Coy. 6/R. Scots, and 1 Coy. 8/H.L.I.) joined the 22nd Bde. from the U.K. on 12/11/14, and was transferred, as Pioneers, to the 51st Div. on 19/8/15.

7/King's joined the 22nd Bde., from 5th Bde., 2nd Div., on 11/11/15, and was transferred to 165th Bde., 55th Div., on 7/1/16.

ARTILLERY :—**No. 7 Pom-Pom Section (A.-A.),** from 25/9/14–20/12/14.

5th Mountain Battery joined from 8th Div. on 26/3/15. and was transferred back to 8th Div. on 20/4/15.

OTHER UNITS :—**No. 10 Sanitary Section** joined from England on 9/1/15, and served with the division until transferred to a Third Army area, by 18/8/17.

7th Divnl. Amb. Workshop joined by 20/6/15, and served until 9/4/16 (transferred to Divnl. Supply Coln.).

———————

The 7th Division was reorganized on a 9-battalion basis on 13/9/18 ; and the pioneer battalion was reorganized on a 3-company basis on 6/5/18.

7TH DIVISION   ORDER OF BATTLE, 1914 - 1918

Dates	Brigades	Battalions and attached Units	Mounted Troops	Art. Brigades	Batteries	Bde. Ammn. Columns	Heavy Artillery	T.M. Medium	T.M. Heavy	Divnl. Ammn. Col.	Field Cos.	Divnl. Signal Coy.	Pioneers	M.G. Units	Field Ambulances	Mobile Vety. Secn.	Divnl. Emplnt. Coy.	Divnl. Train
1914 October (France)	20th	1/G.G.,1 2/S.G.,2 2/Bord., 2/Gord. H.	1/N'berland Hsrs.,3 7th Cyclist Coy.	XIV R.H.A. XXII XXXV	C,4 F, R.H.A. 104, 105, 106 12, 25, 58	XIV R.H.A., B.A.C. XXII B.A.C. XXXV B.A.C.	III5 Hy. Bde. 111H.B., 112H.B.; with Hy. Bty. Ammn. Colns.	...	...	7th D.A.C.	54th 56th5	7th	...	...	21st 22nd 23rd	12th7	...	7th8
	21st	2/Bedf., 2/Gr. How., 2/R.S.F., 2/Wilts.																
	22nd	2/Queen's, 2/R. War., 1/R.W.F., 1/S. Staff.																
1915 Sept. (France)	20th	2/Bord., 2/Gord. H., 8/Devon,10 9/Devon,11 6/Gord. H.12	A. Sqdn., 1/N'berland Hsrs.,14 7th Cyclist Coy.15	XIV R.H.A. XXII XXXV XXXVII (H.),16	F, T,17 R.H.A. 104, 105, 106 12, 25, 58 31 (H.) 35 (H.)	XIV R.H.A., B.A.C. XXII B.A.C. XXXV B.A.C. XXXVII (H.), B.A.C.	...	...	...	7th D.A.C.	54th 95th18 2/High'nd19	7th	...	...	21st 22nd 23rd	12th	...	7th
	21st9	2/Bedf., 2/Gr. How., 2/R.S.F., 2/Wilts, 4/Cam. H.13																
	22nd	2/Queen's, 2/R. War., 1/R.W.F., 1/S. Staff.																
1916 June (France)	20th	2/Bord., 2/Gord. H., 8/Devon, 9/Devon; 20th Bde. M.G. Coy.,21 20th T.M. Bty.22	...	XIV R.H.A.,26 XXII XXXV	F, T, R.H.A. D (H.),16 & 26 104, 105, 106; 35 (H.),16 12, 25, 58; 31 (H.)16	27	...	X.728 Y.728 Z.728	V.728	7th D.A.C.27	54th 95th 3/Durham30	7th	24/Manch.31 (P.)	...	21st 22nd 23rd	12th	...	7th
	22nd	2/R. War., 2/R. Ir. Rgt.,23 1/R.W.F., 20/Manch.;24 22nd Bde. M.G. Coy.,21 22nd T.M. Bty.22																
	91st20	2/Queen's,25 1/S. Staff.,25 21/Manch., 22/Manch.; 91st Bde. M.G. Coy.;21 91st T.M. Bty.22																
1917 June (France)	20th	2/Bord., 2/Gord. H., 8/Devon, 9/Devon; 20th M.G. Coy.; 20th T.M. Bty.	...	XXII XXXV	104, 105, 106; 35 (H.) 12, 25, 58; 31 (H.)	...	...	X.7 Y.7 Z.7	V.7	7th D.A.C.	54th 95th 528th (8/Durham)	7th	24/Manch. (P.)	220th M.G. Coy.33	21st 22nd 23rd	12th	210th34	7th
	22nd	2/R. War., 1/R.W.F., 20/Manch., 2/1/H.A.C.;32 22nd M.G. Coy.; 22nd T.M. Bty.																
	91st	2/Queen's, 1/S. Staff., 21/Manch., 22/Manch.; 91st M.G. Coy.; 91st T.M. Bty.																
1918 April (Italy)	20th	2/Bord., 2/Gord. H., 8/Devon, 9/Devon;35 20th T.M. Bty.	...	XXII XXXV	104, 105, 106; 35 (H.) 12, 25, 58; 31 (H.)	...	...	X.736 Y.736	37	7th D.A.C.	54th 95th 528th	7th	24/Manch. (P.)	No. 7 Battn. M.G.C.38	21st 22nd 23rd	12th	210th	7th
	22nd	2/R. War., 1/R.W.F., 20/Manch.,35 22nd T.M. Bty.																
	91st	2/Queen's, 21/Manch.,35 22/Manch.; 91st T.M. Bty.																
1918 October (Italy)	20th	2/Bord., 2/Gord. H., 8/Devon; 20th T.M. Bty.	...	XXII XXXV	104, 105, 106; 35 (H.) 12, 25, 58; 31 (H.)	...	...	X.7 Y.7	...	7th D.A.C.	54th 95th 528th	7th	24/Manch. (P.)	No. 7 Battn., M.G.C.	21st 22nd 23rd	12th	210th	7th
	22nd	2/R. War.,1/R.W.F.,2/1/H.A.C.; 22nd T.M. Bty.																
	91st	2/Queen's, 1/S. Staff., 22/Manch., 91st T.M. Bty.																

NOTES ON ORDER OF BATTLE

1 Transferred on 4/8/15 to 3rd Gds. Bde. (on formation of Guards Div.).

2 Transferred on 8/8/15 to 3rd Gds. Bde. (on formation of Guards Div.).

3 On 12/4/15, B. Sqdn. was transferred to the 1st Div., and C. Sqdn. to the 8th Div. A. Sqdn. (and m. g. sec.) remained with the 7th Div.

4 Transferred to 3rd Cav. Div. on 19/10/14.

5 Transferred on 4/3/15 to G.H.Q. Artillery, and then to No. 2 Group H.A.R.

6 Transferred on 1/9/15 to Guards Div. (on formation).

7 Joined division in England on 16/9/14, and crossed to Zeebrugge on 7/10/14.

8 39th, 40th, 42nd, and 86th Coe., A.S.C.

9 Bde. (less 4/Cam. H.) transferred to 30th Div. on 19/12/15; it was replaced by 91st Bde.

10 Joined from England on 4/8/15.

11 Joined from England on 8/8/15.

12 Joined from G.H.Q. Troops on 5/12/14. Transferred to L. of C. Troops on 5/1/16.

13 Joined from 24th Bde., 8th Div., on 8/4/15, and was transferred to the 91st Bde. on 20/12/15. The Bn. was transferred to 154th Bde., 51st Div., on 7/1/16, and was sent on 26/2/16 to the Base to be drafted.

14 Transferred to XIII Corps Cav. Regt. on 13/5/16.

15 Transferred to XV Corps Cyclist Bn. on 11/5/16.

16 Joined from IV Corps Artillery on 24/8/15 (55 (H.) had been transferred to CXXXVIII (H.) 8th Div. on 10/5/15). XXXVII (H.) was broken up on 17/5/16; and 31 (less 1 sec.) went to XXXV, and 35 (less 1 sec.) to XXII. 1 sec. 31 and 1 sec. 35 formed D (H.) of XIV R.H.A. 509 (H.) joined XIV R.H.A. on 7/10/16; and on 13/2/17 509 (H) was broken up to complete 31 and 35 to 6 hows. each.

17 Joined from Egypt on 21/12/14.

18 Joined from England on 30/8/15.

19 Joined from England on 17/1/15, and was transferred to 51st Div. on 24/1/16.

20 91st Bde. (20/, 21/, 22/, and 24/March.) joined from 30th Div. on 20/12/15.

21 20th formed on 10/2/16; 22nd on 24/2/16; and 91st joined from England on 14/3/16.

22 20th formed on 14/2/16; 22nd on 14/4/16; and 91st in May, 1916.

23 Joined from 11th Bde., 4th Div., on 22/5/16; transferred to 49th Bde., 16th Div., on 14/10/16.

24 Transferred from 91st Bde. on 20/12/15.

25 Transferred from 22nd Bde. on 20/12/15.

26 Became an Army Bde., R.H.A., on 10/2/17. B/CLXIX joined on 18/2/17 and became C/XIV. 1 sec. of C/CLXIX made D/XIV up to 6 hows. F. & T. were re-armed with 18-pdrs. on 19/6/15.

27 D.A.C. reorganized on 16/5/16, and B.A.C.'s abolished.

28 X. formed on 25/2/16; Y. & Z. in March, 1916.

29 Formed June, 1916.

30 Transferred from 51st Div. on 30/1/16.

31 Transferred from 91st Bde. to 22nd Bde. on 20/12/16; and became pioneers on 22/5/16.

32 Joined from England on 6/10/16.

33 Joined from England on 25/3/17.

34 12th Divnl. Emplnt. Coy. arrived 21/5/17. 12th was renumbered 210th in June, 1917.

35 Transferred on 13/9/18 to 7th Bde., 25th Div. (France).

36 Z. was absorbed in X. & Y. on 22/2/18.

57 V. was disbanded on 12/11/17.

58 Formed 1/4/18. It consisted of 20th, 22nd, 91st, and 220th M.G. Coe.

7TH DIVISION

FORMATION, BATTLES, AND ENGAGEMENTS

The division had no existence before the outbreak of War ; it was gradually assembled at Lyndhurst between the 31st August and the 4th October, 1914. The 12 infantry battalions included the three remaining unallotted regular battalions left in England, as well as nine battalions brought back from various overseas stations, viz.—Guernsey (1), Gibraltar (2), Malta (2), Cairo (1), Natal (1), and the Transvaal (2). The mounted troops included an existing yeomanry regiment as well as a cyclist company, formed on mobilization. The Field Artillery was made up by one R.H.A. Brigade (XIV., of two batteries), and one R.F.A. Brigade (XXXV.) still left at home, together with one R.F.A. Brigade (XXII.) from the Transvaal. The two heavy batteries were new units formed at Woolwich after the outbreak of War, and the field companies came from Chatham and Pretoria. Three of the A.S.C. companies (39, 40, and 42) came from Gibraltar, Malta, and Pretoria, but the remaining company (86) was a new formation.

The 7th Division embarked at Southampton on the 4th and 5th October, and began disembarkation at Zeebrugge on the 6th October. The division moved to Bruges on the 7th October, and reached Ghent on the 9th October. During the night of 11/12 October, a retirement on Ypres was begun and the place was reached on the 14th. The 7th Division served on the Western Front in France and Belgium until the 17th November, 1917, when it began entraining for the Italian Front, on which it served for the remainder of the War. The 7th Division, between 1914 and 1918, was engaged in the following operations :—

1914

9 and 10 Oct. ...	...Antwerp Operations [IV. Corps].
19 Oct.–5 Nov. ...	...BATTLES OF YPRES
21–24 Oct. ...	...Battle of Langemarck [IV. Corps].
29–31 Oct. ...	...Battle of Gheluvelt [I. Corps].

------

18 Dec.	...Rouges Bancs—Well Farm Attack [IV. Corps].

1915

10-13 Mar. ...	...Battle of Neuve Chapelle [IV. Corps, First Army].
9 May	...Battle of Aubers Ridge [In reserve, IV. Corps, First Army]
15-19 May ...	...Battle of Festubert [I. Corps, First Army].
15 and 16 June ...	...Givenchy [IV. Corps].
25 Sept. -8 Oct. ...	...Battle of Loos [I. Corps, First Army].

1916

BATTLES OF THE SOMME

1–5 July ...	...Battle of Albert [XV. Corps, Fourth Army].
1 July	...Capture of Mametz.
14–17 July ...	...Battle of Bazentin Ridge [XV. Corps, Fourth Army].
20 July	...Attack on High Wood [XV. Corps].
3–7 Sept. ...	...Battle of Guillemont [XV. Corps, Fourth Army].

1917

11-15 Jan., and 21 Feb.-5 Mar. ...	...Operations on the Ancre [V. Corps, Fifth Army].
14 Mar.-5 April ...	...German Retreat to the Hindenburg Line [V. Corps, Fifth Army].
3-16 May ...	...Battle of Bullecourt [V. Corps, Fifth Army].

BATTLES OF YPRES

1-3 Oct.	...Battle of Polygon Wood [X. Corps, Second Army].
4 Oct.	...Battle of Broodseinde [X. Corps, Second Army].
9 Oct.	...Battle of Poelcappelle [X. Corps, Second Army].
26-29 Oct. ...	...Second Battle of Passchendaele [X. Corps, Second Army].

On the 10th November the division was warned that it would be moved to Italy. Entrainment began on the 17th November, and by the 28th detrainment was virtually completed in the neighbourhood of Legnago (on the Adige). The 7th Division then advanced to the Piave Front and became reserve to the XIV. Corps.

1918

On the 19th January the 7th Division took over the right sector of the XIV. Corps front on the Piave, and remained in the line until, on the 23rd February, orders were received that the division was to return to France. On the 4th March the move to France was cancelled, and between the 22nd and 31st March the division took over the left divisional front of the XIV. Corps on the Asiago Plateau. The division then took part in the following operations :—

15 and 16 June ...	...Fighting on the Asiago Plateau [In Reserve, XIV. Corps].

On the 11th September the 7th Division was again warned to return to France in exchange with the 47th Division (2/London). The 7th Division was thereupon reduced to a 9-battalion basis ; but, although the divisional advance parties left for France on the 24th September, the return was indefinitely postponed on the 30th ; and, on the 19th October, the division took over the right of the XIV. Corps front on the Piave. The division then took part in :—

BATTLE OF VITTORIO VENETO

23 Oct.-4 Nov. ...	...Passage of the Piave [XIV. Corps, Tenth (Italian) Army].
23-26 Oct. ...	...Capture of the Grave di Papadopoli.
3 Nov.	...Crossing of the Tagliamento.

By 3 p.m., 4th November (Armistice with Austria), the 7th Division had pushed on beyond the Tagliamento and reached a line about one-third of the way to Udine. The division was withdrawn across the Tagliamento on the 6th and 7th, and then moved back to the neighbourhood of Vicenza where demobilization was carried out.

8TH DIVISION

G.O.C.

19 September, 1914	Major-General F. J. DAVIES.
27 July, 1915	Br.-Gen. R. S. OXLEY (acting).
1 August, 1915...	Major-General H. HUDSON.
10 December, 1916	Major-General W. C. G. HENEKER.

G.S.O. 1.

22 Sept., 1914...Lt.-Col. W. H. ANDERSON.
27 Oct., 1915...Lt.-Col. H. HILL
(killed, 10/9/16).
10 Sept., 1916...Major J. C. FREELAND
(acting).
17 Sept., 1916...Lt.-Col. R. E. H. JAMES.
1 Dec., 1916...Lt.-Col. E. H. L.
BEDDINGTON.
14 Dec., 1917...Lt.-Col. H. S ADAIR.
27 Feb., 1918...Lt.-Col. C. C. ARMITAGE.
5 June, 1918...Lt.-Col. A. G. B. BOURNE.

A.-A. & Q.-M.-G.

19 Sept., 1914...Lt.-Col. A. R. HOSKINS.
13 Nov., 1914...Lt.-Col. H. M. DE F.
MONTGOMERY.
21 Mar., 1915...Lt.-Col. P. P. DE B.
RADCLIFFE.
19 July, 1915...Lt.-Col. H. L. ALEXANDER.
15 Oct., 1916...Lt.-Col. R. Q. CRAUFURD.
8 Feb., 1917...Major L. D. LUARD
(acting).
16 Feb., 1917...Major G. C. KELLY
(acting).
25 Feb., 1917...Lt.-Col. VISCOUNT
FEILDING.
3 Nov., 1918...Lt.-Col. Hon. P. G.
SCARLETT.

B.-G., R.A.

30 Sept., 1914...Br.-Gen. A. E. A. HOLLAND.
21 July, 1915...Br.-Gen. G. H. W.
NICHOLSON.
1 Jan., 1917...Br.-Gen. H. G. LLOYD.
19 Mar., 1918...Br.-Gen. J. W. F. LAMONT.

C.R.E.

30 Sept., 1914...Lt.-Col. W. H. ROTHERHAM
(sick, 19/2/15).
19 Feb., 1915...Major C. E. G. VESEY
(acting).
7 Mar., 1915...Lt.-Col. P. G. GRANT.
9 Nov., 1915...Lt.-Col. F. G. GUGGISBERG
(sick, 22/7/16).
22 July, 1916...Major A. H. BROWN
(acting).
6 Sept., 1916...Lt.-Col. C. M. BROWNE.
9 Nov., 1918...Lt.-Col. C. RUSSELL-
BROWN.

23rd BRIGADE

24 Sept., '14...Br.-Gen. F. A. ADAM.
28 Oct., '14...Br.-Gen. R. J. PINNEY.
27 June, '15...Br.-Gen. T. E. TRAVERS-
CLARKE.
7 Sept., '15...Br.-Gen. H. D. TUSON.
27 Aug., '16...Br.-Gen. E. A. FAGAN.
2 Mar., '17...Lt.-Col. J. HAMILTON HALL
(acting).
12 Mar., '17...Br.-Gen. G. W. ST. G.
GROGAN
(V.C., 27/5/18).

24th BRIGADE

29 Sept., '14...Br.-Gen. F. C. CARTER
(sick, 16/3/15).
17 Mar., '15...Br.-Gen. R. S. OXLEY.
27 July, '15...Lt.-Col. T. S. LAMBERT
(acting).
28 July, '15...Lt.-Col. A. C. BUCKLE
(acting).
1 Aug., '15...Br.-Gen. R. S. OXLEY.
(Bde. transferred to 23rd Div., 18/10/15.)

70th BRIGADE

(Joined from 23rd Div., 18/10/15.)
[11 Sept., '15] Br.-Gen. I. F. PHILIPS
(sick, 5/11/15).
8 Nov., '15...Br.-Gen. H. GORDON.
(Bde. returned to 23rd Div., 16/7/16.)

24th BRIGADE

(Returned to the 8th Div., 15/7/16.)
[11 July, '16] Br.-Gen. A. J. F. EDEN.
14 Jan., '17...Br.-Gen. H. W. COBHAM.
7 Nov., '17...Lt.-Col. C. R. H. STIRLING
(acting).
21 Nov., '17...Br.-Gen. R. HAIG.
4 June, '18...Br.-Gen. L. M. STEVENS.
14 Aug., '18...Lt.-Col. S. S. HAYNE
(acting).
6 Sept., '18...Br.-Gen. R. O'H. LIVESAY.

25th BRIGADE

5 Oct., '14...Br.-Gen. A. W. G. LOWRY
COLE
(killed, 9/5/15).
9 May, '15...Br.-Gen. R. B. STEPHENS.
1 April, '16...Br.-Gen. J. W. H. POLLARD.
11 Jan., '17...Br.-Gen. C. COFFIN
(V.C., 31/7/17).
(to Cd. of 50th Div., tempy., 23/2/18.)
23 Feb., '18...Lt.-Col. A. H. S. HART-
SYNNOT (acting)
(sick, 10/3/18).
10 Mar., '18...Lt.-Col. R. H. HUSEY
(acting).
17 Mar., '18...Br.-Gen. C. COFFIN, V.C.
4 May, '18...Lt.-Col. G. E. M. HILL
(acting).
8 May, '18...Br.-Gen. R. H. HUSEY
(wounded and captured, 27/5/18)
(died of wounds, 30/5/18).
29 May, '18...Major H. P. ALLAWAY
(acting).
3 June, '18...Br.-Gen. J. B. POLLOK-
McCALL.
7 Oct., '18...Br.-Gen. Hon. R. BRAND.

90

GENERAL NOTES

The following Units also served with the 8th Division :—

INFANTRY :—13/Lond., joined 25th Bde. from England on 13/11/14 ; and was transferred to G.H.Q. Troops on 20/5/15.

4/Cam. H., joined 24th Bde. from U.K. on 23/2/15 ; and was transferred to 21st Bde., 7th Div., on 8/4/15.

6/Sco. Rif., joined 23rd Bde. from U.K. on 24/3/15 ; and was transferred to 154th Bde., 51st Div., on 2/6/15.

7/D.L.I.(P.), joined from 50th Div. on 20/6/18 (see Note 32).

ARTILLERY :—No. 12 A.-A. Section (18-Pdrs.), from 28/11/14–8/12/14.

5th Mountain Battery, from 3/3/15 (from 3rd Div.)–26/3/15 (transferred to 7th Div.) ; and from 20/4/15 (from 7th Div.)–30/5/15 (transferred to Second Army).

7th Mountain Battery, from 13/12/14 (from England)–24/12/14 (transferred to 1st Div.).

No. 8 T.M.Bty. (first called U.8) was formed 5/6/16 and was disbanded 8/8/16 (part of its personnel was transferred to Y.8).

OTHER UNITS :—No. 14 Sanitary Section, joined from England on 9/1/15, and served with the division until 16/4/17 (transferred to XV. Corps).

8th Divnl. Amb. Workshop was mobilized on 19/10/14 ; joined the 8th Division on 20/10/14, and was transferred to the Divnl. Supply Coln. by 9/4/16.

On 3/2/18 the division was reorganized on a 9–battalion basis ; and on 7/3/18 the pioneer battalion was reorganized on a 3-company basis.

8TH DIVISION   ORDER OF BATTLE, 1914 - 1918

Dates	INFANTRY Brigades	Battalions and attached Units	Mounted Troops	Artillery Brigades	Batteries	Bde. Ammn. Columns	Heavy Artillery	T.M. Medium	T.M. Heavy	Divnl. Ammn. Col.	Field Cos.	Divnl. Signal Coy.	Pioneers	M.G. Units	Field Ambulances	Mobile Vety. Secn.	Divnl. Emplnt. Coy.	Divnl. Train
1914 Nov.	23rd. / 24th / 25th	2/Devon, 2/W. York., 2/Sco. Rif., 2/Midd'x. / 1/Worc., 2/E. Lanc., 1/Sher. For., 2/North'n. / 2/Linc., 2/R. Berks., 1/R. Ir. Rif., 2/R.B.	1/Northants. Yeo.1 / 8th Cyclist Coy.	V, R.H.A. / XXXIII. / XI.v	G,2 O, Z,2 R.H.A. / 32, 33, 36 / 1, 3, 5	V, R.H.A., B.A.C. / XXXIII B.A.C. / XI.v B.A.C.	VIII Hy.Bde.3 / 118 H.B. / 119 H.B. & Hy. Bty. Ammn. Colns.	...	...	8th D.A.C.	2nd / 15th	8th	...	...	24th (1/ W's'x)1 / 25th (2/ W's'x) / 26th (3/ W's'x)	15th4	...	8th5
1915 Sept.	23rd. / 24th6 / 26th	2/Devon, 2/W. York., 2/Sco. Rif., 2/Midd'x., 7/Midd'x.7 / 1/Worc., 2/E. Lanc., 1/Sher. For., 2/North'n, 5/B.W.8 / 2/Linc., 2/R. Berks., 1/R. Ir. Rif., 2/R.B., 8/Midd'x.,9 1/Lond.10	C. Sqdn., 1/N'berland Hsrs.11 / 8th Cyclist Coy.12	V, R.H.A. / XXXIII. / XLIV. / CXXVIII (H.)13	O,Z, R.H.A. / 32, 33, 36 / 1, 3, 5 / 55 (H.), 57 (H.)	V, R.H.A., B.A.C. / XXXIII B.A.C. / XLIV B.A.C. / CXXVIII (H.) B.A.C.	...	...	...	8th D.A.C.	2nd / 15th / 1/1/Home Counties14	8th	...	...	24th / 25th / 26th	15th	...	8th
1916 June	23rd. / 25th / 70th15	2/Devon, 2/W. York., 2/Sco. Rif., 2/Midd'x.; 23rd Bde. M.G. Coy.;16 23rd T.M. Bty.17 / 2/Linc., 2/R. Berks., 1/R. Ir. Rif., 2/R.B.; 25th Bde. M.G. Coy.;16 25th T.M. Bty.17 / 11/Sher. For., 8/K.O.Y.L.I., 8/Y. & L., 9/Y. & L.; 70th Bde. M.G. Coy.;16 70th T.M. Bty.17	...	V, R.H.A.18 / XXXIII. / XLIV.	O, Z, R.H.A.; D (H.)13 / 32, 33, 36; 55 (H.)13 / 1, 3, 5; 57 (H.)13	19	...	X.820, Y.820, Z.820	W.821	8th D.A.C.19	2nd / 15th / 1/1/Home Counties	8th	22/D.L.I. (P.)22	...	24th / 25th / 26th	15th	...	8th
1917 June	23rd. / 24th23 / 25th	2/Devon, 2/W. York., 2/Sco. Rif.,34 2/Midd'x.; 23rd M.G. Coy.; 23rd T.M. Bty. / 1/Worc., 2/E. Lanc.,25 1/Sher. For., 2/North'n.; 24th M.G. Coy.; 24th T.M. Bty. / 2/Linc.,26 2/R. Berks., 1/R. Ir. Rif.,27 2/R.B.; 25th M.G. Coy.; 25th T.M. Bty.	...	XXXIII. / XLIV.	32, 33, 36 / 55 (H.) / 1, 3, 5 / 57 (H.)	...	...	X.8, Y.8, Z.8	W.8	8th D.A.C.	2nd / 15th / 490th (Home Counties)	8th	22/D.L.I. (P.)	218th M.G. Coy.28	24th / 25th / 26th	15th	211th29	8th
1918 March	23rd. / 24th. / 25th.	2/Devon, 2/W. York, 2/Midd'x.; 23rd T.M. Bty. / 1/Worc., 1/Sher. For., 2/North'n.; 24th T.M. Bty. / 2/E. Lanc.,25 2/R. Berks., 2/R.B.; 25th T.M. Bty.	...	XXXIII. / XLIV.	32, 33, 36 / 55 (H.) / 1, 3, 5 / 57 (H.)	...	...	X.830, Y.830	31	8th D.A.C.	2nd / 15th / 490th	8th	22/ D.L.I.32 (P.)	No. 8 Bn.,33 M.G.C.	24th / 25th / 26th	16th	211th	8th

NOTES ON ORDER OF BATTLE

1 Transferred: A Sqdn. to 4th Div. on 13/4/15; B. Sqdn., H.Q., and M.G. Sec., to 6th Div. on 14/4/15; and C. Sqdn. to 5th Div. on 12/4/15. Replaced by C. Sqdn., 1/Northumberland Hussars (from 7th Div.).

2 G. was transferred to 3rd Cav. Div. on 24/11/14. Z. had been reduced on 24/12/13; the Bty. was re-formed on 9/10/14.

3 Transferred to II H.A.R. on 5/3/15.

4 Joined, 16/10/14.

5 41, 84, 85, and 87 Cos., A.S.C.

6 24th Bde. (less 5/B.W.) was transferred to the 23rd Div. on 18/10/15. It was replaced by the 70th Bde. (23rd Div.).

7 Joined from England on 15/8/15. Amalgamated with 8/Midd'x. on 23/6/15; resumed separate formations on 2/8/15. Transferred to 167th Bde., 56th Div. on 8/2/16.

8 Joined from U.K. on 13/11/14. Became pioneers, 18/10/15. Transferred to 154th Bde., 51st Div., 6/1/16, then transferred to 118th Bde., 39th Div., on 29/2/16. Composite Bn. of 4/B.W. and 5/B.W. formed, 15/3/16, and called 4/5/B.W. (118th Bde.).

9 Joined from 85th Bde., 28th Div., on 21/6/15, and amalgamated with 7/Midd'x. Resumed separate formation, 2/8/15. Transferred to 25th Bde., 27/8/15, and then to 70th Bde. on 23/10/15; and to 167th Bde., 56th Div., on 8/2/16.

10 Joined from England 14/3/15. Transferred to 167th Bde., 56th Div., on 8/2/16.

11 Joined, 12/4/16. Transferred to XIII Corps Cav. on 13/5/16.

12 Transferred to III Corps Cyclist Bn. on 12/5/16.

13 Bde. H.Q. formed at Woolwich, 6/7/15; joined 8th Div. on 5/8/15, and took over 55(H.). (XXXVII, 4th Div.) and 57(H.). (XLII, 1st Div.). CXXXVIII (H.) was broken up 18/5/16, and 56(H.) was transferred to XXXIII; 57(H.) to XLV; and D (H.) (formed on 8/5/16 from 1 sec. of 55 and 1 sec. of 57) to V, R.H.A. D (H.) was broken up and secs. returned to 55 and 57 on 13/1/17.

14 Joined from G.H.Q. Troops on 2/2/15.

15 70th Bde. (11/Sher. For., 8/K.O.Y.L.I., 8/Y. & L., and 9/Y. & L.) was transferred from 23rd Div. on 18/10/15. It rejoined 23rd Div. on 16/7/16.

16 23rd was formed on 15/1/16, 25th on 10/1/16, and 70th in Jan., 1916.

17 23rd and 70th formed in Jan., 1916, and 25th in Feb., 1916.

18 Became an Army Bde., R.H.A., on 13/1/17. D (H.) was broken up and secs. rejoined 55 and 57. B/CLXXXVIII joined V, R.H.A., to complete establishment, and was then renamed A/V; it was renumbered 402 on 1/6/17. O. and Z., R.H.A., had been re-armed with 18-pdrs. on 8/6/15.

19 D.A.C. was reorganized, 10-24/5/16, and B.A.C.'s were abolished.

20 X., Y., and Z. were formed in May, 1916.

21 W. was formed in mid-May, 1916.

22 Joined from England and temporarily attached to 19th Div. on 20/6/16; transferred to 8th Div. on 2/7/16.

23 Bde. rejoined from 23rd Div. on 15/7/16.

24 Transferred to 59th Bde., 20th Div., on 3/2/18.

25 Transferred to 25th Bde. on 3/2/18.

26 Transferred on 3/2/18 to 62nd Bde., 21st Div. (and joined on 4/2/18).

27 Transferred on 3/2/18 to 107th Bde., 36th Div. (and joined 4/2/18).

28 Joined from England on 23/3/1917.

29 The Divnl. Emplnt. Coy. joined from England in May, 1917, and was renumbered 211th Divnl. Emplnt. Coy. in June, 1917.

30 Z. was absorbed in X. & Y. on 3/2/18.

31 W.8 and V.50 formed V/VIII H.T.M.B. on 11/2/18.

32 7/D.L.I. (P.) joined on 20/6/18 from 50th Div., and on 8/7/18 it absorbed and replaced 22/D.L.I. (P.).

33 Formed 20/1/18. It consisted of the 23rd, 24th, 25th, and 218th M.G. Cos.

8TH DIVISION

FORMATION, BATTLES, AND ENGAGEMENTS

The division had no existence before the outbreak of War. The first units to arrive (from Malta) assembled on Baddesley Common (near Southampton), and on 2nd October, 1914, Divisional H.Q. and available units moved to Hursley Park (near Winchester), where concentration was effected. The arrival of the 2/E. Lanc. R. on the 30th October completed the division. The 12 infantry battalions had all been brought back from various overseas stations, viz :—India (3), S. Africa (1), Aden (1), Egypt (3), Malta (3), and Bermuda (1). The mounted troops included an existing yeomanry regiment and a cyclist company, which was formed on mobilization. The Field Artillery was made up by one Horse Artillery Bde. (3 batteries), and the two Field Artillery Bdes., which still remained at home. The two Heavy Batteries were new units formed at Woolwich after the outbreak of War, and the Field Companies came from Cairo and Gibraltar. The three Field Ambulances of the Wessex Division (T.F.) were used ; and of the four A.S.C. Companies, one (41) came from Cairo, and the other three were new formations.

The division embarked at Southampton on the 4th and 5th November, and disembarked at Havre on the 6th and 7th ; it began entraining for the Front on the 8th November, and completed its assembly around Merville by the 12th.

Throughout the remainder of the War the 8th Division served on the Western Front in France and Belgium, and was engaged in the following operations :—

1914

18 Dec. ... ...Neuve Chapelle (Moated Grange Attack) [IV. Corps].

1915

10–13 Mar. ... ...Battle of Neuve Chapelle [IV. Corps, First Army].

9 May ... ...BATTLE OF AUBERS RIDGE

Attack at Fromelles [IV. Corps, First Army].

25 Sept. ... ...Bois Grenier [III. Corps, First Army].

1916

BATTLES OF THE SOMME

1 July ... ...Battle of Albert [III. Corps, Fourth Army].

23–30 Oct. ... ...Attack on le Transloy [XIV. Corps, Fourth Army].

94

1917

4 Mar.	...**Bouchavesnes** [XV. Corps, Fourth Army].
14 Mar.–5 April ...	...**German Retreat to the Hindenburg Line** [XV. Corps, Fourth Army].

BATTLES OF YPRES

31 July and 1 Aug.	...**Battle of Pilckem Ridge** [II. Corps, Fifth Army].
31 July	...**Attack on Westhoek.**
16–18 Aug. ...	...**Battle of Langemarck** [II. Corps, Fifth Army].

---

2 Dec.	...**Assault of Southern Redoubt, Passchendaele** (25th Bde.) [VIII. Corps, Second Army].

1918

FIRST BATTLES OF THE SOMME

23 Mar.	...**Battle of St. Quentin** [XIX. Corps, Fifth Army].
24 and 25 Mar. ...	...**Actions at the Somme Crossings** [XIX. Corps, Fifth Army].
26 and 27 Mar. ...	...**Battle of Rosières** [XIX. Corps, Fifth Army].

---

24 and 25 April ...	...**Villers Bretonneux** [III. Corps, Fourth Army].
27 May–6 June ...	...**Battle of the Aisne** [IX. Corps, Sixth (French) Army].

THE ADVANCE TO VICTORY

SECOND BATTLES OF ARRAS

26–30 Aug. ...	...**Battle of the Scarpe** [VIII. Corps, First Army].

THE FINAL ADVANCE IN ARTOIS

7 and 8 Oct. ...	...**Forcing the Rouvroy-Fresnes Line** [VIII. Corps, First Army].
17 Oct.	...**Capture of Douai** [VIII. Corps, First Army].

By 11 a.m. on the 11th November, the 8th Division (the right division of the VIII. Corps) had reached a line 3–4 miles to the N.N.E. of Mons. On the 15th November, the 8th Division was relieved by the 52nd Division on the Armistice Line ; and on the 16th the 8th Division (now transferred to the III. Corps, Second Army) moved back to Tournai. Here, on the 7th December, the division (now in the Fifth Army) was visited by H.M. the King. The division advanced into the Ath–Enghien area, completing the move by the 18th December. Here demobilization was finally carried out and the division passed out of existence on the 20th March, 1919.

27TH DIVISION

G.O.C.

19 November, 1914	Major-General T. D'O. SNOW.
16 July, 1915	Major-General G. F. MILNE.
13 January, 1916	Br.-Gen. S. W. HARE (acting).
7 February, 1916	Major-General W. R. MARSHALL.
14 September, 1916	Br.-Gen. H. D. WHITE-THOMSON (acting).
15 September, 1916	Major-General H. S. L. RAVENSHAW.
30 November, 1916	Br.-Gen. G. A. WEIR (acting).
22 December, 1916	Major-General G. T. FORESTIER-WALKER (invalided, 9/3/19).
10 March, 1919	Major-General W. M. THOMSON (tempy.).
10 May, 1919	Major-General G. N. CORY.

G.S.O. 1.

19 Nov., 1914...Lt.-Col. H. L. REED, V.C.
18 June, 1915...Lt.-Col. G. N. CORY.
20 Dec., 1915...Lt.-Col. F. G. FULLER.
23 Jan., 1916...Lt.-Col. A. L. C. CLARKE (invalided, 10/6/16).
10 June, 1916...Major E. A. PLUNKETT (acting).
16 June, 1916...Lt.-Col. Sir E. I. B. GROGAN, Bt.
28 May, 1917...Lt.-Col. L. HOLLAND.
10 Oct., 1918...Major C. C. GRATTON-BELLEW (acting).
6 Dec., 1918...Lt.-Col. C. C. GRATTON-BELLEW.

A.-A. & Q.-M.-G.

17 Nov., 1914...Colonel H. J. EVERETT.
18 Jan., 1916...Capt. G. R. F. LEVERSON (acting).
25 Jan., 1916...Lt.-Col. E. J. F. VAUGHAN.
17 Aug., 1917...Lt.-Col. G. R. F. LEVERSON (sick, 6/7/18).
6 July, 1918...Major G. WILKS (acting).
18 July, 1918...Major H. R. HOBSON (acting).
13 Sept., 1918...Lt.-Col. G. R. F. LEVERSON.

B.-G., R.A.

18 Nov., 1914...Br.-Gen. A. STOKES.
5 June, 1915...Br.-Gen. G. G. S. CAREY.
9 Sept., 1915...Br.-Gen. H. D. WHITE-THOMSON.
23 Sept., 1916...Br.-Gen. W. R. EDEN (sick, 2/8/18).
2 Aug., 1918...Lt.-Col. O. S. CAMERON (acting).
9 Sept., 1918...Br.-Gen. V. ASSER.

C.R.E.

23 Nov., 1914...Lt.-Col. S. KEEN (sick, 21/1/15).
21 Jan., 1915...Major C. E. P. SANKEY (acting).
11 Feb., 1915...Lt.-Col. H. J. M. MARSHALL.
17 Mar., 1915...Lt.-Col. F. A. WILSON (tempy.).
22 Mar., 1915...Lt.-Col. G. WALKER (sick, 17/6/16).
17 June, 1916...Major R. B. DUTTON (acting).
25 June, 1916...Lt.-Col. G. WALKER.
28 June, 1916...Major R. B. DUTTON (acting).
10 July, 1916...Lt.-Col. R. B. DUTTON.
30 April, 1919...Lt.-Col. R. B. PITT.

80th BRIGADE

19 Nov., '14...Col. G. H. THESIGER
(acting).
22 Nov., '14...Br.-Gen. Hon. C. G.
FORTESCUE.
25 Mar., '15...Br.-Gen. W. E. B. SMITH.
1 July, '16...Lt.-Col. W. J. LONG
(acting).
7 July, '16...Br.-Gen. A. C. ROBERTS
(leave to U.K., 27/3/17).
27 Mar., '17...Lt.-Col. J. H. BAILEY
(acting).
18 June, '17...Br.-Gen. H. L. KNIGHT.
21 Aug., '17...Lt.-Col. J. H. BAILEY
(acting).
25 Aug., '17...⎫ Br.-Gen. W. J. N. COOKE-
24 Sept., '19...⎭   COLLIS.*

*Note.—After the disbandment of the
division, Br.-Gen. Cooke-Collis remained
in command of the 80th Bde. until 12th
August, 1920.

81st BRIGADE

19 Nov., '14...Br.-Gen. D. A.
MACFARLANE.
21 Mar., '15...Br.-Gen. H. L. CROKER.
25 May, '16...Br.-Gen. B. F.
WIDDRINGTON
(leave to U.K., 9/11/18).
9 Nov., '18...Lt.-Col. R. R. FORBES
(acting).
15 Jan., '19...Lt.-Col. R. H. STEWART
(acting).
3 April, '19...⎫ Br.-Gen. F. S. MONTAGU-
15 Sept., '19...⎭   BATES.

82nd BRIGADE

18 Nov., '14...Br.-Gen. L. A. M. STOPFORD
(sick, 9/1/15).
9 Jan., '15...Lt.-Col. J. R. LONGLEY
(acting).
13 Jan., '15...Br.-Gen. J. R. LONGLEY.
20 Dec., '15...Br.-Gen. S. W. HARE.
13 Jan., '16...Lt.-Col. J. D. MATHER
(acting).
7 Feb., '16...Br.-Gen. S. W. HARE
(injured, 29/2/16).
29 Feb., '16...Lt.-Col. J. D. MATHER
(acting).
13 Mar., '16...Br.-Gen. S. W. HARE.
1 April, '16...Br.-Gen. C. R. I. BROOKE.
30 Nov, '16...Lt.-Col. J. H. BAILEY
(acting).

12 Jan., '17...Br.-Gen. C. C. M. MAYNARD
(sick, 22/12/17).
23 Dec., '17...Lt.-Col. J. W. C. KIRK
(acting).
9 Jan , '18...Br.-Gen. R. E. SOLLY-
FLOOD.
25 Sept., '18...Br.-Gen. K. M. DAVIE.
15 June, '19...Br.-Gen. P. L. HANBURY.
29 July, '19...Lt.-Col. H. M. EDWARDS
(acting).
12 Aug., '19...Lt.-Col. S. MATHEWS
(acting).
25 Aug., '19...⎫ Lt.-Col. A. P. DENE
14 Sept., '19...⎭   (acting).

GENERAL NOTES

The following also served with the 27th Division :—

19th **INFANTRY BRIGADE** (2/R.W.F., 1/Sco. Rif., 1/Midd'x, 2/A. & S.H., and 5/Sco. Rif.), under Br.-Gen. Hon. F. Gordon until 14/6/15, then under Br.-Gen. P. R. Robertson—was attached from 31/5/15 until 19/8/15 (transferred to 2nd Division). (Also see General Notes, 6th Division.)

OTHER UNITS :—Cavalry :—D. Sqdn., Derby. Yeo., from 26/3/16 until June, 1916 (transferred to 7th Mtd. Bde.).

Artillery :—XV. Bde. R.F.A. (11, 52, 80 B'ties), from 5th Div., was attached from 7/1/15 until 9/2/15, when the Bde. returned to the 5th Div., leaving behind 11th Bty. (see note 19).

130 How. Bty., R.F.A. (from 3rd Div.), from 8/1/15–21/2/15.

61 How. Bty., R.F.A. (from 5th Div.), from 21/2/15–June, 1915 (transferred to Second Army, and then to Meerut Div. on 23/6/15).

2nd Mountain Bty., from 17/7/15 (from 12th Div.)–26/7/15 (transferred to II. Corps).

Bute Mtn. Bty. (IV. Highland Mtn. Bde.), from 22/7/18 (from 28th Div.)–8/9/18 (to XII. Corps) ; and from 23/9/18 (from XII. Corps)–25/9/18 (rejoined IV. Highland Mtn. Bde., with 14th Greek Div.).

Infantry :—9/A. & S.H., joined 81st Bde. on 23/2/15, and was transferred to 10th Bde., 4th Div., on 21/5/15 (see p. 59).

7th Sanitary Section, formed at Bailleul on 8/1/15, and joined the division on 14/1/15.

27th Divnl. Motor Amb. Workshop, joined the division by 7/2/15 ; and on 7/12/15 was left behind in France, on the division moving to Salonika.

On 22/6/1918 the division completed its reorganization on a 9-battalion basis. The pioneer battalion remained a 4-company organization.

On 25 and 26/9/1918, owing to sickness, the infantry brigades were reorganized into battalions of 2 companies each.

Dates	INFANTRY			ARTILLERY						Engineers	Signal Service	Pioneers	M.G. Unit	Field Ambulances	Mobile Vety. Secn.	Divnl. Emplnt. Coy.	Divnl. Train
	Brigades	Battalions and attached Units	Mounted Troops	Field Artillery			Trench Mortar Batteries		Divnl. Ammn. Col.	Field Coy.	Divnl. Signal Coy.						
				Brigades	Batteries	Bde. Ammn. Columns	Medium	Heavy									
1914 Dec. (France)	80th.	2/K.S.L.I., 3/K.R.R.C., 4/K.R.R.C., 4/R.B., P.P.C.L.I.[4]	A Sqdn., 1/Surrey Yeo.[5] 27th Cyclist Coy.[6]	I7.......	98, 132, 133	I B.A.C.	...	...	27th D.A.C.[8]	1/S. Midland[9] 1/Wessex[10] 2/Wessex[10]	Wessex[11]	...	...	81st[12] (1/HomeCo's) 82nd[12] (2/HomeCo's) 83rd[12] (3/HomeCo's)	16th[13]	...	27th[14]
	81st2.	1/R. Scots, 2/Glouc., 2/Cam. H., 1/A. & S.H.		XIX7.	95, 96, 131	XIX B.A.C.											
	82nd3	1/R. Ir. Rgt., 2/D.C.L.I., 2/R. Ir. Fus., 1/Leins.		XX7.	67, 99, 364	XX B.A.C.											
1915 Sept. (France)	80th.	2/K.S.L.I., 3/K.R.R.C., 4/K.R.R.C., 4/R.B., P.P.C.L.I.[15]	A Sqdn., 1/Surrey Yeo.; 27th Cyclist Coy.	I	11,19 9s, 132, 13320	I B.A.C.	...	...	27th D.A.C.	17th24 1/Wessex 2/Wessex	Wessex	...	...	81st 82nd 83rd	16th	...	27th25
	81st.	1/R. Scots, 2/Glouc., 2/Cam. H., 9/R. Scots,16		XIX	39,21 95,22 96, 131	XIX B.A.C.											
	82nd.	1/R. Ir. Rgt., 2/D.C.L.I., 2/R. Ir. Fus., 1/Leins., 1/Camb.17		XX.	67, 99, 148,19 36425	XX B.A.C.											
				CXXIX (H.)18	A (H.),18 B (H.),18 C (H.)18	CXXIX (H.) B.A.C.											
1916 July (Macedonia)	80th.	2/K.S.L.I., 3/K.R.R.C., 4/K.R.R.C., 4/R.B.; 80th M.G. Coy.;26 80th T.M. Bty.27	A Sqdn., 1/Surrey Yeo.,32 27th Cyclist Coy.33	I	11, 98,34 132,34D(H.),35	I B.A.C.	...	...	27th D.A.C. 40	17th 1/Wessex41 2/Wessex41	Wessex	26/ Middlesex42 (P.)	...	81st 82nd 83rd	16th	...	27th45
	81st.	1/R. Scots, 2/Glouc.,28 2/Cam. H., 1/A. & S.H.; 81st M.G. Coy.;26 81st T.M. Bty.27		XIX	39, 96, 131	XIX B.A.C.											
	82nd.	1/R. Ir. Rgt.,29 2/D.C.L.I.,30 1/Leins.;31 82nd M.G. Coy.;26 82nd T.M. Bty.27		XX.	67, 99, 148,36 D (H.)37	XX B.A.C.											
				CXXIX	95,38 133,20 364,38 D (H.)39	CXXIX B.A.C.											
1917 July (Macedonia)	80th.	2/K.S.L.I., 3/K.R.R.C., 4/K.R.R.C.,44 4/R.B.; 80th T.M. Bty.; M.G. Coy.; 80th S.A.A. Sec. Ammn. Coln.45	...	I	11, 98,34 D (H.)	I B.A.C.	...	...	...	17th 500th (1/Wessex) 501st (2/Wessex)	Wessex	26/ Middlesex (P.)	...	81st 82nd 83rd	16th	818th49	27th50
	81st.	1/R. Scots, 2/Cam. H., 1/A. &S.H., 13/B.W.;46 81st M.G. Coy.; 81st T.M. Bty.; 81st S.A.A. Sec. Ammn. Coln.45		XIX	39, 96, 131 D (H.)	XIX B.A.C.											
	82nd.	2/Glouc.,28 2/D.C.L.I., 10/Hants.,47 10/Cam. H.;48 82nd M.G. Coy.; 82nd T.M. Bty.; 82nd S.A.A. Sec. Ammn. Coln.45		XX.	67, 99; D (H.)	XX B.A.C.											
				CXXIX...	95,38 133; D (H.)	B.A.C.											
1918 August (Macedonia)	80th.	2/K.S.L.I., 3/K.R.R.C., 4/K.R.R.C., 4/R.B.; 80th M.G. Coy.; 80th T.M. Bty.; 80th S.A.A. Sec. Ammn. Coln.	...	I	11, 98; D (H.)	I B.A.C.	...	...	...	17th 500th 501st	Wessex	26/ Middlesex (P.)	...	81st 82nd 83rd	16th	818th	27th
	81st.	1/R. Scots, 2/Cam. H., 1/A. & S.H.; 81st M.G. Coy.; 81st T.M. Bty.; 81st S.A.A. Sec. Ammn. Coln.		XIX	39, 96, 131 D (H.)	XIX B.A.C.											
	82nd.	1/Glouc., 2/D.C.L.I., 10/Hants.; 82nd M.G. Coy.; 82nd T.M. Bty.; 82nd S.A.A. Sec. Ammn. Coln.		XX.	67, 99; D (H.)	XX B.A.C.											
				CXXIX...	95, 133; D (H.)	CXXIX B.A.C.											

NOTES ON ORDER OF BATTLE

1 Formed at Winchester on 17/11/14. The 4 regular battalions came from India and reached Winchester on 19/11/14.

2 Formed at Winchester on 17/11/14. 2/Glouc. (from Tientsin) arrived on 13/11/14, and the other 3 battalions (from India) on 20/11/14.

3 Formed at Winchester on 17/11/14. 2/D.C.L.I. (from Hong Kong) arrived on 18/11/14; and the other 3 battalions (from India) on 18/11 (1/Leins.), 19/11 (1/R. Ir. Rgt.), and 20/11 (2/R. Ir. Fus.)

4 Arrived at Winchester from Salisbury on 16/11/14. Joined 80th Bde. on 24/12/14.

5 Joined at Winchester on 21/11/14

6 Formed at Winchester on 28/11/14

7 I (in Aug., 1914, 13, 67, 69 Bties. at Edinburgh) was re-formed on 23/11/14 at Winchester with 98 (from XX), 182 (formed of left ⅓ of 90), and 133 (formed of left ⅓ of 98).

XIX joined at Winchester on 19/11/14 (with 95, 96, and 97) from India. 97 was transferred to CLXVII (29th Div.), and XIX was reorganized with 95, 96, and 131 (formed of left ⅓ of 95).

8 XX joined at Winchester on 19/11/14 (with 98, 99, and 100) from India. 98 was transferred to I, and 100 to XXXI (28th Div.); and XX was reorganized with 67 (from original I, and made up with 1 sec. of 100), 99, and 364 (formed from 1 sec. of 99 and 1 sec. of 100).

On 30/11/14 nine 18-pdr. guns, etc., arrived to complete batteries to 4 guns each. (In Aug., 1914, XXXI (131, 132, and 133) was at Sheffield.)

9 Joined at Winchester in Dec., 1914 (from IV Home Counties (How.) Bde. R.F.A. of Home Counties Div., T.F.).

10 Joined at Winchester on 20/11/14.

11 Joined at Winchester on 20/11/14.

12 Joined at Winchester : 81st on 17/11, and 82nd and 83rd on 13/11/14.

13 Joined at Winchester.

14 Formed in Nov., 1914; and consisted of 95, 96, 97, and 98 Cos., A.S.C. (The Train was made up from Home Counties Divl. T. & S. Coln.)

15 Left on 8/11/15. On formation of 3rd Cdn. Div. it joined 7th Cdn. Bde. on 24/12/15.

16 Joined from U.K. on 28/2/15; left on 24/11/15 on transfer to 14th Bde., 5th Div.; transferred on 25/1/16 to Third Army Troops, and on 1/3/16 to 154th Bde., 51st Div.

17 Joined from England on 18/2/15; early in March it joined 82nd Bde. It was transferred to VII Corps Trps. 15/11/15, and on 29/2/16 to 118th Bde., 39th Div.

18 Formed 26/8/15. A/LIII (H.) joined 14/6/15 (from 9th Div.) and became A (8/9/15). A/XCII (H.) joined 10/8/15 (from 20th Div.) and became B (8/9/15). C/LXV (H.) joined 11/6/15 (from 12th Div.) and became C (8/9/15). CXXIX (H.) was reorganized on 25/7/16. A (H.) became D (H.). B (H.) was transferred to I and became D/I ; C went to XX and became D/XX. 183 joined from I, 95 from XIX, and 364 from XX.

19 Transferred from XV (5th Div.) on 9/2/15. 1 Sec. 11 and 1 Sec. 39 formed 11A Bty. on 10/2/15. 11A was numbered 148 on 23/2/15. It had joined XX on 10/2/15.

20 Transferred to CXXIX on 25/7/16.

21 Joined from XIV (4th Div.) on 9/2/15. (Also see note 19.)

22 Transferred to CXXIX on 25/7/16.

23 Transferred to CXXIX on 25/7/16.

24 Transferred from 5th Div. on 26/3/15.

25 Became 55th Divnl. Train on 1/1/16.

26 Formed 16/5/15.

27 30th formed on 2/9/16 ; 81st on 16/10/16 ; and 82nd on 31/7/16.

28 Transferred to 82nd Bde. on 3/11/16.

29 Transferred to 30th Div., on 3/11/16.

30 Transferred to 31st Bde., 10th Div., on 2/11/16.

31 Transferred to 29th Bde., 10th Div., on 2/11/16.

32 Transferred on 27/12/16 to XVI Corps Cav. Regt.

33 Transferred on 7/12/16 to XVI Corps Cyclist Bn.

34 98 was broken up and 1 sec. joined 11 and 1 sec. 182 on 28/12/16 ; 132 was then renumbered 98.

35 Formerly B/CXXIX (see note 18).

36 148 was broken up and 1 sec. joined 67 and 1 sec. 99 on 27/12/16.

37 Formerly C/CXXIX (see note 18).

38 95 was broken up and 1 sec. joined 133 and 1 sec. 364 on 27/12/16 ; 364 was then renumbered 95.

39 Formerly A/CXXIX (see note 18).

40 The D.A.C. was abolished on 8/1/17. It formed B Section of XVI Corps Ammn. Coln. on 17/1/17.

41 Renumbered 500th and 501st on 1/2/17.

42 Joined from England on 26/8/16.

43 Train (483, 484, 485, 486 Cos., A.S.C.) embarked at Devonport on 16/1/16, reached Salonika on 21/2/16, and became 27th Divnl. Train. The Train was reorganized in pack and wheel echelons in April, 1916 ; and 862, 863, 864, and 855 Cos. were added to it later.

44 Transferred on 12/6/18 to B.E.F. (France), and joined 151st Bde., 50th Div., on 16/7/18.

45 S.A.A. Secs. were attached to Bdes. from 28/9/16.

46 13/B.W. (Scottish Horse Bn.) joined 1/11/16, and on 11/6/18 it was transferred to B.E.F. (France), and joined 149th Bde., 50th Div., on 15/7/18.

47 Joined on 2/11/16, from 29th Bde., 10th Div.

48 10/Cam. H. (Lovat's Scouts) : 1/1 and 1/2/Lovat's Scouts Yeo. were amalgamated at Cairo on 27/9/16 and became 10/Cam. H. (Lovat's Scouts). The Bn. reached Salonika on 20/10/16 and joined 82nd Bde. on 1/11/16. It was transferred on 22/6/18 to B.E.F. (France), and joined I. of C. Troops on 6/7/18. The Bn. was disbanded on 17/4/19.

49 Formed 14/9/17.

50 Reorganized in Nov., 1917. 852 Coy. absorbed 853 Coy. on 23/11/17 ; and, on the same day, 854 and 855 Cos. (pack echelon) left the Train and became A.T. Pack Bde. Cos. (unallotted).

27TH DIVISION

FORMATION, BATTLES, AND ENGAGEMENTS

The division had no existence before the outbreak of the Great War.

The division assembled and mobilized at Magdalen Hill Camp (2 miles east of Winchester) during November and December, 1914. The 13 infantry battalions of which it was composed came from India (10 from ten different stations), Hong Kong, Tientsin, and Canada (P.P.C.L.I.) ; the infantry brigades were formed at Winchester. The mounted troops included a cavalry squadron from an existing yeomanry unit and a cyclist company, which was formed at Winchester. Of the field artillery brigades : I. was originally at Edinburgh, whilst XIX. and XX. came from India ; but all three were extensively re-organized and re-formed at Winchester (see note 7, Order of Battle Table). The field companies, signal company, field ambulances, and train came from territorial force divisions.

The 27th Division embarked at Southampton on the 19th–21st December, disembarked at le Havre between the 20th–23rd December, and concentrated between Aire and Arques by the evening of the 25th December.

The 27th Division served on the Western Front in France and Belgium until November, 1915. In the following month it embarked for the Macedonian Front, on which it served for the remainder of the War.

Between 1914 and 1918 the division was engaged in the following operations :—

1914

1915

14 and 15 March...   ...**St. Eloi** [V. Corps, Second Army].

BATTLES OF YPRES

22 and 23 April ...   ...**Battle of Gravenstafel Ridge** [V. Corps, Second Army].

24 April–4 May ...   ...**Battle of St. Julien** [V. Corps, Second Army, until 28/4 ; then Plumer's Force].

8–13 May   ...   ...**Battle of Frezenberg Ridge** [V. Corps, Second Army].

24 and 25 May   ...   ...**Battle of Bellewaarde Ridge** [V. Corps, Second Army].

On the 1st November the division was warned to be ready to entrain for Marseille on the 10th November. Entrainment began on the 15th, and embarkation for the Macedonian Front on the 17th ; but it was not until the 13th February, 1916, that the last of the division disembarked at Salonika.

1916

30 Sept.–2 Oct. ...   ...**Capture of the Karajaköis** [XVI. Corps].
3 and 4 Oct. ...   ...**Capture of Yeniköi** [XVI. Corps].
17 Nov. ; & 6 & 7 Dec. ...**Tumbitza Farm** (82nd Bde.).

1917

14 Oct. ...   .**Capture of Homondos** [XVI. Corps].

1918

1–30 Sept. ...   ...**THE OFFENSIVE.**
1 and 2 Sept. ...   ...**Capture of the Roche Noire Salient** [XII. Corps].
22–30 Sept. ...   ...**Passage of the Vardar, and Pursuit to the Strumica Valley** [XII. Corps until 25/9 ; Army Reserve until 27/9 ; then XVI. Corps].

At noon on 30th September, Bulgaria concluded an armistice, and hostilities ceased. The 27th Division had then reached the area Kosturino–Rabrovo–Cestovo. The advance was continued, and Krupnik was passed by the end of October. On the 2nd November the division was ordered to move back down the Struma to the Orlyak area (W. of L. Tahinos), and it remained there until it embarked in December for the Black Sea. Constantinople was reached on the 19th, and the 80th Bde., with I. Bde., R.F.A., 17th Fd. Coy. R.E., and 82nd Fd. Amb., reached Batum on the 22nd December. Detachments were sent to Poti (N. of Batum), and Tiflis ; and on the 19th January, 1919, Divisional H.Q. opened at Tiflis. By the 31st January the last shipload of the division disembarked at Batum. By May, 1919, detachments had been sent to the following places in Azerbaijan, Georgia, and Armenia :—Baku, Krasnovodsk (in Trans-Caspia), Petrovsk, Shusha, Julfa, Erivan, Kars, Tiflis, Batum, and Gagri ; Divisional H.Q. were in Tiflis.

On the 15th August, 1919, the withdrawal of the British Troops began from Trans-Caucasia, and on the 7th September, Divisional H.Q. opened at Batum. On the 14th and 15th September, the 81st and 82nd Bdes. were disbanded. The division was disbanded on the 24th September, 1919, and the divisional commander and the general staff left for Constantinople, after handing over to the military governor of Batum (Br.-Gen. W. J. N. Cooke-Collis, Comdg. 80th Infantry Brigade). On the 4th March, 1920, Br.-Gen. Cooke-Collis was appointed to command the Inter-Allied Force at Batum. This force was withdrawn from Batum by the 14th July, 1920.

28TH DIVISION

G.O.C.

17 December, 1914	Major-General E. S. BULFIN (sick, 11/10/15).
12 October, 1915	Major-General C. J. BRIGGS.
18 May, 1916	Br.-Gen. H. S. L. RAVENSHAW (acting).
21 May, 1916	Major-General H. L. CROKER.
27 January, 1917	Br.-Gen. E. M. MORRIS (acting).
8 March, 1917	Major-General H. L. CROKER.
8 November, 1920	Major-General T. O. MARDEN.
19 March, 1923	Colonel-Commandant A. S. COTTON.

G.S.O. 1.

18 Dec., 1914...Major H. S. DE BRETT (acting).
21 Dec., 1914...Lt.-Col. LORD LOCH.
27 May, 1915...Lt.-Col. R. H. HARE.
12 Nov., 1916...Lt.-Col. R. F. GROSS.
8 Jan., 1918...Lt.-Col. A. P. BLACKWOOD.
20 Nov., 1918...Major M. J. T. REILLY (acting).
19 May, 1919...Lt.-Col. E. S. W. TIDSWELL (sick, 22/12/20).
22 Dec., 1920...Captain M. S. ADSHEAD (acting).
8 Jan., 1920...Major E. L. MORRIS (acting).
20 Jan., 1920...Lt.-Col. E. S. W. TIDSWELL.
3 Feb., 1920...Major E. L. MORRIS (acting).
9 April, 1920...Lt.-Col. S. J. P. SCOBELL.
2 May, 1923...Major E. F. NORTON (acting).

A.-A. & Q.-M.-G.

17 Dec., 1914...Lt.-Col. L. W. ATCHERLEY.
22 April, 1915...Lt.-Col. R. HENVEY.
28 Oct., 1918...Major F. J. COLLAS (acting).
1 Nov., 1918...Lt.-Col. C. E. HOLLINS.
23 Sept., 1919...Major F. J. COLLAS (acting).
20 May, 1920...Col. H. NEEDHAM.
(returned to U.K. in 1921 and D.A.A.G. deputised.)
22 Sept., 1922...Lt.-Col. H. R. G. STEVENS.

B.-G., R.A.

17 Dec., 1914...Lt.-Col. A. L. WALKER (acting).
29 Dec., 1914...Br.-Gen. A. W. GAY.
9 May, 1915...Br.-Gen. D. ARBUTHNOT.
14 Jan., 1916...Br.-Gen. H. E. T. KELLY.
28 July, 1916...Lt.-Col. H. H. BOND (acting).
9 Sept., 1916...Lt.-Col. P. P. E. DE BERRY (acting).
22 Sept., 1916...Br.-Gen. H. E. T. KELLY.
7 Dec., 1916...Lt.-Col. P. P. E. DE BERRY (acting).
11 Jan., 1917...Br.-Gen. H. E. T. KELLY.
12 Jan., 1917...Lt.-Col. P. P. E. DE BERRY (acting).
15 Mar., 1917...Br.-Gen. P. P. E. DE BERRY.
4 Aug., 1919...Lt.-Col. H. E. MARSH (acting).
1 Oct., 1919...Br.-Gen. P. P. E. DE BERRY.
29 Sept., 1922...Col.-Cdt. A. S. COTTON.

C.R.E.

18 Dec., 1914...Col. H. J. W. JEROME.
10 May, 1915...Major F. M. BROWNE (acting).
25 May, 1915...Lt.-Col. A. R. WINSLOE.
4 Oct., 1915...Lt.-Col. E. S. SANDYS.
(By) 22 Sept., 1922...Lt.-Col. C. B. O. SYMONS.
(By) 6 Feb., 1923...Col. P. T. DENIS DE VITRÉ.

83rd BRIGADE

26 Dec., '14...Br.-Gen. R. C. BOYLE
(sick, 13/5/15)

13 May, '15...Lt.-Col. T. O. MARDEN
(acting).

19 May, '15...Br.-Gen. H. S. L. RAVENSHAW.

18 May, '16...Lt.-Col. W. A. BLAKE
(acting).

21 May, '16...Br.-Gen. H. S. L. RAVENSHAW.

14 Sept., '16...Lt.-Col. G. E. BAYLEY
(acting).

25 Sept., '16...Br.-Gen. F. S. MONTAGUE-BATES.

13 Nov., '16...Br.-Gen. R. H. HARE.

10 Mar., '19...Br.-Gen. F. C. NISBET.

1 April, '19...Lt.-Col. W. MILLER
(acting).

23 May, '19...Lt.-Col. R. C. DOBBS
(acting).

27 May, '19...Br.-Gen. F. C. NISBET.

21 Sept., '19...Lt.-Col. R. TYRER (acting).

26 Sept., '19...Br.-Gen. F. S. MONTAGUE-BATES.

26 Feb., '20...Br.-Gen. D. I. SHUTTLEWORTH.

84th BRIGADE

25 Dec., '14...Br.-Gen. F. WINTOUR
(sick, 23/2/15).

23 Feb., '15...Lt.-Col. W. B. WALLACE
(acting).

24 Feb., '15...Br.-Gen. L. J. BOLS.

7 Sept., '15...Br.-Gen. T. H. F. PEARSE.

13 Oct., '15...Br.-Gen. G. A. WEIR.

1 Dec., '16...Lt.-Col. F. A. GREER
(acting).

14 Feb., '17...Br.-Gen. G. A. WEIR.

23 Mar., '18...Br.-Gen. F. C. NISBET.

8 Mar., '19...Br.-Gen. R. H. HARE.

3 April, '19...Lt.-Col. H. R. A. HUNT
(acting).

28 June, '19...Br.-Gen. R. H. HARE.

14 Aug., '19...Lt.-Col. R. C. DOBBS (acting).

9 Oct., '19...Lt.-Col. J. L. FURNEY
(acting).

17 Oct., '19...Br.-Gen. R. H. HARE.

25 Oct., '19...Lt.-Col. J. L. FURNEY
(acting).

5 Nov., '19...Lt.-Col. A. H. YATMAN
(acting).

21 Dec., '19...Col. H. A. V. CUMMINS
(acting).

29 Dec., '19...Lt.-Col. A. H. YATMAN
(acting).

2 Jan., '20...Col. C. BONHAM-CARTER
(acting).

29 Feb., '20...Br.-Gen. W. B. EMERY.
(On 25/9/1922, the 84th became an Army Brigade, directly under G.H.Q., British Forces in Turkey.)

85th BRIGADE

24 Dec., '14...Br.-Gen. A. J. CHAPMAN.

18 May, '15...Br.-Gen. C. E. PEREIRA
(wounded, 26/5/15).

26 May, '15...Capt. C. J. DEVERELL
(acting).

29 May, '15...Lt.-Col. C. W. COMPTON
(acting).

10 June, '15...Br.-Gen. C. E. PEREIRA
(wounded, 27/9/15).

27 Sept., '15...Lt.-Col. A. C. ROBERTS
(acting).

29 Sept., '15...Br.-Gen. B. C. M. CARTER.

24 Oct., '17...Br.-Gen. K. M. DAVIE.

23 Sept., '18...Lt.-Col. W. Y. MILLER
(acting).

27 Sept., '18...Br.-Gen. R. E. SOLLY-FLOOD.

25 Feb., '19...Lt.-Col. W. Y. MILLER
(acting).

26 Mar., '19...Br.-Gen. F. C. NISBET
(tempy.).

5 May, '19...Br.-Gen. R. E. SOLLY-FLOOD.

19 Sept., '19...Lt.-Col. A. H. YATMAN
(acting).

22 Sept., '19...Br.-Gen. F. C. NISBET
(tempy.).

25 Sept., '19...Lt.-Col. A. H. YATMAN
(acting).

4 Nov., '19...Br.-Gen. R. E. SOLLY-FLOOD.

29 Nov., '19...Lt.-Col. A. B. GOSSET
(acting).

17 Dec., '19...Lt.-Col. O. H. DELANO-OSBORNE (acting).

18 Jan., '20...Lt.-Col. A. B. GOSSET
(acting).

29 Jan., '20...Lt.-Col. O. H. DELANO-OSBORNE (acting).

29 Feb., '20⎱
Nov., 1920 ⎰Br.-Gen. A. T. BECKWITH.

(The 85th Bde. disappeared in Nov., 1920, when the 28th Div. was reorganized. Br.-Gen. Beckwith then became Col. on the Staff, Turkish Gendarmerie.)

85th Brigade

(The 85th Bde. was re-formed on 25/9/22.)

25 Sept., '22...Col. A. E. GLASGOW
(tempy.).

6 Oct., '22...Col.-Cdt. A. T. BECKWITH.

GENERAL NOTES

83rd Inf. Bde., transferred to the 5th Division from 3/3/15–7/4/15 ; and was replaced temporarily by the 15th Bde., 5th Div. (q.v.).

84th Inf. Bde., transferred to the 5th Division from 23/2/15–7/4/15 ; and was replaced temporarily by the 13th Bde., 5th Div. (q.v.).

85th Inf. Bde., transferred to the 3rd Division from 19/2/15–2–6/4/15 ; and was replaced temporarily by the 9th Bde., 3rd Div. (q.v.).

A Composite Brigade (consisting of 2/Buffs, 2/N.F., 2/Ches., 1/Welsh, 1/Y. & L.), under Br.-Gen. L. J. Bols, 84th Bde., was formed on 14/5/15. The Composite Bde. was dissolved on 19/5/15, its place being taken by the 85th Bde. ; and the 84th Bde. resumed its independent formation.

The following units also served with the 28th Division :—

INFANTRY :—3/Monmouth, joined 83rd Bde. on 3/3/15 (from England). On 27/5/15, it was amalgamated (in 84th Bde.) with 1/Mon. and 2/Mon. 3/Mon. resumed its independent formation and rejoined 83rd Bde. on 11/8/15. It was transferred to 49th Div. on 2/9/15, and became divnl. pioneers on 18/9/15.

1/Monmouth, joined 84th Bde. on 27/2/15 (from England). Amalgamated 27/5 (see 3/Mon.), and resumed independent formation 11/8/15. On 3/9/15, 1/Mon. was transferred to the 46th Div. as divnl. pioneers.

2/Monmouth, transferred to 84th Bde. from 12th Bde., 4th Div., for amalgamation (see 3/Mon.), and resumed independent formation 24/7/15. It rejoined 12th Bde., 4th Div., 25/7/15.

12/London (Rangers), joined division on 30/1/15 (from England). Posted to 84th Bde. on 8/2/15, transferred to G.H.Q. troops on 20/5/15, and to 56th Div. on 12/2/16.

8/Middlesex, joined 85th Bde. on 11/3/15 (from England), transferred on 20/6/15 to 8th Division, and joined on 21/6/15.

ARTILLERY :—VIII. (H.) Bde., R.F.A. (37 (H) and 65 (H)), from 5th Div., was attached from 21/2–23/6/15.

7th Mountain Battery (disembarked on 29/12/15 at Salonika, from France), joined division on 30/12/15, and served with the division until 18/6/16 (formation of III. Mtn. Arty. Bde.).

IV. Highland Mtn. Arty. Bde. (Ross and Cromarty, Argyll, and Bute Mtn. Bties. and B.A.C.), from December, 1916–22/7/18, when Bute Mtn. Bty. went to 27th Div. IV. Mtn. Arty. Bde. (less Bute Bty.) left 28th Div. on 10/9/18 (transferred to XVI. Corps).

III. Mtn. Arty. Bde. (2nd, 5th, and 7th Mtn. Bties. and B.A.C.), from 16/9/18–Armistice.

ENGINEERS :—2/1/N. Midland Fd. Coy., from 19/6/15 (from 5th Div.)–10/7/15 (transferred to 46th Div.).

OTHER UNITS :—15 (London) Sanitary Section, joined at Winchester and served throughout the War with the division.

28th Divnl. Amb. Workshop, joined in France on 27/1/15 ; it was left behind in France on the division moving to Salonika.

On 26/6/1918 the division completed its reorganization on a 9-battalion basis. The pioneer battalion remained a 4-company organization.

228th Inf. Bde. (Br.-Gen. W. C. Ross), although it was really attached to Army Troops or Corps Troops during its period of existence, was associated with the 28th Division from March, 1917, until its dissolution in January, 1919 (for the composition of the 228th Bde., see Order of Battle Table of the 28th Division for August, 1918).

Dates	Brigades	Battalions and attached Units	Mounted Troops	Brigades (F.A.)	Batteries	Bde. Ammn. Columns	T.M.B. Medium	T.M.B. Heavy	Divnl. Ammn. Coln.	Field Cos.	Divnl. Signal Coy.	Pioneers	M.G. Units	Field Ambulances	Mobile Vety. Secn.	Divnl. Emplnt. Coy.	Divnl. Train
1915 January (France)	83rd1 84th2 85th3	2/K.O., 2/E. York., 1/K.O.Y.L.I., 1/Y. & L. 2/N.F., 1/Suff., 2/Ches. 1/Welsh, 3/R.F., 2/E. Surr., 3/Midd'x.	B Sqdn., 1/Surrey Yeo.4 28th Cyclist Coy.5	III16 XXXI17 CXLVI8	18, 62, 365 69, 100, 103 75, 366, 367	III B.A.C. XXXI B.A.C. CXLVI B.A.C.	…	…	28th D.A.C.9	3/London10 1/Northumbrian11 1/N. Midland12	Home C'ties13	…	…	84th14 (2/London) 85th14 (3/London) 86th14 (2/Northumbrian)	17th15	…	28th16
1915 Sept. (France)	83rd. 84th. 85th.	2/K.O., 2/E. York., 1/K.O.Y.L.I., 1/Y. & L., 5/K.O.18 2/N.F., 1/Suff., 6/Welsh.18 2/Buffs, 3/R.F., 2/E. Surr., 3/Midd'x.	B Sqdn., 1/Surrey Yeo. 28th Cyclist Coy.	III. XXXI. CXLVI. CXXX (H.)19	18, 22,20 62, 365 69, 100, 103 75, 149,22 366, 367 A (H.)23, B (H.)24, C (H.)25	III B.A.C. XXXI CXLVI CXXX (H.) B.A.C.	…	…	28th D.A.C.	38th26 2/1/Northumbrian27 1/7/Hants.28	Home C'ties.	…	…	84th 85th 86th	17th	…	28th29
1916 July (Macedonia)	83rd. 84th. 85th.	2/K.O., 2/E. York., 1/K.O.Y.L.I., 1/Y. & L.; 83rd M.G. Coy.,30 83rd T.M. Bty.,31 83rd S.A.A. Sec. Ammn. Coln.32 2/N.F., 1/Suff., 2/Ches.; 1/Welsh; 84th M.G. Coy.,30 84th T.M. Bty.,31 84th S.A.A. Sec. Ammn. Coln.32 2/Buffs, 3/R.F., 2/E. Surr.; 3/Midd'x.; 85th M.G. Coy.,30 85th T.M. Bty.,31 85th S.A.A. Sec. Ammn. Coln.32	B Sqdn., 1/Surrey Yeo.33 28th Cyclist Coy.34	III. XXXI. CXXX35 CXLVI.	18, 62, 365 69, 100, 103,36 D (H.)37 22,118, 149,38 D (H.)35 75, 366,367,39 D (H.)40	III B.A.C. XXXI CXXX CXLVI B.A.C.	…	…	28th D.A.C.41	38th 2/1/Northumbrian42 1/7/Hants.42	Home C'ties.	23/Welsh43 (P.)	…	84th 85th 86th	17th	…	28th44
1917 July (Macedonia)	83rd. 84th. 85th.	2/K.O., 2/E. York.,45 1/Y. & L.; 1/K.O.Y.L.I.; 83rd M.G. Coy.; 83rd T.M. Bty.; 83rd S.A.A. Sec. Ammn. Coln. 2/N.F.,46 1/Suff., 2/Ches.; 1/Welsh; 84th M.G. Coy.; 84th T.M. Bty.; 84th S.A.A. Sec. Ammn. Coln. 2/Buffs, 3/R.F.,47 2/E. Surr.; 3/Midd'x.; 85th M.G. Coy.; 85th T.M. Bty.; 85th S.A.A. Sec. Ammn. Coln.	…	III. XXXI. CXXX CXLVI49	18, 62, 36549 69, 100; D (H.) 22, 118; D (H.) 75, 366; D (H.)48	III B.A.C. XXXI CXXX CXLVI B.A.C.	…	…	…	38th 449th (Northumbrian) 506th (Wessex)	Home C'ties.	23/Welsh (P.)	…	84th 85th 86th	17th	819th50	28th51
1918 August (Macedonia)	83rd. 84th. 85th.	2/K.O., 2/E. York.; 1/Y. & L.; 83rd M.G. Coy.; 83rd S.A.A. Sec. Ammn. Coln. 1/Suff., 2/Ches., 1/Welsh; 84th S.A.A. Sec. Ammn. Coln. 2/Buffs, 2/E. Surr., 3/Midd'x.; 85th S.A.A. Sec. Ammn. Coln.	…	III. XXXI. LIV52 CXXX	18, 62; D (H.)48 69, 100; D (H.) A, B, C 22, 118; D (H.)	III B.A.C. XXXI LIV B.A.C. CXXX B.A.C.	…	…	…	38th 449th 506th	Home C'ties.	23/Welsh (P.)	…	84th 85th 86th	17th	819th	28th

228th Bde.
(Br.-Gen. W. C. Ross, 1/3/17—6/1/1919.)

2/Garr. Bn., King's b (28/8/17);
2/5 Garr. Bn., D.L.I. (1/5—14/10/17, & 10/3/1918a);
1/Garr. Bn., Sea. H. (1/3/1917);
2/Garr. Bn., R. Ir. Fus. (1/3–6/8/17);
277th M.G. Coy. b (formed 11/9/17);
228th T.M. Bty. (formed 17/9/17);
228th Bde. Sig. Sec. (15/3/17);
84th M.G. Coy. (15/3/17);
143rd Fd. Amb. (19/3/17);
22/R.B. (1/3/17);
228th Bde. Train (1061 Coy.).

Note a. From 14/10/17—10/3/18 the Bn. was with 84th Bde.

Note b. 228th M.G. Coy. was renumbered 277th on 20/11/1917.

Note.—228th Bde. was formed on 26/2/17, and it assembled on 1/3/17. G.H.Q. orders to break up the Bde. were issued on 4/10/18, and the Bde. was disbanded on 6/1/1919.

NOTES ON ORDER OF BATTLE

1 Formed at Winchester. 1/K.O.Y.L.I. (arrived in U.K. from Singapore on 8/11/14) reached Winchester on 13/12/14; 2/K.O. and 2/E. York. on 23/12; and 1/Y. & L. on 24/12/14.

2 Formed at Winchester. 1/Suff. (arrived in U.K. from Egypt on 23/10/14) reached Winchester on 7/12/14; 2/N.F. and 1/Welsh on 23/12/14; and 2/Ches. on 24/12/14.

3 Formed at Winchester. 2/Buffs arrived on 23/12/14; and 3/R.F., 2/E. Surr., and 3/Midd'x. on 24/12/14.

4 Joined at Winchester on 22/12/14.

5 Formed at Winchester on 29/12/14.

6 In Aug., 1914, III (18, 62, and 75 Bties.) was at Jullundur. It arrived in England on 16/11/14, and reached Winchester on 19/11/14. On arrival it formed III and CXLVI: 18 became 18 and 385; 62 became 62 and 366; and 75 became 75 and 367. III was then reorganized with 18, 62, and 385 (each of 4 guns).

7 In Aug., 1914, XXXI (131, 132, and 133 Bties.) was at Sheffield. The Bties. joined the 27th Div. (q.v.), and XXXI was reorganized and re-formed at Winchester on 22 and 23/12/14 with 3 4-gun Bties., viz. 69 (from I, and made up partly from 103), 100 (from XX), and 103 (from XXI).

8 The Bde. of 3 4-gun Bties. was formed at Winchester on 22/12/14, and comprised 75 (from III), 366 (including left ‡ of 62 of III), and 367 (including left ‡ of 75).

9 Mobilized at Slough on 29/12/14, and embarked at Southampton on 17/1/15.

10 Arrived at Winchester on 28/12/14, and transferred to 47th Div. on 6/4/15.

11 Arrived Winchester on 26/12/14; transferred to 50th Div. on 2/6/15.

12 Arrived Winchester on 28/12/14, and transferred to 46th Div. on 6/4/15.

13 Arrived at Winchester on 5/1/15.

14 Arrived at Winchester on 21/12/14.

15 Joined at Winchester.

16 Arrived at Winchester on 21/12/14. It consisted of 170, 171, 172, and 173 Cos., A.S.C. (The Train was formed by 56th (1/London) Divnl. T. & S. Coln.)

17 Joined from England on 3/3/15. Transferred to 2nd Bde., 1st Div., on 21/10/15.

18 Joined from I. of C. on 5/7/15. Transferred to 3rd Bde., 1st Div., on 23/10/15, and became pioneers on 15/5/16.

19 Formed on 8/9/15 from A/XLIX (H.), B/LXXXIX (H.), and A/LXXXIII (H.).

20 Joined (from XXXIV, 2nd Div.) on 4/2/15, and posted to III on 20/2/15.

21 Joined (from XXVI, 1st Div.) on 7/2/15, and posted to XXXI on 17/2/15.

22 Formed in France from 1 sec. 22 and 1 sec. 118, and called 22A on 11/2/15. Redesignated 149 and joined CXLVI on 5/3/16.

23 A/XLIX (H.) (14th Div.) landed in France 20/5/15. Joined 28th Div. on 17/8/15, and became A/CXXX (H.) on 8/9/15.

24 B/LXXXIX (H.) (19th Div.) landed in France 18/7/15. Joined 28th Div. on 7/8/15, and became B/CXXX (H.) on 8/9/15.

25 A/LXXXIII (H.) (15th Div.) landed in France 9/7/15. Joined 28th Div. on 7/8/15, and became C/CXXX (H.) on 8/9/15.

26 Joined on 8/4/15 (from 6th Div.).

27 Joined on 10/7/15 (from England).

28 Arrived in France from England on 20/10/15, and joined 25/10/15.

29 170, 171, 172, and 173 Cos. became 33rd Divnl. Train on 18/11/15. On 25/11/15, 172 Coy. joined 2nd Divnl. Train in exchange for 8 Coy.

30 83rd M.G. Coy. was formed on 21/5/16 ; 84th and 86th on 18/5/16 (85th had been formed provisionally on 13/3/16).

31 83rd was formed as 4th T.M.B. on 12/9/16, and joined Bde. on 1/10/16 ; 84th joined by 7/11/16 ; and 85th (formed as 5th T.M.B. in Septr. 1916) joined Bde. on 1/10/16, and became 85th T.M.B. on 8/12/16.

32 S.A.A. Secs. were attached to Bdes. from beginning of May, 1916.

33 Joined XVI Corps Cav. Regt. on 27/12/16.

34 Joined XVI Corps Cyclist Bn. on 8/12/16.

35 The Bde. was reorganized between 19-25/7/16. 22 was transferred from III on 20/7: 118 from XXXI, and 367 from CXLVI on 25/7; and C/CXXX became D/CXXX on 25/7. 367 was transferred to CXLVI on 27/7/16 in exchange with 149/CXLVI.

36 103 was broken up on 25/12/16; ‡ went to 69 and ‡ to 100.

37 Formerly A/CXXX ; transferred to XXXI on 25/7/16.

38 149 was broken up on 28/12/16 ; ‡ went to 22, and ‡ to 118.

39 367 was broken up on 27 and 28/12/16 ; ‡ went to 75 and ‡ to 366.

40 Formerly B/CXXX ; transferred to CXLVI on 25/7/16.

41 28th D.A.C. was abolished on 17/1/17, and became C Section of XVI Corps Ammn. Coln. on 17/1/17.

42 2/1/Northumbrian was renumbered 449th by 1/5/17 ; and 1/7/Hants was renumbered 506th (Wessex) on 1/2/17.

43 Raised at Porthcawl 27/9/15, sailed 13/8/16, reached Salonika 24/8/16, and joined the division on 31/8/16.

44 Train (120, 121, 122, 123 Cos.) was raised as 13th Divnl. Train. Embarked on 1/11/15, disembarked at Alexandria 16/11/15, joined 28th Div. as its Train on 10/11/15, and reached Salonika on 10/12/15. Reorganized on 9/10/16 in pack and wheel echelons ; and by 15/11/16, 856, 857, 858, 859 Cos. were added to the Train. (Practical tests of the new establishment were made in March, 1916.)

45 Transferred on 20/6/18 to B.E.F. (France), and joined 151st Bde., 50th Div., on 15/7/18.

46 Transferred on 21/6/18 to B.E.F. (France), and joined 150th Bde., 50th Div., on 16/7/18.

47 Transferred on 26/6/18 to B.E.F. (France), and joined 149th Bde., 50th Div., on 15/7/18.

48 Bde. (75 and 366 Bties.) left the division and embarked on 11-13/8/1917. It reached Alexandria 15-22/8/17. D/CXLVI was transferred to III on 10/8/17 and became D/III.

49 365 was broken up 11/8/17 ; ‡ went to 18 and ‡ to 62.

50 Formed 14/9/17, and allotted to 28th Div.

51 Train was reorganized on 26/10/17 ; 856 absorbed 859, and 857 and 858 Cos. became A.T. Pack Bde. Cos.

52 The Bde. (A, B, and C Bties., 4 guns each) joined from 10th Div., 29/8/17. LIV amalgamated with XCVIII (then with 28th Div.) on 9-29/10/19.

28TH DIVISION

FORMATION, BATTLES, AND ENGAGEMENTS

The division had no existence before the outbreak of the Great War.

The division assembled and mobilized at Hursley, Pitt Hill, and Magdalen Hill Camps (around Winchester) during December, 1914, and January, 1915. The 12 infantry battalions, of which it was composed, came from India (10 from nine different stations), Singapore (1), and Egypt (1) ; the brigades were formed at Winchester. The mounted troops included a cavalry squadron from an existing yeomanry unit, and a cyclist company, which was formed at Winchester. Of the field artillery brigades : in August, 1914, III. was in India and XXXI. was at Sheffield, whilst CXLVI. was only formed at Winchester in December, 1914 ; and III. and XXXI. were both extensively reorganized at Winchester (see notes 6, 7, and 8, Order of Battle Table). The field companies, signal company, field ambulances, and train, were territorial force units.

The 28th Division embarked at Southampton on the 15th–18th January, 1915, disembarked at le Havre between the 16th–19th January, and concentrated between Bailleul and Hazebrouck by the 22nd January.

The 28th Division served on the Western Front in France and Belgium until the middle of October, 1915. It embarked for Egypt in October and November, and, on arrival, it encamped in the neighbourhood of Alexandria. On the 17th November, orders were received for the division to embark for Salonika as soon as possible. Embarkation began on the 20th November, but it was not until the 4th January, 1916, that all the units had completed disembarkation at Salonika. (The XXXI. and CXLVI. Brigades, R.F.A., proceeded direct from Marseille to Salonika, sailing on the 17th November ; these two brigades arrived : XXXI. on 27th November, and CXLVI. on the 2nd December.)

Between 1915 and 1918 the division was engaged in the following operations :—

1915

BATTLES OF YPRES

22 and 23 April ...	...**Battle of Gravenstafel Ridge** [V. Corps, Second Army].
24 April–4 May ...	...**Battle of St. Julien** [V. Corps, Second Army, until 28/4 ; then Plumer's Force].
8–13 May ...	...**Battle of Frezenberg Ridge** [V. Corps, Second Army].
24 and 25 May ...	...**Battle of Bellewaarde Ridge** [V. Corps, Second Army].

---

27 Sept.–5 Oct. ...	...**Battle of Loos** [I. Corps, First Army].

At noon on the 19th October, the division was ordered to be ready to entrain in 48 hours for an unknown destination. On 21st October, the division began to entrain for Marseille, and on 24th October the first units sailed from that port. Units began to reach Alexandria on 29th October, and the division (less XXXI. and CXLVI. Bdes., R.F.A., see above) reached Egypt by 22nd November.

The 28th Division was then sent from Alexandria to Macedonia, and the last unit (the Divnl. Train) completed its disembarkation at Salonika on the 4th January, 1916.

110

1916

2 Oct.	...	...	...**Occupation of Mazirko** (84th Bde.) [XVI. Corps].
31 Oct.	...	...	...**Capture of Bairakli Jum'a** [XVI. Corps].

1917

15 May	...	...	...**Capture of Ferdie and Essex Trenches** (near Bairakli Jum'a) [XVI. Corps].
16 Oct.	...	...	...**Capture of Bairakli and Kumli** [XVI. Corps].

1918

18 and 19 Sept.	...		...**Battle of Dojran** [XVI. Corps].
22–28 Sept.		...	...**Pursuit to the Strumica Valley** [XII. Corps].

At noon on 30th September, Bulgaria concluded an armistice and hostilities ceased. At this time the leading brigade (83rd, then under XVI. Corps) had reached Trnovo (in the Strumica Valley, and 18 miles north of Dojran). By the end of October the division had been drawn back to Güvezne. Then early in November the division (less the 85th Bde., the artillery, and the pioneers) was sent to occupy the Dardanelles Forts, and it disembarked in the Narrows on the 12th. On the 14th, the 85th Bde. reached Constantinople, and at the end of November the 84th Bde. moved from the Kilid Bahr-Maidos area to the Gallipoli-Bulair area ; Divisional H.Q. still remained at Chanaq.

28TH DIVISION

ORDER OF BATTLE, TURKEY, 1919 - 1923

Dates	INFANTRY				FIELD AND PACK ARTILLERY				Engineers	Signal Service	Pioneers	Medical		Mobile Vety. Secn.	Divisional Train
	Brigades	Battalions and attached Units	Attached Battalions and other Units	Mounted Troops	Brigades	Batteries	Bde. Ammn. Colns.	Divnl. Ammn. Coln.	Field Cos.	Divnl. Signal Coy.		Field Ambulances	Sanitary Section		
1919 April (Turkey)	83rd........ 84th........ 85th........	9/K.O., 9/E. Lanc., 9/S. Lanc.; 83rd M.G. Coy. 12/Ches., 7/S.W.B., 11/Welsh 25/Punjabis; 84th M.G. Coy. 11/R.W.F., 9/Border, 10/Hants, 31/Punjabis, 39/Garhwal Rif.; 85th M.G. Coy.	2/Garr. Bn., King's; 1/Garr. Bn., Sea. H.; 130t Bn. Tirailleurs Sénégalais; Detnt. R.M.L.I.	...	LIV .... CXXX	A, B, C 22, 118; D (H.)	...	28th D.A.C.	38th 100th 449th 506th	28th	23/Welsh (P.)	84th 85th 86th 110th (Ind.) 143rd	...	17th	28th (121, 122, & 123 H.T. Cos. and 605 M.T. Coy.)
1920 April (Turkey)	83rd........ 84th........ 85th........ Dardanelles Defences	2/Ches.; 84/Punjabis, 95/ Russel's Inf.; 83rd M.G. Coy. 2/R.D.F.; 2/Rajput L.I. 24/ Punjabis, 54/Sikhs; 84th M.G. Coy. 2/R.S.F., 2/E. Surr.; 2/4/Gurkha Rif., 31/Punjabis, 39/Garhwal Rif.; 85th M.G. Coy. 67/Punjabis.	123rd Bn. Tirailleurs Sénégalais	...	XXVIII .... XXXIX	122, 123, 124; 65 (H.); 46, 51, 54; 30 (H.)	XXVIII B.A.C. XXXIX B.A.C.	...	26th [72nd] 54th [100th] 55th [99th]	28th	123/Sikh (P.)	84th 85th 110th (Ind.)	...	17th	28th (121 H.T. Coy.)
1920 15 Nov. (Turkey)	83rd........ 84th........ 85th........ Dardanelles Defences	1/Hants.; 2 Cos., 2/97 Deccan Inf. 1/Gord. H., 2/R.D.F.; 25/Punjabis, 1 Coy., 2/128 Pioneers 20/Hussars; Anatolian M.I. 50/Kumaon Rif.; 1 Coy., 2/128 Pioneers; Thracian M.I. 2/97/Deccan Inf. (less 2 Cos.); 1 Sec., 54th Fd. Coy., R.E. C. Sec., 110th Ind. Fd. Amb.	Z. Coy., M.G.C. Armoured Train "Marlborough" 2/4 Greek Archipelago Regt.	(See 84th & 85th Bdes.)	X .... XXVIII	46, 51, 54; 30 (H.); 122, 123, 124; 65 (H.)	X B.A.C. XXVIII B.A.C.	...	26th 54th 55th	28th	2/128 Pioneers (see 84th and 85th Bdes.)	85th 110th (Ind.)	...	...	28th (121 H.T. Coy.)
1920 December (Turkey)	83rd........ 84th........	1/Hants. 50/Kumaon Rif., 2/97/Deccan Inf. 1/Gord. H.; 25/Punjabis, 2/128/ Pioneers.	...	20/Hsrs.	X	46, 51, 54; 30 (H.)	X B.A.C.	...	55th	28th	(See 84th Bde.)	85th 110th (Ind.)	...	...	28th (121 H.T. Coy.)
1922 May (Turkey)	83rd........ 84th........	1/Irish Gds., 1/Buffs, 1/Loyal. 2/Essex, 2/Sher. For.	...	3/Hsrs.	XIX	39, 96, 97; 29 (H.)	XIX B.A.C.	...	55th	28th	...	85th	...	...	28th (121 H.T. Coy.)
1922 18 October (Chanak and Gallipoli)	83rd........ 85th........	2/R.F., 2/R. Suss., 1/Loyal, 1/Gord. H. 1/K.O.S.B., 2/Sher. For., 2/H.L.I., 2/R.B.	...	B. Sqdn. (less 1 Trp.), 3/Hsrs.	XVII .... XIX .... V Pack	13, 26; 92 (H.); 96; 29 (H.); 1 (H.), 5 (H.), 7 (H.) 14 (H.) (3·7in. H.)	XVII B.A.C. XIX B.A.C. V Pack B.A.C.	...	12th	2nd	...	83rd 86th	85th	7th (by 18/11/22)	121 H.T. Coy. 780 M.T. Coy.
1923 February (Chanak and Gallipoli)	83rd........ 85th........	2/R. Suss., 1/Loyal. 1/K.O.S.B., 2/H.L.I., 2/R.B.	2/R.F.	B Sqdn, 3/Hsrs. (less 1 Troop with 1st Gds. Bde.)	XVII .... XIX .... V Pack	13, 26; 92 (H.); 96; 29 (H.); 1 (H.), 14 (H.) (3·7in. H.)	XVII B.A.C. XIX B.A.C. V Pack B.A.C.	...	12th	2nd	...	83rd 86th	85th	7th	121 H.T. Coy. 780 M.T. Coy. "E" Supply Coy.
1923 June (Chanak and Gallipoli)	83rd........ 85th........	1/Buffs, 2/R.F., 2/R. Suss. 1/K.O.S.B., 2/H.L.I., 2/R.B.	...	B Sqdn, 3/Hsrs. (less 1 Troop with 1st Gds. Bde.)	XVII .... V Pack	13, 26; 92 (H.); 1 (H.), 14 (H.) (3·7in. H.)	XVII B.A.C. V Pack B.A.C.	...	12th	2nd	...	...	...	...	...

28TH DIVISION, 1919 - 1920

DARDANELLES DEFENCES

(By) 6 Feb., '20...Br.-Gen. P. P. E. DE
            BERRY (B.-G., R.A.).
(By) 7 April, '20...Lt.-Col. J. H. M.
            CORNWALL.
(By) 14 July, '20...Col. H. A. V. CUMMINS.
(By) 25 July, '20...Major H. L. COLAN.
(By) 15 Sept., '20...Lt.-Col. G. WATKINS.
(By) 6 Nov., '20...Lt.-Col. J. MARTIN.

22–27 Sept., '22 ...Col.-Cdt. D. I.
            SHUTTLEWORTH.

(On 27/9/22, the G.O.C. 28th Division
took over command of the Dardanelles
Defences, and the Dardanelles Force,
under Col.-Cdt. Shuttleworth, became
83rd Inf. Bde., 28th Div.)

242nd BRIGADE

30 Mar., '20...Br.-Gen. F. S. MONTAGUE-
            BATES.
30 Aug., '20...⎫ Br.-Gen. H. A. V.
 3 Oct., '20...⎭   CUMMINS.

(The 242nd Bde. was attached to the
28th Div. from 6/6–15/9/20). For the
composition of the 242nd Bde., see Note
under April, 1920, below.)

ATTACHED UNITS AND NOTES

APRIL, 1919.

Military Operating Staff, Anatolian Railways.
M.T. Detnt., Arab Concentration Camp.
3rd Cav. Bde., Mule Corps.
28th Casualty Clearing Station.
Field Bakery.
Supply Depot.
Graves Registration Unit.

NOTE.—28th Divnl. Ammn. Coln. was disbanded on 7/8/1919.

APRIL, 1920.

Military Operating Staff, Anatolian Railways.
Detnt., Navy and Army Canteen Board.
Detnt., 780th M.T. Coy.
21st Stationary Hospital.
52nd Ambulance Train.
Detnt., 34th Motor Ambulance Convoy (787 Coy., M.T.).
22nd Advanced Depot, Medical Stores.

NOTE.—242nd Inf. Bde. (formed on 30/3/1920, under Br.-Gen. F. S.
   Montague-Bates) was attached to 28th Div. from 6/6/20–15/9/20.
   The Bde. consisted of 1/Gord. H., 1/10/Jats, 1/21, and 1/25 Punjabis ;
   and attached to it were 20/Hsrs., Anatolian M.I., 51st Bty., R.F.A.,
   26th Fd. Coy., R.E., 1 Coy., 2/128 Pioneers, 1 Sec. " Z." M.-G. Coy.,
   84th Fd. Amb., and " A " and " B " Echelons, R.A.S.C. The Brigade
   was around Izmid.

15 NOVEMBER, 1920.

Military Operating Staff, Anatolian Railways.
Detnt., Navy and Army Canteen Board.
Detnt., 780th M.T. Coy.
7th Sanitary Section.
21st Stationary Hospital.
52nd Ambulance Train.
Detnt., 34th Motor Ambulance Convoy (787 Coy., M.T.).
22nd Advanced Depot, Medical Stores.
Indian Base Depot.

ATTACHED UNITS AND NOTES—*Continued*

18 OCTOBER, 1922.

NOTES :—(1) **1st Guards Bde.** (Col.-Cdt. J. McC. Steele)—2/G.G., 3/C.G., 1/Ir. G., and Bde. Sig. Sec., assembled at Constantinople by 10/10/22. The transport with 2/G.G. lay off Chanaq from 2–4/10/22, and that with 3/C.G. from 8–9/10/22. 2/G.G. disembarked at Constantinople on 6/10/22, Bde. H.Q. on 9/10/22, and 3/C.G. on 10/10/22. The 1st Guards Bde. then became an Army Bde., directly under G.H.Q., B.F.T.

(2) **84th Inf. Bde.** (Col.-Cdt. W. B. Emery)—1/Buffs, 2/Essex, 1/N. Staff., and 84th Bde. Sig. Sec. ; with 3/Hsrs. (less B. Sqdn.), 39 and 97 Bties., R.F.A., and 11/R.M.L.I. (attached), was on the Asiatic shore of the Bosporus, with Bde. H.Q. at Haidar Pasha. 84th Bde. had become an Army Bde. on 25/9/22 (under G.H.Q., B.F.T.).

On 18/10/22, the following units were attached to the 28th Div.:—

ARTILLERY—I. Heavy Bde., R.G.A. (1st, 2nd, 3rd, and 4th Hy. Bties.—8in. Hows.) ;
III. Medium Bde., R.G.A., (10 (H.), 33 (H.), 34, and Comp. Bty. (1/2 Hows.)—6in. Hows. and 60-pdrs.) ;
V. Medium Bde., R.G.A. (3, 18, 20, and 22 Bties.—6in. Hows.);
Survey Coy., R.A. ; and 13, 6in. ; 6, 4in. ; and 15, 12-pdrs. (naval) ; and 24th Fortress Coy., R.E. ; 85th C.C.S. ; and 3 Sqdns. R.A.F. (36 machines).

FEBRUARY, 1923.

I. Heavy Bde., R.G.A. (1st, 2nd, 3rd, and 4th Hy. Bties.—8in. Hows.).
III. Medium Bde., R.G.A. (6th and 10th Med. Bties.—6in. Hows., and 2nd Med. Bty.—60-pdrs.) ;
V. Medium Bde., R.G.A. (3rd, 18th, 20th, and 22nd Med. Bties.—6in. Hows.);
" S " Coast Battery, R.G.A. (late Composite Bty.) ;
Survey Coy., R.A.
24th Fortress Coy., R.E.
85th Casualty Clearing Station ; and 21st Stationary Hospital.
R.A.F.—4th Squadron (12 Bristol Fighters).

JUNE, 1923.

I. Heavy Bde., R.G.A. (1st, 2nd, 3rd, and 4th Hy. Bties.) ;
III. Medium Bde., R.G.A. (2nd, 6th, and 10th Med. Bties.) ;
V. Medium Bde., R.G.A. (3rd, 18th, 20th, and 22nd Med. Bties.) ;
Survey Coy., R.A.

NOTES :—(1) The **84th Inf. Bde.** (2/E. York., 1/Duke's, 1/Gord. H.), was in the Izmid Peninsula, and attached to it were 3/Hsrs. (less B. Sqdn.), XIX. R.F.A. Bde. (39, 96, 97, and 29 (H). Bties), and 55 Fd. Coy., R.E.

(2) The **1st Guards Bde.** (2/G.G., 3/C.G., 1/Ir. G., and 11/R.M.L.I.), was in Constantinople, with 1 troop, B. Sqdn., 3/Hsrs., attached to it.

28TH DIVISION IN TURKEY, 1919 - 1923

NARRATIVE

In March, 1919, the 84th Bde. moved to the Haidar Pasha area, and in April, Divisional H.Q. were transferred to Moda (south of Haidar Pasha), and LIV. and CXXX. Bdes., R.F.A., were transferred to Constantinople and Haidar Pasha. In November, 1919, so as to guard the Anatolian Railway, the 83rd Bde. was moved from the Chanaq area to Izmid, Eski Shehr, and Afiun Qarahisar. In March, 1920, 83rd Bde. H.Q. were transferred from Izmid to Constantinople, but the three infantry battalions remained in Anatolia and were transferred to the 84th Bde. At the end of March, 1920, a new infantry brigade (242nd—under Br.-Gen. F. S. Montague-Bates) was formed from three battalions of the 28th Division (10/Jats, 21/ and 25/Punjabis), with headquarters at Izmid ; the 242nd Bde. came directly under G.H.Q. from 2nd April (see notes Order of Battle Table). At the beginning of April the 28th Division had two brigades (83rd and 85th) in and around Constantinople, with one battalion (67/Punjabis of the 83rd Bde.) at Chanaq, the remaining brigade (84th) was at Haidar Pasha ; the artillery had one brigade (XXVIII.) at Constantinople, whilst the other brigade (XXXIX.) had three batteries in Anatolia and one battery (temporarily) at Batum. In September, 1920, the Greek Army took over the Izmid front, enabling the British Army of Occupation to be greatly reduced, and troops were sent to Mesopotamia and other theatres where they were more needed. By the end of November the 28th Division (with its H.Q. in Constantinople) was reorganized into two brigades—83rd at Constantinople and Chanaq and 84th at Haidar Pasha—with one cavalry regiment, one field artillery brigade, and one field company (see Order of Battle Table).

In December, 1920, the Venizelist Government fell, King Constantine re-ascended the throne, and the Greeks, ceasing to be allies, at once began operations against the Kemalists in Asia Minor.

By September, 1921, the Greeks, after severe fighting, had established themselves on the Baghdad Railway round Eski Shehr and Afiun Qarahisar. During the period Allied G.H.Q. had declared neutral zones on both sides of the Dardanelles and Bosporus ; and the 28th Division had been mainly occupied in suppressing brigandage within these areas and in constructing a defensive line about 15 miles east of the Bosporus.

By May, 1922, the four Indian battalions had left for India, and they were replaced by three British battalions, and, with the exception of the engineers, all the other British units were also relieved. (See Order of Battle Table.)

Negotiations for peace which had been taking place between the Greeks and the Kemalists came to nothing, and in July, 1922, a Greek Army Corps advanced into Western Thrace and threatened Constantinople. Thereon the 28th Division (less the Irish Guards and a field battery) was sent to occupy the Chatalja Lines, a position 15 miles in length and some 25 miles to the west of Constantinople ; the French and Italian contingents were also moved up, the whole force being placed under command of the French.

In late August the Kemalists delivered an attack on the weakened Greek army in Anatolia ; and, breaking through, they drove the Greeks back to Smyrna and the Sea of Marmara.

It was in this pursuit that the Kemalist forces first came into contact with the few British troops at Chanaq. On the 11th September, the 83rd Bde. headquarters moved down to Chanaq and formed a brigade from the forces located and arriving there ; and on the 27th September the G.O.C., 28th Division, took over the command of the Dardanelles Defences, and the division was formed from the 83rd Bde. and the 85th Bde. (re-formed on the 25th September). But the situation had been so menacing that infantry and artillery had been hurried over from Egypt, and they were followed by units from Malta, Gibraltar, and England ; and between the 25th September and the

NARRATIVE—*Continued*

11th October, eight battalions, three field batteries, four pack batteries, four heavy batteries, eight medium batteries, and four squadrons, R.A.F., reached the threatened theatre. As an additional precaution the transport with 2/G.G. (Guards Bde. from Aldershot) on board, lay off Chanaq from the 2nd–4th October, and the ship with 3/C.G. on the 8th and 9th October, before going on to Constantinople. Guards Brigade H.Q. reached Constantinople on the 9th and 3/C.G. on the 10th October, 1922 (see notes on Table).

The tension was eased by an agreement which was reached on the 8th October at Mudania (Anatolia), whereby the Kemalist forces withdrew 10 kilometres from the Dardanelles, and were not to approach Constantinople within 30 miles from the Asiatic shore. For their part, the Allies undertook that the Greeks should leave Thrace, and two battalions from the 83rd Bde. (2/R. Sussex and 1/Gordon Highldrs.) from Chanaq, and one battalion from the 84th Bde. (1/Buffs) formed the British contingent for this task; and 1/Buffs remained as part of the inter-allied guard on the River Maritsa until peace was concluded. Gradually the Chanaq garrison was withdrawn, and by February, 1923, it had been reduced to five battalions (see Table).

Peace with Turkey was eventually concluded on the 24th July, 1923, and this was ratified at Angora on the 23rd August. The evacuation of the Allied troops had been worked out, and on the 24th August the first embarkation of British troops began, and continued steadily thereafter.

On the 2nd October, 1923, the final ceremony of evacuation took place at 11-30 a.m., at the Dolma Baghche Palace, on the Bosporus, and at 3 p.m., on the same day, the last British transport left Constantinople. The nine years' war existence of the 28th Division had come to an end.

29TH DIVISION

G.O.C.

18 Jan., 1915 (Mobilization)	Major-General F. C. SHAW.
10 March, 1915	Major-General A. G. HUNTER-WESTON.
4 June, 1915	Major-General H. DE B. DE LISLE.
15 August, 1915...	Major-General W. R. MARSHALL (tempy.).
24 August, 1915...	Major-General H. DE B. DE LISLE.
12 March, 1918	Br.-Gen. R. M. JOHNSON (acting).
19 March, 1918	Major-General D. E. CAYLEY.
10 August, 1918...	Br.-Gen. H. H. S. KNOX (acting).
25 August, 1918...	Major-General D. E. CAYLEY.

G.S.O. 1.

20 Jan., 1915...Col. O. C. WOLLEY-DOD.
11 June, 1915...Lt.-Col. C. J. PERCEVAL.
13 Aug., 1915...Lt.-Col. C. G. FULLER.
12 Oct., 1917...Lt.-Col. J. MOORE.
28 Dec., 1917...Lt.-Col. H. E. R. R. BRAINE.
15 July, 1918...Lt.-Col. P. B. O'CONNOR.
14 Nov., 1918...Lt.-Col. J. S. DREW.

A.-A. & Q.-M.-G.

18 Jan., 1915...Lt.-Col. C. J. PERCEVAL.
11 June, 1915...Lt.-Col. C. G. FULLER.
13 Aug., 1915...Lt.-Col. L. H. ABBOTT.
8 Nov., 1917...Lt.-Col. R. Q. CRAUFURD.

B.-G., R.A.

14 Feb., 1915...Br.-Gen. R. W. BREEKS (invalided, 30/5/15).
30 May, 1915...Br.-Gen. H. A. D. SIMPSON-BAIKIE (invalided, 3/9/15).
3 Sept., 1915...Br.-Gen. H. E. STOCKDALE (sick, 10/10/15).
10 Oct., 1915...Lt.-Col. F. A. WYNTER (acting).
11 Oct., 1915...Br.-Gen. F. B. JOHNSTONE (tempy.).
15 Oct., 1915...Br.-Gen. H. E. STOCKDALE (sick, 23/3/16).
23 Mar., 1916...Lt.-Col. W. P. MONKHOUSE (acting).
11 April, 1916...Br.-Gen. H. E. STOCKDALE.
22 April, 1916...Br.-Gen. M. PEAKE.
20 Dec., 1916...Br.-Gen. E. B. ASHMORE.
28 July, 1917...Br.-Gen. G. H. A. WHITE.
1 Sept., 1917...Br.-Gen. E. H. STEVENSON (wounded, 30/11/17).
30 Nov., 1917...Lt.-Col. E. R. BURNE (acting).
12 Dec., 1917...Br.-Gen. R. M. JOHNSON.

C.R.E.

1 Feb., 1915...Lt.-Col. G. B. HINGSTON (wounded, 6/6/15; died of wounds, 16/6/15).
6 June, 1915...Capt. (tempy. Lt.-Col.) R. K. A. MACAULAY (acting).
30 June, 1915...Lt.-Col. A. J. SAVAGE (invalided, 26/10/15).
26 Oct., 1915...Major (tempy. Lt.-Col.) R. K. A. MACAULAY (acting).
2 Nov., 1915...Lt.-Col. W. M. PYNE.
10 June, 1916...Lt.-Col. H. BIDDULPH.
10 Jan., 1918...Lt.-Col. W. GARFORTH.
22 Mar., 1918...Lt.-Col. R. K. A. MACAULAY.

86th BRIGADE

11 Jan., '15...Lt.-Col. H. V. S. ORMOND
(acting).
1 Feb., '15...Br.-Gen. S. W. HARE
(wounded, 25/4/15).
25 April, '15...Col. O. C. WOLLEY-DOD
(tempy.).
27 April, '15...Lt.-Col. D. E. CAYLEY
(acting).
30 April, '15 ⎱ Lt.-Col. H. G. CASSON
4 May, '15 ⎰ (acting).

———

(On 4/5/15, the 86th Bde. was temporarily split up : 2/R.F. and 1/L.F. were attached to 88th Bde. ; and 1/R.M.F. and 1/R.D.F. to 87th Bde. The 86th Bde. was re-formed on 6/6/15.)

———

6 June, '15...Br.-Gen. O. C. WOLLEY-
DOD
(invalided, 13/8/15).
13 Aug., '15...Br.-Gen. D. E. CAYLEY
(tempy.).
14 Aug., '15...Br.-Gen. C. J. PERCEVAL.
20 Dec., '15...Br.-Gen. W. DE L.
WILLIAMS.
29 April, '17...Br.-Gen. R. G. JELF
(invalided, 16/8/17).
16 Aug., '17...Lt.-Col. H. NELSON
(acting).
24 Aug., '17...Br.-Gen. G. R. H. CHEAPE.

88th BRIGADE

27 Jan., '15...Br.-Gen. H. E. NAPIER
(killed, 25/4/15).
25 April, '15...Lt.-Col. H. C. SMITH
(acting)
(killed, 25/4/15).
26 April, '15...Lt.-Col. O. G. GODFREY-
FAUSSETT (acting).
29 April, '15...Lt.-Col. W. DE L. WILLIAMS
(acting).
26 May, '15...Br.-Gen. W. DORAN
(invalided, 7/6/15).
7 June, '15...Br.-Gen. D. E. CAYLEY.
1 Oct., '17...Br.-Gen. H. NELSON.
22 Jan., '18...Br.-Gen. B. C. FREYBERG,
V.C.

87th BRIGADE

24 Jan., '15...Br.-Gen. W. R. MARSHALL.*
27 April, '15...Lt.-Col. R. O. C. HUME
(acting).
28 April, '15...Lt.-Col. H. G. CASSON
(acting).
29 April, '15...Br.-Gen. W. R. MARSHALL..
24 July, '15...Lt.-Col. Q. G. K. AGNEW
(acting).
8 Aug., '15...Br.-Gen. W. R. MARSHALL..
15 Aug., '15...Lt.-Col. C. H. T. LUCAS
(acting).
24 Aug., '15...Br.-Gen. C. H. T. LUCAS.
7 Dec., '16...Br.-Gen. R. N. BRAY
(invalided, 14/2/17).
14 Feb., '17...Lt.-Col. A. J. WELCH
(acting).
3 April, '17...Br.-Gen. C. H. T. LUCAS.
20 Oct., '17...Lt.-Col. A. J. ELLIS
(acting).
12 Nov., '17...Br.-Gen. C. H. T. LUCAS.
16 Jan., '18...Lt.-Col. G. T. RAIKES
(acting).
20 Jan., '18...Br.-Gen. G. H. N. JACKSON.

———

*On 27/4/15, Br.-Gen. W. R. Marshall was placed in command of all troops ashore at Helles. He did not resume command of the 87th Bde. until 29/4/15.

GENERAL NOTES

The following units also served with the 29th Division:

INFANTRY :—29th **Indian Infantry Bde.** (Br.-Gen. H. V. Cox)—14/K.G.O. Ferozepore Sikhs, 69/Punjabis, 89/Punjabis, and 6/Gurkha Rif., with 108th Ind. Field Amb., 23rd Mule Corps (S. and T.), and S. and T. Corps, landed at Helles on 1/5/15, and joined 29th Div. On 3/6/15, 5/Gurkha Rif. and 2/10/Gurkha Rif. landed and joined 29th Ind. Bde. The 29th Ind. Bde. served with the 29th Div. until 7/7/15, and on 10/7/15 the Bde. left Helles for Imbros. (VII. Mtn. Arty. Bde. was employed at Anzac.)

125th (Lancashire Fusilier) Inf. Bde. (Br.-Gen. H. C. Frith)—5/L.F., 6/L.F., 7/L.F., and 8/L.F., and Sec. E. Lanc. Divnl. Sig. Coy., of 42nd (E. Lanc.) Div., was attached to 29th Div. at Helles from 5/5–8/5/15. The Bde. then joined the Composite Division.

New Zealand Inf. Bde. (Colonel F. E. Johnston)—Auckland Bn., Canterbury Bn., Otago Bn., and Wellington Bn., and Sec. N.Z. and A. Divnl. Signal Coy., of A. and N.Z. Div., landed from Anzac on 6/5/15 at W. Beach (Helles), and served with the 29th Div. until the Bde. returned to Anzac on 19/5/15.

Plymouth Bn., R.M.L.I. (R.N. Div.), was attached to the 29th Div. from 15/4 to 4/5/15, for beach duties during the landing at Helles. On 4/5/15 the Bn. joined the Comp. Naval Bde.

Anson Bn. (R.N. Div.), was attached to the 29th Div. from 15/4 to 2/5/15, for beach duties during the landing at Helles. Anson Bn. rejoined 2nd Bde., R.N.D., on 2/5/15.

Drake Bn. (R.N. Div.), landed at W. Beach (Helles) at 8.30 p.m. 26/4/15, and relieved Anson Bn. on beach duties with 29th Div. On 2/5/15 Drake Bn. joined Comp. Nav. Bde.

2/1/London R., joined 88th Bde. on 9/9/15, and remained with the 29th Div. until it reached Egypt in January, 1916. The Bn. returned to France and arrived at Marseille on 24/4/16. In May, 1916, the Bn. was broken up in France and drafted.

2/3/London R., joined 86th Bde. on 24/9/15, and remained with the 29th Div. until it reached Egypt in January, 1916. The Bn. returned to France and arrived at Marseille on 24/4/16. In May, 1916, the Bn. was broken up in France and drafted.

ARTILLERY :—I. **(N.S.W.) Field Arty. Bde.** (1st, 2nd, and 3rd B'ties.), landed at Helles on 4/5/15, and joined 29th Div. On reorganization of the Artillery on 19/8/15, the Bde. joined Right Group, VIII. Corps. On 30/9/15 the Bde. returned to Anzac.

6th Bty., Aus. Field Arty., and 3rd Bty., N.Z. Field Arty. These two batteries landed at Helles on 4/5/15, and were attached to the 29th Div. until 17/8/15, when both batteries returned to Anzac.

5/E. Lanc. Bty. (42nd Div.), landed at Helles on 14/5/15, and was attached to the 29th Divnl. Arty. On 19/8/15 the Bty. was transferred to Right Group, VIII. Corps.

6/E. Lanc. Bty. (42nd Div.), landed at Helles on 6/7/15, and was attached to the 29th Divnl. Arty. On 19/8/15 the Bty. was transferred to Right Group, VIII. Corps.

43rd Siege Battery (4, 6-in. Mk. VII Guns). — The Bty. began mobilization at Woolwich on 8/7/15, embarked at Devonport on 21/7/15, arrived Alexandria 2/8/15, left on 6/9/15, and landed at Helles on 11/9/15. The Bty. joined XXIV. Siege Bde., and on 14/9/15 was attached to 29th Divnl. Arty. After the evacuation the Bty. reached Alexandria on 18/1/16. It left Egypt for Salonika on 5/3/16, and on 12/6/16 it joined XX. Heavy Bde.

OTHER UNITS :—1 Sec., 10 Sqdn., R.N.A.C.D. (6 light Vickers guns), was attached to the 29th Div. from 5/5/15–20/6/15 ; it was then transferred to VIII. Corps.

16 Sanitary Section, embarked at Avonmouth on 20 and 22/3/15. It was transferred to IV. Corps on 2/4/17.

29th Divnl. Amb. Workshop (a) : Embarked at Avonmouth on 22/3/15. The workshop unit was left at Alexandria and only reached W. Beach (Helles) on 3/9/15. On the 29th Div. returning to France, in March, 1916, the workshop unit was left in Egypt.

(b). A fresh workshop unit for the 29th Div. came from England and arrived at Rouen on 4/4/16. This unit joined the 29th Div. on 10/4/16. By 16/4/16 the workshop unit was absorbed by the Divnl. Supply Column.

By 11/2/18 the reorganization of the division on a 9-battalion basis was completed ; and on 1/3/18 the pioneer battalion (2/Monmouth) was reorganized on a 3-company basis.

Dates	INFANTRY Brigades	Battalions and attached Units	Mounted Troops	Horse, Field, and Mountain Artillery — Brigades	Batteries	Bde. Ammn. Columns	Heavy & Siege Batteries	T.M. Medium	T.M. Heavy	Divnl. Ammn. Col.	Engineers Field Cos.	Signal Service Divnl. Signal Coy.	Pioneers	M.G. Units	Field Ambulances	Mobile Vety. Secn.	Divnl. Emplnt. Coy.	Divnl. Train
1915 April (Galli-poli)	86th[1] 87th[3] 88th[4]	2/R.F.,[1] 1/L.F., 1/R.M.F.,[2] 1/R.D.F.; 2/S.W.B., 1/K.O.S.B., 1/R. Innis. F., 1/R.; 4/Worc., 2/Hants., 1/Essex, 5/R. Scots.[5]	C Sqdn., Surrey Y.co.;[6] 29th Divnl. Cyclist Coy.[7]	XV R.H.A.[8] XVII[9] .... CXLVII[10] IV (High-land)[11] Mtn. Bde.	B, L, Y; 13, 26, 92; 10, 97, 368; 460 (H.)[12]; Argyll Bty., Ross & Cromarty Bty.	XV R.H.A. B.A.C.; XVII B.A.C.; CXLVII B.A.C.; How. Bty. A.C.; IV (Higld.) Mtn. B.A.C.	90 H.B.[13] & H.B.A.C.; 14 S.B.[14] & S.B.A.C.	...		29th D.A.C.[15]	2/London[16] & 2/Lowland[16] 1/W. Riding[18]	1/ L'd'n[17]	...	...	87th[18] (1/W. Lanc.) 88th[18] (1/E. A'glin.) 89th[18] (1/High-land)	18th[19]	...	29th[20]
1916 June (France)	86th. 87th[26] .... 88th.	2/R.F., 1/L.F., 16/Midd'x.[21] 1/R.D.F.; 86th Bde. M.G. Coy.;[22] 86th Bde. T.M Bty[23]; 2/S.W.B., 1/K.O.S.B., 1/R. Innis. F., 1/Bord.; 87th Bde. M.G. Coy.;[22] 87th T.M. Bty.[23]; 4/Worc., 2/Hants., 1/Essex, R.Newf'dld Bn.[24] 88th Bde. M.G. Coy.;[22] 88th Bde. T.M. Bty.[23]	...	XV R.H.A.[25] XVII[26] .... CXXXII[27] CXLVII[28]	B, L, Y[29]; 13, 26, 92; 460 (H.); 369, 370, 371; D (H.); 10, 97, 368; D (H.)	...[30]	...	X.29[31] Y.29[31] Z.29[31]	V.29[32]	29th D.A.C.[30]	2/London; 1/W. Riding; 3/Kent[33]	1/ L'd'n[34]	2/Mon-m'th[34] (P.)	...	87th 88th 89th	18th	...	29th[35]
1917 June (France)	86th. 87th .... 88th.	2/R.F., 1/L.F., 16/Midd'x.[36] 1/R.D.F.[37] 86th M.G. Coy.; 86th T.M. Bty.; 2/S.W.B., 1/K.O.S.B., 1/R. Innis. F.,[38] 1/Bord.; 87th M.G. Coy.; 87th T.M. Bty.; 4/Worc., 2/Hants., 1/Essex,[39] R.Newf'dl'd. Bn.; 88th M.G. Coy.; 88th T.M. Bty.	...	XV R.H.A. XVII	B, L; 1/Warwick;[40] 460 (H.)[41]; 13 26, 92; D (H.)[42]	...	...	X.29 Y.29 Z.29[43]	V.29[44]	29th D.A.C.	455th[45] (W. Riding) 497th[45] (Kent) 510th[45] (London)	1/ L'd'n	2/Mon-mouth (P.)	227th M.G. Coy.[46]	87th 88th 89th	18th	226th[47]	29th
1918 March (France)	86th. 87th .... 88th.	2/R.F., 1/L.F., 1/R. Guernsey L.I.;[48] 86th T.M. Bty.; 2/S.W.B., 1/K.O.S.B., 1/Bord.; 87th T.M. Bty.; 4/Worc., 2/Hants., R.Newf'd'd. Bn.;[49] 88th T.M. Bty.	...	XV R.H.A. XVII	B, L; 1/Warwick: 460 (H.); 13, 26, 92; D (H.)	...	...	X.29 Y.29	...	29th D.A.C.	455th 497th 510th	1/ L'd'n	2/Mon-mouth (P.)	No. 29 Bn, M.G.C.[50]	87th 88th 89th	18th	226th	29th
1918 May (France)	86th. 87th .... 88th.	2/R.F., 1/L.F., 1/R.D.F.[51] 86th T.M. Bty.; 2/S.W.B., 1/K.O.S.B. 1/Bord.; 87th T.M. Bty.; 4/Worc., 2/Hants., 2/Leins.;[52] 88th T.M. Bty.	...	XV R.H.A. XVII	B, L; 1/Warwick: 460 (H.); 13, 26, 92; D (H.)	...	...	X.29 Y.29	...	29th D.A.C.	455th 497th 510th	1/ L'd'n	2/Mon-mouth (P.)	No. 29 Bn, M.G.C.	87th 88th 89th	18th	226th	29th

NOTES ON ORDER OF BATTLE

1 Bde. formed on 9/1/15 at Nuneaton. The Bns. arrived on 11 and 12/1/15. 2/R.F. 1/L.F, and 1/R.D.F. came from India; and 1/R.M.F. from Burma.

2 1/R.M.F. transferred on 25/4/16 to L. of C.; and on 28/5/16 joined 48th Bde. 16th Div.

3 Bde. formed on 11/1/15 at Rugby and Coventry. The Bns. arrived between 11/1 and 19/1/15. 2/S.W.B. came from Tsintao; 1/Bord. from Burma; and 1/K.O.S.B. and 1/R. Innis. F. from India.

4 Bde. formed on 12/1/15 at Stratford and Banbury. The Bns arrived: 2/Hants. (from Mhow) on 13/1/15; 1/Essex (from Mauritius), 18/1/15; 4/Worc. (from Burma), 18/1/15; and 5/R. Scots (Edinburgh) on 11/3/15.

5/R.S absorbed the bulk of 6/R.S.

6 Joined Jany, 1915. Transferred to XV Corps Cav. Regt. 11/5/16; and on 21/5/16 Transferred to III Corps Cav. Regt.

7 Formed in Jany, 1915, from units of the division. B.A.C. began mobilization on 19/1/15. (B'ties, 4, 18-pdrs. each.)

Transferred on 11/5/16 to VIII Corps Cyclist Bn.

In Aug., 1914, B. was formed at Leamington in Jany, 1915. XV R.H.A. was formed at Leamington in Jany, 1915. R.H.A. at Mhow; L. (reformed after Néry 1/9/14) was quartered at St. John's Wood, until embarkation at Avonmouth. (B'ties, 4, 18-pdrs each.)

9 In Aug., 1914, XVII (10, 26, 92) was at Allahabad. 10 (transferred to CXLVII) was replaced by 13 (formerly in I at Edinburgh). XVII began mobilization on 19/1/15. (B'ties, 4, 18-pdrs each.)

10 Bde. formed at Leamington on 1/1/15. B.A.C. began to mobilize on 7/1/15. 10 (transferred from XVII), and 97 (transferred from XIX, St. Thomas's Mount) completed Bde. with 368, which was formed at Leamington from left secs. of 10 and 97 on 6/1/15. (B'ties, 4, 18-pdrs. each.)

11 Bde. formed at Leamington on 4/8/14, and concentrated at Bedford on 10/8/14. It was allotted to the division 10/3/15, and embkd. at Avonmouth on 16/3/15. It was transferred to 11th Div. (for Suvla) on 29/7/15; and on 13/8/15 it was transferred at Suvla to the 10th Division.

12 Bty. (4, 4.5in. H.) was formed at Stowmarket; and was allotted to the division on 1/2/15.

13 The Bty. (4, 60-pdrs.) in Aug., 1914, was quartered at Nowgong (C.I.), and on 10/3/15 it was allotted to the division. It was transferred at Helles on 1/6/15 to Group IV, VIII Corps Arty. It went from Egypt to France with XXXIV Hy. Bde. on 8/4/16, and joined III Corps, Fourth Army, on 17/4/16.

14 The Bty. (4, 6-in. H.) was allotted to the division on 10/3/15. It mobilized and equipped at Woolwich, 12/19/3/15, and embarked from Avonmouth. It was transferred at Helles on 1/6/15 to Group IV, VIII Corps Arty. It went from Egypt to France with XXIV Siege Bde. on 8/4/16, and joined VIII Corps, Fourth Army, on 17/4/16.

15 Formed in 1915, and embkd. with Div. from Avonmouth. The D.A.C. was left in Egypt; and in October it was transferred to 10th Div. (for Salonika). It sailed in *MARQUETTE* (torpedoed off Salonika on 23/10/15). The D.A.C. lost 100 men and all equipt. The D.A.C. was completed from B.A.C.'s and 42nd D.A.C.

16 The Fd. Cos. mobilized at Crowborough, Southam, and Kineton; and joined the Div. in Jany, Febry, and March. 2/Lowland was transferred on 24/2/16 to 52nd (Lowland) Div.

17 Joined the Div. in Febry, 1915.

18 Mobilized in the divisional area.

19 Formed at Woolwich, 8/1/15, and joined 5/2/15.

20 Divnl. Train (Wessex) joined the Div. in Febry, 1915, and was converted into a regular basis. It consisted of 246, 247, 248, and 249 Cos, A.S.C. In Egypt, on 12/3/16, it was transferred to 53rd (Welsh) Div.

21 Joined on 25/4/16 from G.H.Q. Troops.

22 M.G. Cos. formed: 86th on 28/2/16 (at el Kubri); 87th on 16/2/16 (at Suez); and 88th on 21/2/16 (at Suez).

23 Bde. T.M.B.'s arrived: 86th by 21/4/16; 87th by 28/4/16; and 88th on 16/4/16.

24 Joined at Suvla on 19/9/15

25 369 (arrived from England on 15/3/16) joined XV Bde. on 31/3/16, and was transferred on 20/5/16 to CXXXII. B. & I. were made up to 6-gun batteries on 12/9/16 by 371/CXXXII; and Y. was completed by 1/2 369/CXXXII on 12/9/16.

460 (H.) (previously D/XVII) joined Bde. on 12/9/16, and it was completed to 6 hows. on 19/1/17 by 1/2 D/XVII.

26 370 (from England on 15/3/16) joined Bde. on 31/3/16; on 20/5/16 it was transferred to CXXXII in exchange for 460 (H.), which then became D/XVII. D/XVII was re-transferred as 460 (H.) on 12/9/16 to XV R.H.A., and its place was taken by D from CXXXII, which then became D/XVII.

On 12/9/16, 13 and 26 were made up to 6-gun batteries by 370/CXXXII, and 92 by 1/2 369/CXXXII. On 19/1/17, D/XVII was broken up and completed 460 (H.) of XV R.H.A., and D/CXLVII. The latter then became D/XVII.

27 LVII (H.) (A, formerly 181/LVII, and D, formed from part of 181) reported to 10th Div. at Suvla on 16/8/15. LVII was transferred on 2/3/16 to 29th Div., and 460 (H.) joined LVII (H.) at Alexandria on 3/3/16.

On 8/3/16 at Alexandria LVII (H.) became CXXXII (H.) and 460 (H.) became C/CXXXII, A/LVII became B/CXXXII, and D/LVII became C/CXXXII.

CXXXII was reorganized on 20/5/16: B. became D/CXLVII, and C/CXXXII became D/CXXXII. 369 (from XV, R.H.A.), 370 (from XVII), and 371 (from CXLVII) joined CXXXII on 20/5/16.

On 12/9/16 CXXXII was broken up, and 369, 370, and 371 were used to complete the 6 batteries of XV R.H.A. and XVII; and D/CXXXII became D/XVII (in place of 460 (H.)—see n. 26).

28 371 (from England on 15/3/16) joined Bde. on 31/3/16; on 21/5/16 it was transferred to CXXXII in exchange for B/CXXXII, which then became D/CXXXII.

On 31/1/17 CXLVII became an A.F.A.: Bde., D/CXLVII was made up to 6 hows. by 1/2 D/XVII, and was then transferred to XVII as D/XVII. A/LXXXI joined the Bde. on 19/1/17, and became A/CXLVII. On 21/1/18 C/CCCXXXII (H.) joined the Bde., and became D(H.)/CXLVII on 14/2/18.

29 Y. was transferred on 27/11/16 to 1st Cav. Div., and joined on 1/12/16.

30 53rd (Welsh) D.A.C. became 29th D.A.C. on 7/4/16 (in France).

On 13/5/16 B.A.C.'s were abolished and the D.A.C. was reorganized.

31 Formed in April, 1916. Z. 29 arrived by 21/4/16

32 From May, 1916.

33 Joined at Suez on 26/2/16 (from 52nd Div.)

34 Joined from L. of C. on 30/1/16 from 12th Div., 4th Div.) to L. of C. on 30/1/16 from 12th Div., 4th Div.). (Transferred to 29th Div. on 24/3/16.

35 Train from England on 20/3/16, and reported to 29th Div. on 24/3/16. Train consisted of 225, 226, 227, 228 Cos., A.S.C.

36 Disbanded 11/2/18.

37 Transferred on 19/10/17 to 48th Bde., 16th Div.

38 Transferred on 5/2/18 to 109th Bde., 36th Div.

39 Transferred on 4/2/18 to 112th Bde., 37th Div.

40 1/Warwick R.H.A. (T.F.) Bty. joined on 27/11/16 from 1st Cav. Div.

41 460 (H.) (previously D/XVII) joined Bde. on 12/9/16. Made up to 6 hows. on 19/1/17 by 1/2 D/XVII (formerly D/CXXXII) (See notes 25 and 26.)

42 Formerly D/CXLVII. It was made up to 6 hows. on 19/1/17 by the transfer of 1/2 D/XVII (formerly D/CXXXII). Then D/CXLVII was transferred to XVII as D/XVII.

43 Z. was broken up on 4/2/18; the personnel was transferred to Y.29.

44 V. was broken up on 4/2/18; the R.F.A. personnel was transferred to X.29, and the R.G.A. personnel to VIII Corps Artillery.

45 Field Cos. were renumbered on 1/2/17.

46 Joined 20/7/17.

47 No. 28 Employment Coy., 1/Labour Corps, arrived from the Base on 25/5/17. It was renumbered 229th in June, 1917.

48 Joined division from England on 2/10/17; transferred on 27/4/18 to G.H.Q. Troops.

49 Transferred on 29/4/18 to G.H.Q. Troops; and on 13/9/18 joined 28th Bde., 9th Div.

50 Formed 15/2/18. It included 86th, 87th, 88th, and 227th M.G. Cos.

51 Joined 26/4/18 from 48th Bde., 16th Div.

52 Joined 23/4/18 from 47th Bde., 16th Div.

29TH DIVISION

FORMATION, BATTLES, AND ENGAGEMENTS

The division had no existence before the outbreak of the Great War. Between January and March, 1915, the division assembled and mobilized in the Midlands, in the area Nuneaton–Rugby–Banbury–Stratford, with headquarters at Leamington. The 12 infantry battalions of which the division was composed were collected from Asia (10), Africa (1), and Europe (1). Of these 12 battalions, one came from China, three from three different stations in Burma, six from six different stations in India, one from Mauritius, and the remaining battalion was an existing T.F. battalion from Edinburgh. The brigades were formed in the mobilization area. The mounted troops included a cavalry squadron from an existing yeomanry unit, and a cyclist company which was formed in the mobilization area. Of the artillery brigades, XV. R.H.A. was formed at Leamington, in January, 1915, two of its batteries came from India, and it was completed by a battery which had returned to England from the Western Front to be re-formed; XVII. R.F.A. was in India in August, 1914, and CXLVII. R.F.A. was formed at Leamington, in January, 1915. During mobilization, both field artillery brigades were extensively reorganized (see Order of Battle Table, notes 9 and 10). The Highland Mountain Bde. was an existing T.F. formation, the 90th Heavy Bty. came from Nowgong (C.I.); and 14 Siege Battery and 460 (H.) Battery were new formations. The field companies, signal company, field ambulances, and train, were territorial force units.

The division embarked at Avonmouth on the 16th–22nd March, and proceeded via Malta (22nd March) to Alexandria, where the first transport arrived on the 28th March. The division disembarked at Alexandria, and on the 7th April re-embarkation began for Mudros (actually before the disembarkation of the whole division had been completed). On the evening of the 23rd April the ships of the covering force sailed from Lemnos and spent the following day anchored off Tenedos.

The landing on the Gallipoli Peninsula began about 7 a.m. on the 25th April. For the rest of the year the 29th Division served on the Gallipoli Peninsula and took part in the following operations :—

1915

THE BATTLES OF HELLES

25 and 26 April	...The Landing at Cape Helles.
26 April	...Capture of Sedd el Bahr.
28 April	...First Battle of Krithia.
1 and 2 May ...	...Eski Hissarlik.
6–8 May... ...	...Second Battle of Krithia.
12 May	...Gurkha Bluff (29th Ind. Inf. Bde.).
4 June	...Third Battle of Krithia [VIII. Corps].

---

28 June–2 July ...	...Gully Ravine [VIII. Corps].
6–13 August ...	...Krithia Vineyard [VIII. Corps].

Between 16-21 August, 29th Divnl. H.Q. ; 86th, 87th, 88th Inf. Bdes. ; 2/London, 2/Lowland, 1/W. Riding Fd. Cos. ; 1/London Sig. Coy. ; 87th, 88th and 89th Fd. Ambces moved to Suvla and came under IX. Corps. The 29th Divnl. Artillery (see Order of Battle Table) remained at Helles under VIII. Corps.

THE BATTLES OF SUVLA

21 August ...	...Battle of Scimitar Hill [IX. Corps].

Night 19/20 December	...Evacuation of Suvla (88th Inf. Bde.) [IX. Corps].

The 87th Inf. Bde. returned to Helles on 1/10/15, and 2/Lond. Fd. Coy. on 2/11/15. After the Evacuation of Suvla, Divnl. H.Q., with 86th and 88th Inf. Bdes., and the two Fd. Cos. returned to Helles between 16–22 December, and came again under VIII. Corps. (The three field ambulances were left at Mudros and Imbros.)

1916

Night of 7/8 January	...Evacuation of Helles [VIII. Corps].

After the Evacuation of Helles, the 29th Division moved to Egypt and was concentrated at Suez. On 25th February orders were received for the early move of the division to France. Embarking in March, the division disembarked at Marseille, and between 15–29 March it effected its concentration on the Somme, east of Pont Remy. For the rest of the Great War the 29th Division served on the Western Front in France and Belgium.

THE BATTLES OF THE SOMME

1 July	...Battle of Albert [VIII. Corps, Fourth Army].
10–18 October ...	...Battle of the Transloy Ridges (88th Bde. with 12th Div.) [XV. Corps, Fourth Army].

1917

| 27 January | ... | ...Le Transloy (87th Bde.) [XIV. Corps, Fourth Army]. |
| 28 February | ... | ...Saillisel (86th Bde.) [XIV. Corps, Fourth Army]. |

THE BATTLES OF ARRAS

12–14 April	...	...First Battle of the Scarpe [VI. Corps, Third Army].
23 and 24 April		...Second Battle of the Scarpe [VI. Corps, Third Army].
3 and 4 May	...	...Third Battle of the Scarpe [VI. Corps, Third Army].

THE BATTLES OF YPRES

16–18 August	...	...Battle of Langemarck [XIV. Corps, Fifth Army].
4 October	...	...Battle of Broodseinde [XIV. Corps, Fifth Army].
9 October	...	...Battle of Poelcappelle [XIV. Corps, Fifth Army].

BATTLE OF CAMBRAI

| 20 and 21 November | ...The Tank Attack [III. Corps, Third Army]. |
| 30 Nov.–3 Dec. ... | ...German Counter-Attacks [III. Corps, Third Army]. |

1918

THE BATTLES OF THE LYS

10 and 11 April	...Battle of Estaires (less 88th Inf. Bde.) [XV. Corps, First Army].
10 and 11 April	...Battle of Messines (88th Inf. Bde., with 25th Div. on 10/4, and with 34th Div., 11/4) [IX. Corps, Second Army].
12 and 13 April	...Battle of Hazebrouck (less 88th Inf. Bde.) [XV. Corps, Second Army].
13 and 14 April	...Battle of Bailleul (88th Bde. with 34th Div.) [IX. Corps, Second Army].

THE ADVANCE TO VICTORY

| 18 August | ... | ...Capture of Outtersteene Ridge (87th Bde.) [XV. Corps, Second Army]. |
| 4 September | ... | ...Capture of Ploegsteert and Hill 63 (86th and 88th Bdes.) [XV. Corps, Second Army]. |

THE FINAL ADVANCE IN FLANDERS

| 28 Sept.–2 Oct. ... | ...Battle of Ypres [II. Corps, Second Army]. |
| 14–19 October ... | ...Battle of Courtrai [II. Corps, Second Army]. |

The 29th Division was withdrawn to rest on the 24th October, and on the 7th November it was transferred to the X. Corps (via XV. Corps) and moved south into the Tourcoing area. On the night 7/8, the 88th Bde. took over part of the X. Corps Front Line along the Schelde (east of St. Genois), and on the next night the brigade established a line of posts on the right bank. On the 11th November the 88th Bde. was ordered to seize the Dendre crossings at Lessines. The Brigadier was at Flobecq at 9-30 a.m., and galloping forward from there with A. Sqdn., 7th Dragoon Guards (attached from 3rd Cavalry Division), the bridges at Lessines were captured and secured by 11 a.m., when the Armistice brought hostilities to an end.

The 29th Division was ordered to the Rhine and it began its march on the 18th November. During this advance the division crossed the fields of Waterloo (on the 23rd) and Ramillies (on the 27th). On the 4th December, the division entered Germany at Malmédy, and arrived on the 9th at Cologne. On Friday, the 13th December, the 29th Division crossed the Rhine by the Hohenzollern Bridge, and it completed its occupation of the bridgehead on the 16th.

On the 15th March, 1919, the 29th Division ceased to exist.

APPENDIX I

THE CHANGES IN THE COMPOSITION OF A BRITISH DIVISION ON THE WESTERN FRONT DURING THE GREAT WAR, 1914-1918

AUGUST, 1914.	JUNE, 1915.	SEPTEMBER, 1916.
Divnl. H.Q.	Divnl. H.Q.	Divnl. H.Q.
Infantry : 3 Brigades (12 Inf. Battns., with 2 Vickers Guns each).	**Infantry :** 3 Brigades (12 Inf. Battns., with 4 Vickers Guns each).	**Infantry :** 3 Brigades (12 Inf. Battns., with Guns each) ; 3 Bde. M.G. Cos. (16 Vickers M.G. each) ; 3 Bde. Light T.M. B'ties. (8, 3″ Stokes Mortars
Mounted Troops : 1 Sqdn., Divnl. Cavy. 1 Divnl. Cyclist Coy.	**Mounted Troops :** 1 Sqdn., Divnl. Cavy. 1 Divnl. Cyclist Coy.	
Artillery : H.Q. Divnl. Artillery. 3 Field Artillery Bdes. (18-pdrs.) and 3 B.A.C.'s ; 1 Field Artillery (How.) Bde. (4·5″ H.) and 1 (How.) B.A.C. ; 1 Heavy Bty. (60-pdrs.) and Hy. Bty. A.C. 1 Divisional Ammn. Coln.	**Artillery :** H.Q. Divnl. Artillery. 3 Field Artillery Bdes. (18-pdrs.) and 3 B.A.C.'s ; 1 Field Artillery (How.) Bde. (4·5″ H.) and 1 (How.) B.A.C. 1 Divisional Ammn. Coln.	**Artillery :** H.Q. Divnl. Artillery. 4 Field Artillery Bdes. (18-pdrs. and 4·5″ H.); 3 Medium T.M. B'ties. (4, 2″ T.M. each) ; 1 Heavy T.M. Bty. (4, 9·45″ Mortars). 1 Divisional Ammn. Coln.
Engineers : H.Q. Divnl. Engineers. 2 Field Cos.	**Engineers :** H.Q. Divnl. Engineers. 3 Field Cos.	**Engineers :** H.Q. Divnl. Engineers. 3 Field Cos.
Signal Service : 1 Signal Coy.	**Signal Service :** 1 Signal Coy.	**Signal Service :** 1 Signal Coy.
		Pioneers : 1 Pioneer Battalion (8 Lewis Guns).
3 Field Ambulances.	3 Field Ambulances. 1 Sanitary Section.	3 Field Ambulances. 1 Sanitary Section.
1 Mobile Vety. Section.	1 Mobile Vety. Sec.	1 Mobile Vety. Section.
	1 Workshop for Motor Amb. Cars.	
1 Divisional Train (4 Horse-Transport Cos., A.S.C.).	1 Divisional Train (4 H.-T. Cos., A.S.C.).	1 Divisional Train (4 H.-T. Cos., A.S.C.).

W.E. STRENGTH :

	1914.	1915.	1916.
All Ranks	18,179	18,122	
Horses	5,594	5,174	
Guns	76	56	
18-pdrs	54	48	48
4·5″ H.	18	8	16
60-pdrs	4		
Trench Mortars			
Stokes			24
Medium (2″)			12
Heavy (9·45″)			4
Machine Guns	24	48	
Vickers	24	48	48
Lewis Guns			152
Carts and Vehicles	877	834	
Cycles	382	521	
Motor Cycles	9	17	
Motor Cars	9	11	
Motor Lorries		5	
Motor Ambulance Cars		21	

Authority : Based on W.E. (Part I), Jany., 1914.	Compiled from W.E. of 29th, 52nd, and Cdn. Divs., 1915.	W.E. (Part VII), Sept.,

	APRIL, 1917.	OCTOBER, 1918.

APRIL, 1917.
Divnl. H.Q.

Infantry :
3 Brigades
(12 Inf. Battns. with 16 Lewis Guns each) ;
3 M.G. Cos.
(16, Vickers M.G. each) ;
3 Light T.M. B'ties.
(8, 3″ Stokes Mortars each).

Artillery :
H.Q. Divnl. Artillery.
2 Field Artillery Bdes.
(18-pdrs. and 4·5″ H.) ;
3 Medium T.M. B'ties.
(4, 2″ T.M. each) ;
1 Heavy T.M. Bty.
(4, 9·45″ Mortars).

1 Divisional Ammn. Coln.

Engineers :
H.Q. Divnl. Engineers.
3 Field Cos.

Signal Service :
1 Signal Coy.

Pioneers :
1 Pioneer Battalion
(8 Lewis Guns).

Machine-Gun Unit :
1 Machine-Gun Company
(16 Vickers M.G. each).

3 Field Ambulances.
1 Sanitary Section.

1 Mobile Vety. Section.

1 Divisional Train
(4 H.-T. Cos., A.S.C.).

(left margin: 12 Lewis ... each).)

OCTOBER, 1918.
Divnl. H.Q.

Infantry :
3 Brigades
(9 Inf. Battns. with 36 Lewis Guns each) ;

3 Light T.M. B'ties.
(8, 3″ Stokes Mortars each).

Artillery :
H.Q. Divnl. Artillery.
2 Field Artillery Bdes.
(18-pdrs. and 4·5″ H.) ;
2 Medium T.M. B'ties.
(6, 2″ T.M. each).

1 Divisional Ammn. Coln.

Engineers :
H.Q. Divnl. Engineers.
3 Field Cos.

Signal Service :
1 Signal Coy.

Pioneers :
1 Pioneer Battalion
(12 Lewis Guns).

Machine-Gun Unit :
1 Machine-Gun Battalion
(4 Cos., with 16 Vickers M.G. each).

3 Field Ambulances.

1 Mobile Vety. Section.

1 Divnl. Employment Coy.

1 Divisional Train
(4 H.-T. Cos., A.S.C.).

	1917.	**W.E. STRENGTH :** **1918.**
19,372	18,825	16,035......All Ranks.
5,145	4,342	3,838......Horses.
64	48	48......Guns.
	36	36......18-pdrs.
	12	12......4·5″ H.
		60-pdrs.
40	40	36......Trench Mortars.
	24	24......Stokes.
	12	12......Medium (2″).
	4	Heavy (9·45″).
200	264	400......Machine Guns.
	64	64......Vickers.
	200	336......Lewis Guns.
878	845	822......Carts and Vehicles.
372	388	341......Cycles.
24	22	44......Motor Cycles.
13	11	11......Motor Cars.
3	3	3......Motor Lorries.
21	21	21......Motor Amb. Cars.
1916.	W.E. (Part VIIA), April, 1917.	W.E. (Part VII), 31st October, 1918.

INDEX OF FORMATIONS

BRIGADES AND DIVISIONS

BRIGADES

Artillery—

R.H.A.—

III, 4 ; 5 (note 5) ; 6 ; 9 ; 12 ; 13 (note 4).
IV, 17 ; 20 ; 21 (note 10).
V, 92 ; 93 (note 18) ; 94.
VII, 1 ; 4 ; 6.
XIV, 84 ; 85 (note 26) ; 86.
XV (with 3rd Cavalry Div.), 17 ; 20 ; 21 (note 10) ; 22.
XV (with 29th Division), 5 (notes 24 and 28) ; 120 ; 121 (notes 8, 25, and 26) ; 122.
XVII, 21 (note 41).
Royal Canadian Horse Artillery, 20 ; 21 (note 51).

R.F.A.—

I, 100 ; 101 (note 7) ; 102.
II, 76.
III, 108 ; 109 (note 6) ; 110.
VIII (H), 68 ; 69 (note 20) ; 107.
X, 112.
XII (H.), 76 ; 77 (note 15).
XIV, 21 (note 41) ; 60 ; 61 (note 22).
XV, 68 ; 99.
XVII, 112 ; 120 ; 124 (notes 9 and 26) ; 122.
XIX, 100 ; 101 (note 7) ; 102 ; 112 ; 114.
XX, 100 ; 101 (note 7) ; 102.
XXII, 84 ; 86.
XXIII, 52 ; 53 (note 34).
XXIV, 76.
XXV, 36.
XXVI, 36 ; 37 (note 20).
XXVII, 68.
XXVIII, 68 ; 69 (note 29) ; 112.
XXIX, 60.
XXX (H.), 52 ; 53 (note 20).
XXXI, 108 ; 109 (note 7) ; 110.
XXXII, 60.
XXXIII, 92.
XXXIV, 44 ; 45 (note 29).
XXXV, 84 ; 86.
XXXVI, 44.
XXXVII (H.), 60 ; 61 (note 4) ; 84 ; 85 (note 16).
XXXVIII, 76 ; 77 (note 26).
XXXIX, 36 ; 112.
XL, 52.
XLI, 44.
XLII, 52.
XLIII (H.), 36 ; 37 (note 15).
XLIV (H.), 44 ; 45 (note 19).
XLV, 92.
LIV, 108 ; 109 (note 52) ; 112.
LVII (H.), 121 (note 27).
LXI (H.), 28 ; 29 (notes 15 and 28).
LXXIV, 28 ; 29 (notes 13 and 29).
LXXV, 28 ; 29 (notes 14 and 29).
LXXVI, 28 ; 29 (notes 14 and 30).
CXXVII (H.), 60 ; 61 (note 15).
CXXVIII (H.), 92 ; 93 (note 13).
CXXIX (H.), 100 ; 101 (note 18).

R.F.A.—_Continued_

CXXX (H.), 108 ; 109 (notes 19 and 35) ; 112.
CXXXII, 120 ; 121 (note 27).
CXLVI, 108 ; 109 (notes 8 and 48) ; 110.
CXLVII, 120 ; 121 (notes 10 and 28) ; 122.
I Australian (New South Wales), 119.

R.G.A.—

I Group H.A.R., 37 (note 7) ; 45 (note 6) ; 53 (note 5) ; 77 (note 3).
II Group H.A.R., 61 (note 5) ; 85 (note 5) ; 93 (note 3).
II, 37 (note 7) ; 43 ; 45 (note 6).
IV, 53 (note 5) ; 77 (note 3).
XII, 43.
I Heavy, 114.
III Heavy, 84 ; 85 (note 5).
VIII Heavy, 92 ; 93 (note 3).
XIII Heavy, 69 (note 5).
XX Heavy, 119.
III Medium, 114.
V Medium, 114.
XXIV Siege, 119.

Mountain—

III, 107.
IV (Highland), 99 ; 107.

Pack—

V, 112.

Cavalry Brigades—

1st, 2 ; 4 ; 6 ; 7.
2nd, 2 ; 4 ; 6 ; 7.
3rd, 2 ; 4 ; 5 (note 2) ; 6 ; 10 ; 11 ; 12 ; 13 (notes 2, 4, 7 and 10) ; 14 ; 15.
4th, 2 ; 3 ; 4 ; 5 (note 3) ; 6 ; 10 ; 12 ; 13 (note 15) ; 14 ; 15.
5th, 10 ; 12 ; 13 (notes 3, 4, and 8) ; 14 ; 15.
6th, 18 ; 20 ; 21 (notes 2 and 6) ; 22 ; 23.
7th, 18 ; 20 ; 21 (notes 7 and 31) ; 22.
8th, 18 ; 20 ; 21 (notes 20 and 32) ; 22.
9th, 2 ; 4 ; 5 (note 12) ; 7.
Canadian, 18 ; 19 ; 20 ; 21 (note 48).

Infantry Brigades—

1st (Guards) (1st Division, 1914), 34 ; 36 ; 37 (notes 1 and 17) ; 38.
1st Guards (Guards Division), 26 ; 28 ; 29 (notes 1 and 23).
1st Guards (Turkey, 1922-23), 114 ; 116.
2nd Guards, 26 ; 28 ; 29 (notes 3, 5, and 22) ; 31.
3rd Guards, 26 ; 28 ; 29 (notes 6, 7, 8, 9, and 10).
4th (Guards) (2nd Division, 1914), 42 ; 43 ; 44 ; 45 (note 1) ; 46.
4th Guards (1918), 27 ; 29 (note 40) ; 31.
1st, 34 ; 36.
2nd, 34 ; 35 ; 36.
3rd, 34 ; 35 ; 36 ; 39.
5th, 42 ; 43 ; 44 ; 47.

Infantry Brigades—*Continued*

6th, 42 ; 43 ; 44.
7th, 50 ; 52 ; 53 (note 9) ; 54.
8th, 50 ; 51 ; 52 ; 54.
9th, 50 ; 51 ; 52 ; 54 ; 55 ; 107.
10th, 58 ; 59 ; 60 ; 62.
11th, 58 ; 59 ; 60 ; 62.
12th, 58 ; 59 ; 60.
13th, 66 ; 67 ; 68 ; 70 ; 107.
14th, 66 ; 67 ; 68 ; 69 (note 9).
15th, 54 ; 66 ; 67 ; 68 ; 70 ; 107.
16th, 74 ; 75 ; 76 ; 78.
17th, 74 ; 75 ; 76 ; 77 (note 7) ; 78.
18th, 74 ; 76 ; 78.
19th, 42 ; 44 ; 45 (note 15) ; 62 ; 75 ; 99.
20th, 82 ; 83 ; 84.
21st, 82 ; 84 ; 85 (note 9).
22nd, 82 ; 83 ; 84.
23rd, 90 ; 91 ; 92.
24th, 90 ; 91 ; 92 ; 93 (notes 6 and 23).
25th, 90 ; 91 ; 92 ; 95.
29th Indian, 119 ; 123.
70th, 90 ; 92 ; 93 (note 15).
71st, 74 ; 76 ; 77 (note 18) ; 79.
76th, 50 ; 52 ; 53 (note 31).
80th, 98 ; 100 ; 101 (note 1) ; 103.
81st, 98 ; 100 ; 101 (note 2) ; 103.
82nd, 98 ; 100 ; 101 (note 3) ; 103.
83rd, 66 ; 67 ; 106 ; 107 ; 108 ; 109 (note 1) ;
   111 ; 112 ; 115 ; 116.
84th, 66 ; 67 ; 106 ; 107 ; 108 ; 109 (note 2) ;
   111 ; 112 ; 114 ; 115 ; 116.
85th, 50 ; 51 ; 106 ; 107 ; 108 ; 109 (note 3) ;
   111 ; 112 ; 115.
86th, 118 ; 119 ; 120 ; 121 (note 1) ; 123 ; 124.

Infantry Brigades—*Continued*

87th, 118 ; 120 ; 121 (note 3) ; 123 ; 124.
88th, 118 ; 119 ; 120 ; 121 (note 4) ; 123 ; 124.
91st, 82 ; 84 ; 85 (note 20).
95th, 66 ; 68 ; 69 (note 9).
99th, 42 ; 44 ; 45 (note 28) ; 47.
107th, 58 ; 59.
125th (Lancashire Fusilier), 119.
228th, 107 ; 108.
242nd (1920), 113 ; 115.
Composite (28th Div., 1915), 107.
Dardanelles Defences (1920-22), 112 ; 113.
New Zealand, 119.

DIVISIONS

Cavalry—

1st, 1–7 ; 11.
2nd, 9–15 ; 19.
3rd, 17–23.

Infantry—

Guards, 25–31.
1st, 33–39.
2nd, 41–47.
3rd, 49–55.
4th, 57–63.
5th, 65–71.
6th, 73–79.
7th, 81–87.
8th, 89–95.
27th, 97–103.
28th, 105–111 ; in Turkey, 112–116.
29th, 117–124.

Printed under the authority of HIS MAJESTY'S STATIONERY OFFICE
By Charles Birchall & Sons, Ltd., James Street, Liverpool, 2.
943. T51-5245, 770, 1/35, C.B.&S., Ltd.

Lightning Source UK Ltd.
Milton Keynes UK
UKOW03f1125141114

241613UK00001B/13/P